Power-Sprachkurs
DEUTSCH als Fremdsprache

by Christine Breslauer

Assisted by Renate Weber

PONS GmbH
Stuttgart

PONS
Power-Sprachkurs
DEUTSCH als Fremdsprache

by Dr. Christine Breslauer

Assisted by Renate Weber

The contents of this course correspond to those of ISBN 978-3-12-561703-2.

4. Auflage 2016

© PONS GmbH, Stöckachstraße 11, 70190 Stuttgart, 2014
www.pons.de
E-Mail: info@pons.de
All rights reserved.

Editor: Antje Wollenweber, Angela Saur
Logo design: Erwin Poell, Heidelberg
Logo adaptation: Sabine Redlin, Ludwigsburg
Recordings, sound editing and mastering: Ton in Ton Medienhaus, Stuttgart
Additional sound editing: ARTist Tonstudio, Pfullingen
Speakers: Robert Atzlinger, Joachim Bräutigam, Cornelius Dane, Juliana Eitel,
Nathalie Fischer, Karl Gabor, Viola Gabor, Rudolf Guckelsberger,
Susanne Heydenreich, Günter-A. Kopsch, Tamara Mertens, Marcus Michalski,
Claudia Schojan, Inge Spaughton, Luise Wunderlich, Annette Wunsch
Cover design: Beaufort 8, Stuttgart
Cover layout: Anne Helbich, Stuttgart
Cover photograph: Vlado Golub, Stuttgart; background image: Thinkstock/TommL
Illustrations: Walter Uihlein, Altdorf
Layout: one pm, Petra Michel, Stuttgart
Typesetting: Bettina Herrmann, Stuttgart; Digraf.pl – dtp services
Print: Gebr. Geiselberger GmbH, Altötting

ISBN: 978-3-12-561949-4

Introduction

Welcome to your German course!

This course is designed to motivate you to learn German not only fast, but also in an entertaining way - in particular in the areas of everyday German and language which you may need on vacation. During the course you will learn how to communicate confidently in these situations. Using modern, communicative methods which provide practice in authentic contexts, the emphasis is on understanding and speaking. To make this easier, we have included an interesting and motivating running story into the course. At the same time, working through the many varied tasks and exercises, you will acquire a solid foundation in grammar, vocabulary and cultural knowledge. The flexibility of the course means that it is suitable for both learners of German at a beginner's level and those with some previous knowledge of the language. Comprehensive feedback and tips on how to learn more effectively will help you to make really fast progress.

How is the course structured?

The course has 16 units. It also contains four revision sections after every fourth unit to revise and reinforce the contents of those units. Each unit is made up of four sections:

- **Getting started:** This part 'warms you up' prior to the dialogue and main contents of the unit.

- **Listen in:** Each unit is based firmly on the dialogue and running story. Listening and pronunciation skills are practised thoroughly in this section.

- **Practice makes perfect:** This is where you learn grammar, communication and vocabulary-based material in a systematic way. Following that there is motivating practice material using a rich variety of exercises.

- **Finishing up:** Intercultural information, games or further exercises round off the unit enjoyably and effectively.

 Audio CD required. The numbers indicate which of the two audio CDs and which track number you should listen to.

 Useful and interesting information and tips about the German language and culture.

 The number refers to the additional grammatical information which can be found in the appendix.

Check your knowledge with online tests

At the end of each week you can check your knowledge with an online test. To get to the tests, go to

www.pons.de/power

You can either sign up with your email address or do the tests without registration. In that case your results will not be saved. Select **PONS Power-Sprachkurs Deutsch als Fremdsprache** to get to the tests.

The appendix contains

Tapescripts:
There are transcriptions of everything that you hear in the course. If there is anything in the dialogues that you didn't understand, you can always check the translation.

Answer key + tips:
To check your answers, use the answer key, which includes feedback and learning tips.

Grammar overview:
In this section the most important grammar points covered in the course are explained in more depth.

Glossary:
This is a list of all words used in the course, listed alphabetically with translations.

Audio CDs
The two audio CDs contain all dialogues and sound files from the exercises.

INHALT

Main characters

The story takes place in Düsseldorf, a town in Germany.
There, Thomas, Sylvia and Aynur work together in the editorial office of the local newspaper "Blickpunkte".

These are the main figures in the ongoing story:

Thomas Kowalski is from Düsseldorf. He works as an editor of the local newspaper "Blickpunkte". He's interested in computers and in his leisure time he likes visiting art exhibitions or going to concerts.

Sylvia Moser comes from Vienna, Austria. She's the "Blickpunkte" photographer. After work she often goes to the sports club.

Aynur Hartmann studies journalism and is doing a work placement in the editorial office. Her mother is Turkish and her father is German. She likes cycling, but most of all meeting friends.

Other important people in the editorial team:

The "Blickpunkte" editor is **Herr Braun**. He is 50 years old and leads the editorial team extremely well.

Frau Schmidt is the editorial office secretary.

Thomas' family:

Susanne Kowalski is Thomas Kowalski's wife. She is a kind woman and mother. She's planning a picnic for her husband's colleagues.

Lisa is Thomas' and Susanne's daughter. She's seven years old and is in her first year at school. She enjoys school, especially painting and sports. When she grows up she'd like to be an artist.

And last but not least there is **Herr Greiner**, an expert in exotic animals. He's a biology teacher interested in animals from Australia.

1

Hello! Let's start by learning some ways of greeting people in German! Listen and repeat!

 CD 1 – TR. 1

 NICE TO KNOW

Grüß Gott! is used in South Germany and Austria only.

Hallo! – Guten Tag!

Auf Wiedersehen! – Tschüss!

Grüß Gott!

Guten Morgen!

Gute Nacht!

2

Five of the main figures of the story introduce themselves. Four of them work in an editorial office in Düsseldorf. Find out who's who. Listen to the figures introducing themselves.

 CD 1 – TR. 2

 NICE TO KNOW

Düsseldorf is the capital of North-Rhine-Westphalia, one of the 16 federal states of Germany. Insiders simply use the abbreviation **NRW** instead of **Nordrhein-Westfalen**.

Who's who? Fill in the numbers of the pictures.

____ **A** Ich bin Susanne Kowalski.

____ **B** Ich heiße Sylvia Moser. Ich bin Fotografin.

____ **C** Ich bin Thomas Kowalski. Ich bin Redakteur.

____ **D** Ich bin Herr Braun. Ich bin Chefredakteur.

____ **E** Ich heiße Aynur Hartmann. Ich bin Studentin.

CD 1 - TR. 3

○ 3

One Monday in the editorial office: Thomas Kowalski, the local editor, meets his new team with whom he'll work together closely. The editor-in-chief, Mr. Braun, introduces the two new colleagues to Thomas, who likes them at once. Don't worry if you don't understand everything right away.

Now listen again. If you like you can also read the tape script which you can find in the appendix.

○ 4

CD 1 - TR. 3

Listen to the dialogue again. Even if you don't understand every word, the intonation can help you to decide if the statements below are true or false. Read them and mark with a **T** for "true" or an **F** for "false".

	true	false
1. Mr. Kowalski isn't fine.	☐	☐
2. He is meeting Mrs. Moser for the first time.	☐	☐
3. Mrs. Moser is a photographer.	☐	☐
4. Aynur is here on a work placement.	☐	☐
5. Mr. Braun is in a hurry and has to go.	☐	☐
6. Sylvia Moser doesn't want to be called by her first name.	☐	☐
7. Mr. Kowalski doesn't know the name "Aynur".	☐	☐
8. Aynur is a German name.	☐	☐

5

 CD 1 – TR. 4

What do people say when they meet? Here you can repeat some expressions and practise your pronunciation. Listen to the sentences and then repeat them aloud.

Wie heißen Sie?	*What's your name?*
Ich heiße Sylvia Moser.	*My name is Sylvia Moser.*
Guten Morgen, Herr Braun.	*Good morning, Mr. Braun.*
Wie geht es Ihnen?	*How are you?*
Ganz gut, danke.	*Not bad, thank you.*
Das ist Frau Hartmann.	*This is Mrs. Hartmann.*
Freut mich.	*Nice to meet you.*
Auf Wiedersehen!	*Goodbye!*

NICE TO KNOW

Questions like **Wie geht es Ihnen?** or **Wie geht es dir?** are only used when the people know each other well.

Say it aloud! When you practise your pronunciation, feel free to exaggerate and to play with your voice. This is also a good way to learn new vocabulary.

6

 CD 1 – TR. 5

Listen to how the letters of the German alphabet are pronounced and then repeat them.

**a b c d e f g h i j k l m
n o p q r s t u v w x y z**

 NICE TO KNOW

In order to explain letters with umlauts **ä**, **ö** and **ü**, you can say **a Umlaut**, **o Umlaut** and **u Umlaut**. And for the **ß**, as in heißen, we say **eszet** (s + z).

Answering questions like:
- **Wie schreibt man das?** *How do you spell that?*
- **Können Sie das bitte buchstabieren?** *Can you spell that out, please?*
- **Schreibt man das mit „i" oder „y" (am Ende)?**
  Do you spell that with an "i" or a "y" (at the end)?

It's important to know the German alphabet.

Practice makes perfect

 CD 1 – TR. 6

7

When you're on the telephone you may well have to spell your name or something else and also to understand if the caller spells something to you. Listen to how the names of some European capital cities are spelled and write them down. Repeat and spell the names. Then choose some other European cities and try to spell them.

1. _____ 4. _____

2. _____ 5. _____

3. _____ 6. _____

 NICE TO KNOW

To avoid misunderstandings there is a special spelling system, for example **A wie Anton, B wie Berta** and so on.

8

All words have syllables that are stressed. This is the basis of rhythm in the German language. There are words with the stress on the 1st, 2nd, 3rd or 4th syllable, for example:

• **Tho**mas, **schrei**ben
• Stu**dent**in, entschul**dig**en Sie bitte
• Foto**graf**in, Redak**teur**
• fotogra**fie**ren

 CD 1 – TR. 7

Listen carefully and repeat.

schreiben – Studentin   Fotografin – fotografieren

Have you noticed the differences between the stressed and unstressed syllables? The voice becomes a bit slower, clearer and louder on the stressed syllable.

 CD 1 – TR. 8

Listen and repeat.

Thomas – fotografieren – ganz gut
Entschuldigen Sie bitte! – Wie heißen Sie?

CD 1 - TR. 9

9

You have already learnt that each word has a stress pattern and that this is the basis for rhythm in German. Try it with some international words.

stress on the 1. syllable	stress on the 2. syllable	stress on the 3. syllable
_____	_____	_____
_____	_____	_____
_____	_____	_____
_____	_____	_____

> Musik | Computer | Telefon | Hotel | Radio
> Technik | Disco | Kassette

10

You have already encountered most of the personal pronouns (he, you, I ...) in the introductory dialogue. Here you can find them all together and practise some of them right away.

	singular	plural
1st person	ich *(I)*	wir *(we)*
2nd person	du *(you) (familar form)*	ihr *(you) (familar form)*
	Sie *(you) (polite form)*	Sie *(you) (polite form)*
3rd person	er, sie, es *(he, she, it)*	sie *(they)*

NICE TO KNOW

Note that **Sie**, when used as the formal form of you, always starts with a capital letter.

Choose the right personal pronoun and write it into the gap.

> ich | sie | er

1. Das ist Herr Kowalski, _____ ist Redakteur.

2. Wie heißt du? – _____ heiße Aynur.

3. Aynur ist Studentin und _____ studiert Journalismus.

Practice makes perfect

 CD 1 – TR. 10

11

You have probably noticed that the verbs used in the introductory dialogue have various endings, for example:
- **Wie heißen Sie? – Ich heiße Thomas Kowalski.**
- **Wie schreibt man das?**

The present tense of most German verbs is formed by taking the stem (**heiß-, schreib-**) and adding an ending which is related to the person being described (**-en, -e, -t** ...).

Look at the present tense of the verb schreiben. Then listen and repeat each form.

 NICE TO KNOW

The forms of the present tense can have a future meaning. Depending on the context, the meaning of **ich komme** can be I come, I'm coming or I'll be coming. German's not so hard after all!

ich	schreibe	wir schreiben
du	schreibst	ihr schreibt
er, sie, es	schreibt	sie schreiben

The polite form, singular and plural, is **Sie schreiben**.

To memorize the forms of the present tense take other verbs and conjugate them, for example: **machen – ich mache – du machst – er...** (*to make or do*)
Then try it with **sagen** (*to say*) and **kommen** (*to come*).

12

To express sentences like **Ich bin Thomas** (*I'm Thomas*) you need the most common verb in German: **sein** (*to be*).

As in many other languages, the verb **sein** is irregular and you have to learn the different forms by heart.

ich	bin (*I'm*)	wir sind (*we are*)
du	bist (*you are*)	ihr seid (*you are*)
Sie	sind (*polite form*)	Sie sind (*polite form*)
er, sie, es	ist (*he, she, it is*)	sie sind (*they are*)

Read the sentences about Aynur and write the correct form of **sein** in the gaps. Then repeat the complete sentence.

1. Das _____ Aynur Hartmann.

2. Ich _____ Studentin.

3. Thomas, Sylvia und Aynur _____ Kollegen.

° 13

Do you remember how the present tense is formed? You take the stem of the verb and add an ending. Fill in the gaps with the correct form of **studieren**, **heißen** and **sein**. Don't forget that **sein** is irregular. When you have completed the paradigms, repeat the forms.

NICE TO KNOW

The **du-form** has the ending **-st**. But if the stem of the verb ends in **-s** or **-ß** like **heiß-** the ending becomes **-t: du heißt**.

studieren	heißen	sein
Ich studiere	ich	ich bin
du	du heißt	du
er, sie, es	er, sie, es	er, sie, es ist
wir studieren	wir heißen	wir
ihr studiert	ihr heißt	ihr seid
sie / Sie	sie / Sie	sie / Sie

° 14

 CD 1 – TR. 11

For greeting and saying goodbye you have to make a difference between a formal and an informal situation (family, friends etc.).

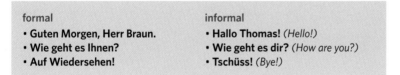

formal	informal
• **Guten Morgen, Herr Braun.**	• **Hallo Thomas!** *(Hello!)*
• **Wie geht es Ihnen?**	• **Wie geht es dir?** *(How are you?)*
• **Auf Wiedersehen!**	• **Tschüss!** *(Bye!)*

° 15

 CD 1 – TR. 12

Listen to some little words and useful expressions that open up the way to a lot of language. Match each one to the correct translation.

1.	*Welcome!*	____	**A**	Interessant!
2.	*Thank you!*	____	**B**	Nein.
3.	*Please!*	____	**C**	Herzlich willkommen!
4.	*No.*	____	**D**	Aha.
5.	*I see.*	____	**E**	Bitte!
6.	*Interesting!*	____	**F**	Wie bitte?
7.	*Great!*	____	**G**	Super!
8.	*Sorry.*	____	**H**	Entschuldigen Sie bitte!
9.	*Excuse me!*	____	**I**	Ja.
10.	*Yes.*	____	**J**	Danke!

Finishing up

° 16

In the hall of the editorial office the secretary Mrs Schmidt meets Aynur. She supposes that Aynur is one of the new employees and starts a short conversation. The dialogue is jumbled up. Can you reconstruct the dialogue between the secretary Mrs Schmidt and Aynur? Write each part into the correct position. Then read the complete dialogue.

> Ich studiere Journalismus.
> Nein. Sylvia Moser ist Fotografin.
> Interessant!
> Guten Tag, ich heiße Aynur Hartmann.
> Aha! Und Sie?
> Und was studieren Sie?
> Ich bin Studentin. Ich mache hier ein Praktikum.
> Guten Tag, ich bin Frau Schmidt.
> Freut mich. Sie sind Fotografin, oder?

° 17

Read the sentences and write the pronouns shown below into the correct gaps. Read carefully about how many people are mentioned and whether they are speaking directly to someone or in the 3rd person about someone. If you need to remind yourself of the meanings of the personal pronouns, see § Personal pronouns.

> wir | sie | Sie | du | ich | ihr | er | es

1. Wer bist _____? – Ich bin Lisa.

2. Entschuldigen _____ bitte, wie schreibt man das?

3. Wie heißt ihr? – Sie heißt Sylvia und _____ heiße Aynur.

4. Das ist Herr Braun, _____ ist Chefredakteur.

5. Aha, _____ seid Kollegen. – Ja, wir sind Kollegen.

6. Aynur ist Studentin, _____ macht ein Praktikum.

7. Hallo, _____ sind Sylvia und Aynur.

8. Wie geht _____ Ihnen? – Danke, gut.

CD 1 – TR. 13

1

Would you like to travel in Europe? Which countries? Have a look at the map.

Hear and read the names of ten European countries and nationalities. Now match the countries and nationalities.

NICE TO KNOW

Germans often say **England** but they really mean Great Britain (**Großbritannien**).

1.	England	____ **A**	österreichisch
2.	Frankreich	____ **B**	englisch
3.	Deutschland	____ **C**	deutsch
4.	Österreich	____ **D**	türkisch
5.	Schweiz	____ **E**	italienisch
6.	Italien	____ **F**	französisch
7.	Polen	____ **G**	polnisch
8.	Spanien	____ **H**	spanisch
9.	Türkei	____ **I**	russisch
10.	Russland	____ **J**	schweizerisch

Listen in!

2

Imagine you are in a German town (town = **die Stadt**). You can find places or buildings that are often landmarks or even symbols of that town.

Look at the pictures and read the German names. Now listen to them and repeat the words.

1. die Brücke   **2.** der Park   **3.** das Museum

4. die Straße   **5.** die Kirche   **6.** der Fluss

7. der Stadtteil   **8.** der Markt

 CD 1 - TR. 15

3

After a short break, Thomas, Sylvia and Aynur continue their conversation to find out more about each other. Aynur's name leads the conversation to the topics of residence, origins and other interesting subjects.

Listen to the dialogue. Don't worry if you don't understand everything. Later we will look at more details.

4

 CD 1 - TR. 15

In the introductory dialogue you heard Thomas, Sylvia and Aynur speaking about nationalities and residences. You are now going to look for
more details. Who lives where? Who's a foreigner?
First read the questions below. What would Aynur, Sylvia and Thomas
answer? Yes or no?
Listen to the dialogue again and answer the questions. Do this for each
person.

	1. Aynur		2. Sylvia		3. Thomas	
	yes	no	yes	no	yes	no
1. Is your mother Turkish?	☐	☐	☐	☐	☐	☐
2. Do you live in Wodan Street?	☐	☐	☐	☐	☐	☐
3. Are you Austrian?	☐	☐	☐	☐	☐	☐
4. Do you live in Düsseldorf?	☐	☐	☐	☐	☐	☐
5. Do you live near a market?	☐	☐	☐	☐	☐	☐

5

As you know from the introductory dialogue, Sylvia gave her business
card (**Visitenkarte**) to Aynur and Thomas. What is written on the card?
Someone has given you an empty form. Can you complete it with the help
of the information on the business card?
Write the missing words into the gaps. Now it's easy to understand the
new words, isn't it?

> **Telefonnummer | Beruf | Sylvia | Nachname | Adresse**

_____: Moser   Vorname: _____

_____: Fotografin

_____: Bäckerstraße 9, 40213 Düsseldorf

_____: 0211/45 06 33

Sylvia Moser
Fotografin
Bäckerstraße 9
40213 Düsseldorf
Tel.: 0211/450633
E-Mail: sylvia.moser@bmx.de

Practice makes perfect

 CD 1 - TR. 16

NICE TO KNOW

The sound of **zwei** and **drei** is similar. To avoid misunderstandings you can say **zwo** instead of **zwei**.

○ **6**

In the introductory dialogue, the telephone numbers and the post code were spoken separately. Of course, you can also group numbers, as you will see in the next few units.

Listen to the numbers and then repeat.

null	eins	zwei	drei	vier

fünf	sechs	sieben	acht	neun

○ **7**

What are the numbers in German? Write the number into the gap.

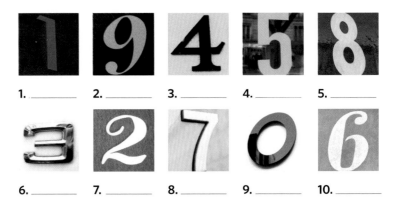

1. _____   2. _____   3. _____   4. _____   5. _____

6. _____   7. _____   8. _____   9. _____   10. _____

8

There are two basic word order patterns:

1. **Normal word order:** the verb comes second.
   A Herr Müller **lebt** in Deutschland. (*Mr Müller lives in Germany.*)
   B Woher **kommst** du? (*Where are you from?*)
   C Hier **ist** meine Visitenkarte. (*Here is my business card.*)
   The first word is A the subject, or B a question word or C another element (so that the subject is placed behind the verb).

2. **Inverted word order.** Yes / no- questions start with the verb followed by the subject.

Kommst du aus Italien?	**Sind Sie Fotografin?**
(*Do you come from Italy?*)	(*Are you a photographer?*)

Listen carefully and concentrate on the intonation:
In the 1st sentence the voice falls at the end while in the 2nd sentence (yes /no-question) the voice rises.

 CD 1 - TR. 17

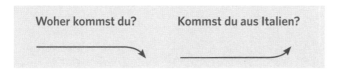

9

Put the words into the correct order.

1. Frau | aus | ist | Müller | Berlin.

_____

2. die | Wo | Wodanstraße? | liegt

_____

3. Aynur | die | fährt | Türkei. | in

_____

4. Sind | aus | Österreich? | Sie

_____

5. nach | Düsseldorf? | Sie | Fahren

_____

Practice makes perfect

10

When you are talking about languages or nationalities, the following expressions can be useful:

 CD 1 - TR. 18

Ich komme aus Österreich. Ich bin Österreicherin.
(I'm from Austria. I'm Austrian (female).)
Welche Sprachen sprechen Sie? – Französisch und Englisch.
(Which languages do you speak? – French and English.)
Sprechen Sie Deutsch? *(Do you speak German?)*
Wie heißt „Bahnhof" auf Französisch?
(What is "Bahnhof" in French?)

 CD 1 - TR. 19

Listen to the question and mark the right answer.

A Ich spreche deutsch.   B Ja, Englisch und Französisch.

 NICE TO KNOW

Unfortunately Turkey and Switzerland are exceptions: **Wo?** ▸ in der Türkei / Schweiz. **Woher?** ▸ aus der Türkei / Schweiz. **Wohin?** ▸ in die Türkei / Schweiz.

Note that German has different words for male and female inhabitants.

Deutschland	Deutscher	Deutsche (!)
England	Engländer	Engländerin
Spanien	Spanier	Spanierin
Frankreich	Franzose	Französin (!)
Griechenland	Grieche	Griechin
Italien	Italiener	Italienerin
Österreich	Österreicher	Österreicherin
Polen	Pole	Polin
Russland	Russe	Russin
Schweiz	Schweizer	Schweizerin
Türkei	Türke	Türkin

Here are the rules for the feminine form:
-e ▸ -in: Türk**e** – Türk**in**   **-er ▸ -erin**: Schweiz**er** – Schweiz**erin**
The exceptions are: **Deutsche, Französin**

11

In a conversation about the place of residence, the country of origin and the destination you can use these questions and answers:

* Place:
    - **Wo** wohnen Sie? *(Where do you live?)*
    - **In** Düsseldorf, **in** Deutschland. **In der** Bäckerstraße 9.
    - **Wo** liegt Düsseldorf? *(Where is Düsseldorf situated?)*
    - **In** Nordrhein-Westfalen. *(In North-Rhine-Westphalia.)*

- Origin:
  - **Woher** kommst du? *(Where do you come from?)*
  - Ich komme **aus** Wien. / **aus** Österreich.
    (I come from Vienna. / from Austria.)

☉	Wo?	in	
☉→	Woher?	aus	+ Stadt/Land
→☉	Wohin?	nach	

- Destination, direction:
  - **Wohin** fährt Anna? *(Where is Anna going?)*
  - Sie fährt **nach** Rom / **nach** Italien.
    (She is going to Rome / Italy.)

Write **in**, **aus** or **nach** into the gaps.

1. Peter fährt oft ＿＿＿＿＿ Frankreich.

2. Bist du Italiener? – Ja, ich komme ＿＿＿＿＿ Rom.

3. Wien liegt ＿＿＿＿＿ Österreich.

12

CD 1 – TR. 20

Imagine this situation: you are sitting in a train from Munich (the capital of Bavaria – **Bayern**) to Hamburg. It's a long journey. Passengers come and go. Sometimes you can hear parts of their conversations.
Listen to six short dialogues about nationalities, countries and residences. Do you understand what the conversation is about? Choose the correct statement.

1. A ☐ Er ist aus Deutschland.
   B ☐ Er ist aus England.
   C ☐ Er ist aus Griechenland.

2. A ☐ Frau Müller fährt nach Bonn.
   B ☐ Frau Müller wohnt in der Gartenstraße 3.
   C ☐ Frau Müller wohnt in der Goethestraße 8.

3. A ☐ Er spricht Deutsch und Französisch.
   B ☐ Er spricht nur Deutsch.
   C ☐ Er spricht Englisch und Deutsch.

4. A ☐ Er ist Schweizer.
   B ☐ Er ist Italiener.
   C ☐ Er ist Franzose.

5. A ☐ Er fährt nach Bayern.
   B ☐ Er fährt nach Erlangen.
   C ☐ Er fährt nach Hamburg.

° 13

Remember the end of the introductory dialogue:
– Dort ist **ein** Museum, oder? *(There is a museum, isn't there?)*
– Ja, **das** Stadtmuseum. *(Yes, the city museum.)*

Nouns in German have an indefinite (a, an) and a definite (the) article. The article indicates the gender of nouns. All German nouns are either masculine, feminine or neuter and are always written with capital letters.

	masculine	feminine	neuter
indefinite	**ein** Fluss	**eine** Straße	**ein** Haus
definite	**der** Fluss	**die** Straße	**das** Haus
	(river)	*(street)*	*(house)*

CD 1 – TR. 21

Read and listen to the sentences.

1. **Das ist ein Haus. Das Haus ist alt.**
   (This is a house. The house is old.)
2. **Das ist eine Straße. Die Straße liegt in Düsseldorf.**
   (This is a street. The street is in Düsseldorf.)
3. **Das ist ein Fluss. Der Fluss heißt „Rhein".**
   (This is a river. The river is called "The Rhine".)

Unfortunately, there is no sure way of telling what gender a noun is. The best thing you can do is to always learn a noun with its article, for example **die** Adresse *(the address)*.

CD 1 – TR. 22

° 14

As you already know, the article (**der**, **die**, **das**) indicates the gender of nouns. Let's have a look at some nouns.
Read the words below. Do you remember the correct article? If you need help, listen to the nouns. Put a circle around the correct article (*der*, *die* or *das*). Repeat them (don't forget the article!) and try to memorize them.

1. der | die | das Bahnhof
2. der | die | das Straße
3. der | die | das Land
4. der | die | das Stadt
5. der | die | das Fluss

6. der | die | das Adresse
7. der | die | das Turm
8. der | die | das Nummer
9. der | die | das Haus
10. der | die | das Telefon

CD 1 – TR. 23

1

Let's see what you can eat and drink at a café.
Look at the pictures and listen to what these delicious things are called in German. Then write the words into the right gaps.

> Schinkentoast | Kuchen | Schokoladentorte | Bier | Mineralwasser
> Kaffee | Tee | Wein | Orangensaft | Cola

1. _____   2. _____   3. _____   4. _____   5. _____

6. _____   7. _____   8. _____   9. _____   10. _____

2

CD 1 – TR. 24

Let's have a look at some phrases you can use when you visit a café (**ein Café**) in a German-speaking country.
Read the sentences and listen to them. What could be their meaning?
Match the English translation to the correct German sentence.

1. Was möchten Sie?

2. Ich hätte gern einen Kaffee.

3. Ich nehme lieber einen Tee mit Zitrone.

4. Ich nehme ein Stück Apfelkuchen.

5. Ich möchte nur etwas trinken.

6. Wir möchten bitte zahlen.

___ **A** *What would you like?*

___ **B** *Can we have the bill, please?*

___ **C** *I'd like a piece of apple pie.*

___ **D** *I'd like to have a coffee.*

___ **E** *I'll just have something to drink.*

___ **F** *I prefer a tea with lemon.*

Listen in!

° **3**

It's still early afternoon. Sylvia and Aynur have visited the editorial office, Thomas has finished his article. Because it's Aynur and Sylvia's first day of work, they have been invited to have a coffee. Now the team is sitting in a café. Thomas hasn't decided yet what to order.

What do Thomas, Sylvia and Aynur say or do during their visit to the café? Listen to the dialogue and look at the pictures.

Now listen to the dialogue again and read the text in the tape script which you can find in the appendix.

How can you understand the gist of a spoken text even if you don't know each word? Before you do a listening activity, look at the task, the questions or the pictures, so that you understand the situation and have an idea of what the text is about. And in real life? Instead of pictures you have gestures and facial expressions that help you to get the gist of a text.

4

CD 1 – TR. 25

Let's have a look at the dialogue a little more closely and find some details. What do Thomas, Sylvia and Aynur drink or eat?
Listen to the dialogue again. Who drinks or eats what? Write the expressions below in the appropriate space.

Sylvia	Aynur	Thomas
_____	_____	_____
_____	_____	_____
_____	_____	_____

> einen Tee mit Zitrone | ein Mineralwasser | einen Kaffee
> | einen Schinkentoast | einen Apfelkuchen

5

CD 1 – TR. 26

We have already talked about the intonation of words. Now we'll look a little closer at the vowels of the stressed syllable. The vowels **a**, **e**, **i**, **u**, **o** and the umlauts **ä**, **ö**, **ü** can be spoken long or short.
To develop an ear for the differences between long and short vowels, listen to the following pairs of words.

1. zahlen – Tasse

2. nehmen – essen

3. vier – bitte

4. Zitrone – kommen

5. gut – Turm

6. Käse – hätte

7. Österreich – möchte

8. Süden – Stück

Sometimes the German spelling shows you how to pronounce the stressed vowel: An h following a vowel makes the sound long like in **zahlen**. The same effect has an e behind an i like in **vier**. Note that in neither case you can hear the h or the e.
A double consonant behind the vowel is a sure sign that the vowel is short like in **kommen**.

Are you ready to try it yourself? Listen to the words again and repeat them aloud.

Practice makes perfect

 CD 1 - TR. 27

 NICE TO KNOW

If you want to know how old somebody is, you can ask **Wie alt sind Sie?** or informally **Wie alt bist du?** You would answer **Ich bin ...** and give your age.

° 6

Note how the numbers from 13 to 19 are spoken. Listen to the numbers and repeat them.

10	**11**	**12**	**13**	**14**
zehn	elf	zwölf	dreizehn	vierzehn

15	**16**	**17**	**18**	**19**
fünfzehn	sechzehn	siebzehn	achtzehn	neunzehn

° 7

How much is a beer? How much is the bill? Look at the pictures and complete the sentences by filling in the correct numbers.

2,10 €

1. Ein Bier? Das macht

zwei Euro _____.

2,16 €

2. Ein Stück Kuchen kostet

zwei Euro _____.

12,15€

3. Das macht zusammen _____

Euro fünfzehn.

8

Unfortunately a number of verbs are irregular, but only in the 2nd and 3rd person singular. For example:

nehmen: Was n**i**mmst du? – Ich nehme einen Tee.
(What do you take? – I'll take a tea.)
essen: Aynur **i**sst gerne Kuchen.
(Aynur likes eating cake.)
sehen: S**ie**hst du die Frau dort?
(Do you see the woman there?)
sprechen: Spr**i**chst du Englisch?
(Do you speak English?)
fahren: Peter f**ä**hrt nach Berlin.
(Peter goes to Berlin.)

 NICE TO KNOW

The verb **haben** (*to have*) has another irregularity, but only in the 2nd and 3rd person singular: **du hast, er hat**. All other persons are regular.

Look again at the examples above and then complete the rules for the verbs with a stem-vowel change.

> Rules: The stem-vowel **e** changes into _____ or **ie** (spoken as a
>
> short or long "i") and the stem-vowel _____ changes into **ä**
> (a Umlaut).

Note that not all verbs with **e** or **a** change the stem-vowel.
You might wonder how to know if the stem-vowel changes or not.
In general, the dictionary will show you the paradigm when the verb is irregular.

9

Choose the correct verb form to complete the sentences.
Remember that a number of verbs changes the stem-vowel in the 2nd and 3rd person singular and that some verbs are irregular.

1. Was *nahm* | *nimmst* | *nehmst* du? – Einen Apfelkuchen.
2. Peter *möchte* | *möchten* | *möchtet* einen Milchkaffee.
3. Wer *zahlt* | *zählt* | *zahlen* die Rechnung? – Ich.
4. Wohin *fahren* | *fahrt* | *fährt* sie? – Nach Düsseldorf.
5. Er *ist* | *isst* | *esst* einen Schinkentoast.
6. Anna *hätte* | *hat* | *hättet* gern eine Tasse Tee.
7. Cola, Bier, Mineralwasser ... – *Hat* | *Hast* | *Haben* du auch Wein?

CD 1 - TR. 28

° **10**

In a café or a restaurant, the waiter would ask you:

Was möchten Sie? *(What would you like?)*
Möchten Sie einen Apfelkuchen mit oder ohne Sahne?
(Would you like an apple pie with or without whipped cream?)
Was hätten Sie gern? *(What would you like to have?)*
Was nehmen Sie? *(What do you take?)*

CD 1 - TR. 29

For your answer you would use the same structure. Listen and fill in the correct form of the verb.

1. Ich _____ einen Apfelkuchen mit Sahne.

2. Ich _____ gern einen Toast.

3. Ich _____ einen Kaffee.

Expressions with **möchte** and **hätte** are very common. That's why it's worth the trouble to learn the forms even if they are quite irregular. Here are the forms:

forms of möchte		forms of hätte	
ich	möchte ein Bier	ich	hätte gern ein Bier
du	möchtest	du	hättest
er, sie, es	möchte	er, sie, es	hätte
wir	möchten	wir	hätten
ihr	möchtet	ihr	hättet
sie	möchten	sie	hätten
Sie	möchten	Sie	hätten

CD 1 - TR. 30

 NICE TO KNOW

In Germany and in Austria, the currency is called **Euro**. One Euro consists of 100 **Cent**. The currency in Switzerland is the **Schweizer Franken** - one Schweizer Franke equals 100 **Rappen**.

° **11**

To call the waiter / waitress you can say **Hallo!** or **Entschuldigung!** *(Excuse me!)*, but the best is eye contact and perhaps to raise your hand slightly and use phrases like
• **Wir möchten bitte zahlen.** *(We'd like to pay, please.)*
• **Die Rechnung, bitte!** *(The bill, please.)*

When the waiter / waitress comes to your table he / she might say
• **Das macht 19 Euro 10.** *(That's 19 Euro 10 Cent.)*
• **Getrennt oder zusammen?** *(Separate (bills) or together?)*
It is common for everyone to pay for him or herself, unless your companion expressly says he / she wants to pay for you.

Listen again to the end of the introducing dialogue. If you want to read the text you'll find it in the appendix.

You are not obliged to leave a tip (**das Trinkgeld**) as it is normally included in the bill, but you usually round up the bill saying **Stimmt so!** *(Keep the change!)* or give 5 – 10 % tip.

12

 CD 1 - TR. 31

Imagine you and your friend are in a café or restaurant. The waiter is speaking to you. Do you know what to answer?
Read and listen to what the waiter says. Then match the correct reaction with the waiter's sentences. Listen again to the sentences and repeat them aloud.

1. Was nehmen Sie?

2. Möchten Sie etwas essen?

3. Wir haben Kaffee, Cappuccino, Espresso …

4. Möchten Sie etwas trinken?

5. Möchten Sie den Kuchen mit oder ohne Sahne?

6. Zahlen Sie getrennt oder zusammen?

7. Das macht 19 Euro.

____ **A** Haben Sie auch Milchkaffee?

____ **B** Zusammen.

____ **C** Ich nehme einen Tee.

____ **D** Ja, wir hätten gern ein Bier und einen Wein.

____ **E** Stimmt so!

____ **F** Nein, danke.

____ **G** Mit Sahne, bitte.

 CD 1 - TR. 32

13

It's time to go to a café to drink and eat something, isn't it?
Listen to the dialogue. What does the waiter say and what does the guest answer? You can also read the dialogue in the appendix. Now try to repeat the sentences aloud.

Finishing up

14

Of course you have noticed the article in sentences like

- Ich möchte **einen** Tee. *(I'd like a tea.)*
- Möchten Sie **den** Tee mit Zitrone oder mit Milch? *(Would you like the tea with lemon or with milk?)*

It's the accusative case. Don't worry, only the masculine form changes:

	masculine	feminine	neuter
indefinite	**einen** Tee	eine Cola	ein Bier
definite	**den** Tee	die Cola	das Bier

Listen and write the correct article into the gap.

> den | ein | einen

1. Nehmen wir ein Bier oder _____ Wein?

2. Siehst du _____ Mann dort?

3. Ich hätte gern _____ Mineralwasser.

15

You already know a lot of nouns, their gender and their articles. Read the sentences and write the correct article into the gaps.

> das | den | der | die | die | ein | eine | einen | einen

Die Studentin macht **(1)** _____ Praktikum.

Ich nehme **(2)** _____ Apfelkuchen und **(3)** _____ Kaffee.

Wir möchten bitte **(4)** _____ Speisekarte.

Zahlst du **(5)** _____ Rechnung?

Hast du auch **(6)** _____ Handynummer?

Ich möchte **(7)** _____ Rathaus und **(8)** _____ Bahnhof fotografieren.

Wer ist **(9)** _____ Mann dort? Das ist Thomas Kowalski.

CD 1 – TR. 34

1

The Rhine is a river full of life and it flows through a beautiful landscape.
Let's have a look at what you can find in, on and along the river Rhine.
Listen to the words and read them. We have always given the plural form.
On the right you can find the singular form of the words.

Häuser   Dörfer   Fische   Schiffe

das Haus – *house*
das Dorf – *village*
der Fisch – *fish*
das Schiff – *ship*
das Tier – *animal*
der Weinberg – *vineyards*
die Burg – *castle*
das Krokodil – *crocodile*

Tiere   Weinberge   Burgen   Krokodile

Now you have a general idea of the Rhine. But what about crocodiles in
the Rhine? This will be an important question in this unit! Go ahead!

2

 CD 1 – TR. 35

 NICE TO KNOW

What do you know about crocodiles and how would you react to a
crocodile in the Rhine?
Listen to four statements about crocodiles. Then write the missing words
into the gaps.

The expression **es gibt** (*there is /are*) is invariable. So you can say **es gibt ein Krokodil** (*there is a crocodile*) and also **es gibt zwei Krokodile** (*there are two crocodiles*).

> gefährlich | möglich | keine | groß

1. Krokodile sind _____ .

2. Ein Krokodil im Rhein? Nicht _____ !

3. Im Rhein gibt es _____ Krokodile!

4. Ich denke, Krokodile sind _____ .

Listen in!

3

What is the daily work of Thomas, Sylvia and Aynur in the editorial office? Well, most of the time they read, write or speak on the phone. Here are some parts of a telephone call. Listen to the sentences.
Can you guess the meaning of the phrases? Match them with the corresponding description in English.

1. Was kann ich für Sie tun?	____ A *Somebody is introducing himself.*
2. Lokalredaktion *Blickpunkte*, Sylvia Moser am Apparat.	____ B *The called person is offering help.*
	____ C *It's the form for closing a phone call.*
3. Danke für den Anruf.	
4. Guten Tag. Mein Name ist Kowalsky.	____ D *Sylvia is answering the phone.*
	____ E *The called person ist thanking for the call.*
5. Auf Wiederhören.	

4

After another day without any special event in the editorial office one morning Thomas receives an interesting call from a lady. He informs Sylvia and Aynur who couldn't hear the whole telephone conversation. Together they decide that it might be a good story for their newspaper "Blickpunkte" (Limelights).
Listen to the dialogue. In the dialogue, you'll hear the word "Benrath". It's a district in the southern part of Düsseldorf.

CD 1 - TR. 37

5

Let's look at the dialogue a little more closely and find out some details. Before listening once more to the dialogue read the statements below. Then you'll know what details to look for and you can pay attention to these points.

After this preparation listen to the dialogue and decide whether these statements are "true" (T) or "false"(F).

	true	false
1. The woman who is calling wants to tell a fictional story.	☐	☐
2. The crocodile swimming in the Rhine is quite big.	☐	☐
3. Thomas doubts the truth of the story.	☐	☐
4. The woman doesn't know where the crocodile is.	☐	☐
5. Aynur and Sylvia are surprised about the news.	☐	☐
6. At the end the team continues on working at the office.	☐	☐

 CD 1 - TR. 38

6

What can you say if you are not sure about something? Let's have a look at the possibilities. You have heard some of them in the introducing dialogue:

That's sure: **Ich weiß.** *(I know.)* and **Ich bin sicher.** *(I'm sure.)*
Quite sure: **Ich denke, wir kommen.** *(I think, we'll come.)*
Less sure: **Vielleicht kommen wir.** *(Maybe we'll come.)*
Unsure: **Ich bin nicht sicher.** *(I'm not sure.)* and
Ich weiß nicht. *(I don't know.)*

Read the questions and listen to the reactions.

1. Sind Sie interessiert? – Ich weiß nicht …, ja, vielleicht.
2. Und? Kommen Sie? – Ja, ich denke, wir kommen.

And the following questions are good for raising doubt:
Sind Sie sicher? *(Are you sure?)*, **Wirklich?** *(Really?)*, **Wie bitte?** *(Sorry?)*

How do people react to the crocodile in the Rhine?
Listen carefully to the intonation.

Wirklich? Das ist doch nicht möglich!
Wie bitte? Im Rhein gibt es doch keine Krokodile!

 NICE TO KNOW

The word **doch** has different meanings. In **das ist doch nicht möglich!** it's used to emphasize. In **im Rhein gibt es doch keine Krokodile**, the speaker wants that the dialogue partner agrees.

 CD 1 - TR. 39

Practice makes perfect

CD 1 - TR. 40

NICE TO KNOW

The farewell **Auf Wiederhören.** instead of **Auf Wiedersehen.** *(goodbye.)* is only used on the phone. In a less formal situation you would say **Tschüss.** *(bye).*

7

In an official situation you usually answer the phone by saying the company's name, department, your name and asking how you can help the caller:

- **Lokalredaktion „Blickpunkte", Kowalski am Apparat. Guten Tag!** *(Local editorial office of "Blickpunkte", Kowalski on the phone. Good morning!)*
- **Was kann ich für Sie tun?** *(What can I do for you?)*

The caller also says who he is:

- **Mein Name ist Kundera.** *(My name is Kundera.)*
- **Hier spricht Maria Kundera.** *(This is Maria Kundera.)*

At the end of the call you say:

- **Danke für den Anruf. Auf Wiederhören!** *(Thanks for calling. Goodbye!)*

CD 1 - TR. 41

Listen to how people answer the phone. You'll find the text in the appendix.

8

Aynur is sitting in the editorial office when the phone rings. It's her friend Claudia who wants to know what's up.

The sentences of the dialogue are mixed up. Put them into the correct order. In the word box you'll find some help with the vocabulary.

Was ist los? – What's up?

Das ist doch nicht möglich! – But that isn't possible!

1. *Aynur:* ____ A Sylvia, Thomas und ich suchen ein Krokodil.
2. *Claudia:* ____ B „Blickpunkte". Aynur Hartmann am Apparat.
3. *Aynur:* ____ C Das ist doch nicht möglich! Ein Krokodil im Rhein!
4. *Claudia:* ____ D Wie bitte? Ein Krokodil?
5. *Aynur:* ____ E Hallo, Aynur. Hier ist Claudia. Was machst du? Was
6. *Claudia:*   ist los?
    ____ F Ja. Eine Frau sagt, im Rhein schwimmt ein Krokodil.

Listen to the dialogue. Focus on the quite neutral intonation of Aynur and the expressive reactions of Claudia. Read the dialogue aloud and try to imitate the intonation.

CD 1 - TR. 42

° **9**

Of course, you remember the plural forms in sentences like:
- **Am Rhein gibt es Dörfer, Burgen und Weinberge.**
  (On the Rhine, there are villages, castles and wineyards.)

And what about the rules?
Good news: The definite article, nominative and accusative, is always **die**:   14
- **Die Dörfer und die Burgen am Fluss sind sehr schön.**
  (The villages and the castles on the river are very pretty.)

Depending on the gender and the ending of the singular there are six different endings for the plural: **-e**, **-n**, **-en**, **-er**, **-s** or no ending. The vowels **a, o, u** mostly become **ä, ö, ü**.

gender	singular	plural	ending
masculine or neuter	der Meter	die Meter	—
	der Fluss	die Flüsse	-e
neuter (1 syllable)	das Dorf	die Dörfer	-er
feminin	die Geschichte	die Geschichten	-n
	die Burg	die Burgen	-en
masc./fem./neuter (foreign words)	das Foto	die Fotos	-s

° **10**

Write the plural of the nouns into the gaps. You don't have to write the article, because it's always **die**.

1. die Zeitung _____

2. das Foto _____

3. der Kuchen _____

4. die Frau _____

5. der Fisch _____

6. das Schiff _____

7. das Haus _____

8. das Tier _____

CD 1 - TR. 43

° 11

To answer questions starting with **Wie ist ... ?** *(What's ... like?)* and to describe people, animals or objects you can use adjectives:

- **Wie ist das Krokodil? – Es ist groß, gefährlich und 2 Meter lang.**
  (What is the crocodile like? – It's tall, dangerous and 2 metres long.)
- **Die Häuser sind alt, klein und hässlich.**
  (The houses are old, small and ugly.)

With **sehr** *(very)* you intensify the characteristics:
- **Der Tee ist sehr heiß und süß.** *(The tea is very hot and sweet.)*

CD 1 - TR. 44   Read and listen to some other very common words:

gut *(good)*, schlecht *(bad)*, kalt *(cold)*, neu *(new)*, jung *(young)*, schön *(beautiful)*, bitter *(bitter)*, langweilig *(boring)*.

° 12

Look at the pictures and complete the sentences by filling in the missing adjectives.

1. Markus ist _____, Stefan ist klein.

2. Der Kaffee ist gut und sehr

_____ .

3. Die Straße ist 300 Meter

_____ .

4. Die Geschichte ist nicht gut, sie ist

_____ .

5. Das Haus Nummer 21 ist _____ und hässlich.

°13

CD 1 – TR. 45

In the introducing dialogue you have seen two possibilities to negate sentences and words:

1. To negate a sentence or a part of it you add **nicht**:
- Ich weiß **nicht**. (*I don't know.*)
- Das ist **nicht** möglich! (*That's not possible!*)

2. To negate a noun with an indefinite article you can use **kein, keine, kei-nen** in the singular. The plural is always **keine**.
- Ein Krokodil? Im Rhein gibt es **kein** Krokodil!
  (*A crocodile? In the Rhine, there isn't a crocodile!*)
- Nimmst du einen Kaffee? – Nein, ich nehme **keinen** Kaffee.
  (*Will you take a coffee? – No, I won't take a coffee.*)
- Zwei Schiffe? Ich sehe **keine** Schiffe. (*Two ships? I don't see any ships.*)

NICE TO KNOW

The verb **wissen** (*to know*) is irregular: **ich weiß, du weißt, er weiß, wir wissen, ihr wisst, sie wissen**; polite form: **Sie wissen.**

Write the correct form of **kein** into the sentences.

> keine | kein | keine | keinen

1. Eine Cola? Nein, ich trinke _____ Cola.

2. Ein Hotel? Nein, dort ist _____ Hotel.

3. Wo sind Fische? Ich sehe _____ Fische.

4. Ich möchte bitte _____ Orangensaft.

nicht + ein = kein
nicht + eine = keine
nicht + einen = keinen

°14

Complete the sentences below by using **nicht** or a form of **kein**, for example: **Ich komme nicht.** or **Das ist kein Schiff.**

1. Einen Fisch? Ich esse _____ Fisch.

2. Die Häuser sind _____ alt.

3. Thomas sucht _____ Krokodil.

4. Nein danke, ich möchte _____ Kaffee.

5. Wir fahren _____ nach Benrath.

6. Dort gibt es _____ Tiere.

Finishing up

 CD 1 – TR. 46

More numbers:
20 zwanzig
21 einundzwanzig
22 zweiundzwanzig
23 dreiundzwanzig
30 dreißig
31 einunddreißig
40 vierzig
50 fünfzig
60 sechzig
70 siebzig
80 achtzig
90 neunzig
100 (ein)hundert
101 (ein)hundert-
eins
102 (ein)hundert-
zwei
200 zweihundert
300 dreihundert

° 15

Listen to the numbers and repeat. Note that the ending **-ig** is spoken as **ich**.

20	**21**	**22**	**30**	**37**
zwanzig	einundzwanzig	zweiund-zwanzig	dreißig	siebenunddreißig

60	**70**	**99**	**100**	**175**
sechzig	siebzig	neunund-neunzig	hundert	hundertfünfund-siebzig

Note two things: The numbers 21 – 99 are formed the other way round from English: "ein + und + zwanzig". For 100 you can say **hundert** or **ein-hundert**.

° 16

Now write the numbers into the gaps.

1. Das Haus ist groß: **24** Meter. _____

2. Das sind **100** Euro. _____

3. Die Adresse ist Mozartstraße **63.** _____

4. Die Straße ist **70** Meter lang. _____

5. Der Fluss ist **850** Meter lang. _____

 CD 1 – TR. 47

 NICE TO KNOW

In the dialects of southern Germany and in Austria people tend not to differentiate between **b**, **d**, **g** and **p**, **t**, **k**. All these letters are pronounced equally and have a "soft" sound.

° 17

Have you noticed that some German letters don't always have the same sound? The sounds of **r**, **b**, **d** and **g** vary depending whether they appear at the beginning, in the middle or at the end of a word.
Listen to the example words and try to repeat the words aloud. At the end of a word, an **r** is hardly heard; **b**, **d**, **g** sound like **p**, **t**, **k**. The ending **-ig** sounds like **ich** and the combination **ng** has only one syllable.

1. **R**hein – Häuse**r**   **4.** **g**ut – Ta**g**
2. le**b**en – lie**b**   **5.** zwanzi**g** – rich**t**i**g**
3. Län**d**er – Lan**d**   **6.** E**ng**land – la**ng**

1

You are already able to communicate in various situations. Let's have a look at a summary of the important communication functions in units 1–4.
Here you have a list of the communication functions you already know. Match them with the corresponding sample sentences.

1. *asking for spelling*
2. *ordering something*
3. *speaking about languages*
4. *introducing someone*
5. *asking for the origin*
6. *saying where you live*
7. *declining an offer*
8. *asking for the bill*
9. *identifying yourself on the phone.*
10. *describing someone or something*

____ **A** Ich spreche Englisch und Russisch.

____ **B** Die Dörfer am Rhein sind klein und sehr schön.

____ **C** Die Rechnung, bitte!

____ **D** Woher kommen Sie?

____ **E** Nein, danke. Ich möchte keinen Kaffee.

____ **F** Das ist Sylvia Moser. Sie ist Fotografin.

____ **G** Guten Tag. Hier spricht Aynur Hartmann.

____ **H** Wie schreibt man das?

____ **I** Ich möchte einen Tee mit Zitrone und einen Kuchen.

____ **J** Ich wohne in Düsseldorf, in der Bäckerstraße.

2

 15

Change sentences 1–3 into questions, e. g.: **Ich nehme einen Kaffee. – Nimmst du einen Kaffee?** and sentences 4–6 into questions with an interrogative: **Er wohnt in Köln. – Wo wohnt er?**
Don't forget to write a capital letter at the beginning of your sentence and a question mark at the end. If you don't remember all the rules of German word order, look it up in the grammar overview.

1. Er spricht Deutsch.
2. Ich möchte ein Bier.
3. Es gibt Kaffee und Kuchen.
4. Ich heiße Peter Müller.
5. Mario kommt aus Italien.
6. Rita und Max leben in Frankreich.

Communication

CD 1 – TR. 48

° 3

You have already practised a lot of situations in which you can answer in German. Here you can repeat six different situations.
Listen to the question and then choose the correct answer.

1. A ☐ Nein, ich bin Franzose.
   B ☐ Nein, ich spreche Englisch.
   C ☐ Nein, ich fahre nach Polen.

2. A ☐ Nein, danke.
   B ☐ Ich nehme ein Glas Weißwein.
   C ☐ Ich möchte einen Apfelkuchen.

3. A ☐ Die Stadt ist groß und sehr schön.
   B ☐ In Deutschland.
   C ☐ Ja, ich fahre nach Köln.

4. A ☐ Er fährt nach Deutschland.
   B ☐ Er wohnt in Düsseldorf.
   C ☐ Er ist aus London.

5. A ☐ Tschüss, Klaus!
   B ☐ Was kann ich für Sie tun?
   C ☐ Ich bin Redakteur.

6. A ☐ Ich weiß nicht.
   B ☐ Krokodile sind gefährlich.
   C ☐ Das ist doch nicht möglich!

° 4

Read the questions and choose the correct answer.

1. Was möchten Sie?
   A ☐ Ich hätte gern ein Bier.
   B ☐ Ich lese die Zeitung.
   C ☐ Ich sehe zwei Fische.

2. Welche Sprachen sprichst du?
   A ☐ Ich bin Italiener.
   B ☐ Ich komme aus Polen.
   C ☐ Ich spreche nur Deutsch.

3. Gibt es ein Krokodil im Rhein?
   A ☐ Ja, danke.
   B ☐ Ich weiß nicht.
   C ☐ Das Krokodil ist groß.

5

Do you remember? The present tense of regular verbs is formed with the stem of the infinitive and the personal ending. Here you can find a summary of the rules and repeat the irregular forms, too.
Read the rules and complete the examples by filling in the correct ending or the missing word.

 19, 22

The present tense

1. Regular forms:

ich komm**e** – du komm_____(1) – er, sie, es komm_____(2) –

wir komm**en** – ihr komm**t** – sie komm_____(3) – Sie komm_____(4)

2. A number of verbs change the stem vowel from **e** to **i** or **ie** and **a** to **ä** in the 2nd and 3rd person singular:

ich n**e**hme – du n**i**mmst – er _____(5) or

ich f**a**hre – du _____(6) – er, sie, es _____(7)

3. The verb **sein** is irregular: *Aynur und Sylvia* _____(8) *Kollegen.*

And also **haben** is irregular: *Sylvia* _____(9) *ein Handy.*

NICE TO KNOW

The pronoun **man** *(one, you)* is used together with the 3rd person singular:
Wie schreibt man das? *(How do you write that?)*

6

Don't worry about the German articles. Here you will get a good overview of the forms and rules.
Complete the rules below by filling in the missing forms.

 3, 4, 11

 NICE TO KNOW

Countries are neuter and used without an article: **Deutschland ist schön** – <u>es</u> ist schön.
Remember two exceptions: <u>Die</u> **Schweiz** / <u>Die</u> **Türkei ist schön** – <u>sie</u> ist schön.

The gender of the noun (masculine, feminine or neuter) is indicated by the article. You have:

- Definite articles: **der**, **die**, **das**. Plural:

  _____.

- Indefinite articles: **ein**, _____, **ein**.

- Negated indefinite articles: **kein**, **keine**, _____. Plural: **keine**.

- In the accusative case, only the masculine article changes, e.g.

  _____ and _____.

- No article is used in front of countries and indefinite nouns in the plural.

Grammar

NICE TO KNOW

The plural of feminine words ending in -in is regular -en, but note the spellling: **die Fotografin – die Fotografinnen; die Türkin – die Türkinnen**. The **n** doubles here.

 13, 14, 12

7

Do you remember how to form plural nouns? Depending on the gender and the ending of the singular there are six types of plural endings.
Read the rules and write the plural form of the nouns into the gaps. Don't forget that **a, o, u** often become **ä, ö, ü**.

rule	singular	plural
Masculine and neuter nouns in **-er/-el/-en** don't get a plural ending:	der Computer	_____
The other masculine and neuter nouns get **-e**	das Telefon	_____
Monosyllabic neuter nouns get **-er**	das Glas	_____
Feminine nouns in **-e** get **-n**	die Tasse	_____
The other feminine nouns get **-en**	die Bedienung	_____
Numerous foreign words get **-s**	das Hotel	_____

Unfortunately there are a lot of exceptions from these rules. Look at the Nice to know box below on the left to see the plural of some very common words.

NICE TO KNOW

some exceptions:
der Mann –
 die Männer
die Mutter –
 die Mütter
der Name –
 die Namen
die Nummer –
 die Nummern

8

In each sentence, the pronoun is missing. Choose the correct pronoun and write it in the gaps.

1. Was machst _____ ? – Ich lese.

> wir | du | Sie

2. Das sind Peter und Franz. _____ sind Kollegen.

> Sie | Er | Ich

3. Kommt ihr nach Paris? – _____ kommen nicht.

> Ich | Wir | Es

Vocabulary

9

You have already learnt a lot of words. Here you can practise their use.
One of the four words doesn't fit into the given sentence or category.
Mark the word which you think is wrong.

1. Der Kaffee ist ...
  A ☐ heiß.
  B ☐ bitter.
  C ☐ langweilig.
  D ☐ süß.

2. Stadt
  A ☐ Häuser
  B ☐ Straßen
  C ☐ Brücken
  D ☐ Dörfer

3. Er ... Frankreich.
  A ☐ fährt in
  B ☐ lebt in
  C ☐ ist aus
  D ☐ kommt aus

4. Im Rhein ... Fische.
  A ☐ sind
  B ☐ schwimmen
  C ☐ gibt es
  D ☐ fahren

5. Visitenkarte

  A ☐ Telefonnummer
  B ☐ Hausnummer
  C ☐ Post
  D ☐ Adresse

6. Welche Sprachen sprichst
du? – Ich spreche ...
  A ☐ Polnisch.
  B ☐ Russin.
  C ☐ Deutsch.
  D ☐ Französisch.

7. Dort sind zwei ...
  A ☐ Tiere.
  B ☐ Flüsse.
  C ☐ Turm.
  D ☐ Dörfer.

8. Peter ... ein Glas Wein.
  A ☐ trinkt
  B ☐ nimmt
  C ☐ möchte
  D ☐ liest

10

You can already say a lot of things about yourself in German. Answer the
questions with your personal data. Try to write complete sentences. On
the right you'll find possible answers.

1. Wie heißen Sie?
2. Wie alt sind Sie?
3. Woher kommen Sie?

4. Und wo wohnen Sie?
5. Welche Sprachen sprechen Sie?
6. Was trinken Sie gerne?

Possible answers:
1. Ich heiße Sarah Baker.
2. Ich bin 36.
3. Ich komme aus London, aus England.
4. In London.
5. Ich spreche Englisch, Französisch und Deutsch.
6. Ich trinke gerne Kaffee und Wein.

° **11**

In units 1–4 you have learnt a lot of words and expressions that are suitable for situations in a café, in the office or in town. Here you can revise them.

Look at the pictures. Which sentence fits to which picture? Write the correct number in the box next to each sentence.

1. A ☐ Hier gibt es Getränke.

   B ☐ Hier ist ein Computer.

   C ☐ Dort ist der Bahnhof.

2. A ☐ Wo wohnen Sie?

   B ☐ Was schreiben Sie?

   C ☐ Was möchten Sie?

3. A ☐ Die Rechnung, bitte!

   B ☐ Dort ist ein Fluss.

   C ☐ Die Zeitung heißt „Blickpunkte".

4. A ☐ Eine Geschichte schreiben.

   B ☐ Kirchen fotografieren.

   C ☐ Einen Kuchen essen.

5. A ☐ Bier und Wein.

   B ☐ Häuser, Straßen, Brücken.

   C ☐ Telefon.

12

You've received a postcard from your colleagues! Read it and write the missing words into the gaps.

Hallo ...,

Wie geht's? Wir sind jetzt 10 Tage hier. Das

Land ist _____ schön.

Die Städte Berlin, Hamburg und Düsseldorf

sind _____ und interessant. Wir fotografie-

ren _____, Brücken und Türme.

Jetzt sind _____ im Café. Wir _____

Kaffee.

Und wir essen Torte und Apfelkuchen. Die Ku-

chen _____ super!

Tschüss

Deine Kollegen

13

How many things can you see in each picture? Complete the gaps with the number and the plural of the objects. Write the numbers as words starting with a small letter, e. g. **zwei Radios**.

1 _____

2 _____

3 _____

4 _____

CD 1 - TR. 49

° 14

Here is a summary of the intonation rules for single letters, words and sentences you have learnt in units 1 – 4.

Read the rules and listen to the examples. Now try it yourself and read the words aloud.

> **e** = stressed   e̲ = long   e = short

1. German words can be stressed on the 1st, 2nd, 3rd or 4th syllable.

> F**i**sche – Caf**é** – Min**e**ralwasser – fotograf**ie**ren

2. There is a difference in the pronunciation of long and short vowels.

> n**eh**men – **e**ssen; Zitr**o**ne – k**o**mmen

3. The umlaut **ä** is similar to **e**, **ö** and **ü** are spoken as **o** and **u** by pursing the lips as if you wanted to kiss someone.

> K**ä**sekuchen; **Ö**sterreich; s**ü**dlich

4. A **-b**, **-d** or **-g** at the end of a word is spoken as **p**, **t** or **k**.

> lieb – Land – Tag

5. The ending **-ig** sounds like **ich**.

> vierzig – richtig

6. The **r** is pronounced differently, depending on its position in the word.

> Rhein – sehr

7. In yes /no questions, the voice goes up at the end of the sentence.

> Sind Sie Herr Müller? ↗

8. In questions with an interrogative and in statements, the voice falls at the end of the sentence.

> Wo wohnen Sie? ↘   Der Kaffee ist heiß. ↘

> Now it's time for the first online test!
> Go to **www.pons.de/power** and test what you have learned!

1

Here you'll learn words you'll need when travelling by train, tram, bus or underground.
Listen to the German words for the activities, means of transport and places and write the missing words into the gaps.

 CD 1 – TR. 50

die U-Bahn – *under-ground train*

die Straßenbahn – *tram*

der Fahrkartenauto-mat – *ticket machine*

die Haltestelle – *stop*

das Gleis – *platform*

entwerten – *to cancel (the ticket)*

einsteigen – *to get on*

aussteigen – *to get off*

1. _____

2. _____

3. _____

4. _____

5. _____

6. _____

 NICE TO KNOW

When travelling on buses, trams or suburban trains in German cities, you can either buy a **Einzelfahrkarte** (*single journey ticket*), or, the reduced rate **Mehrfahrtenkarten** (*multiple journey tickets*).

7. _____

8. _____

> aussteigen | einsteigen | entwerten | Fahrkartenautomat |
> Gleis | Haltestelle | Straßenbahn | U-Bahn

Now listen again and say the new words out loud to memorize them. Look at the word box to see the gender of the nouns and the translation.

Listen in!

 CD 1 - TR. 51

 NICE TO KNOW

To indicate the Intercity and Intercity-express trains the abbreviations **IC** or **ICE** can be used.

2

Let's have a look at the information you can get from a timetable which shows three different connections from Düsseldorf Main Station to Frankfurt Airport.

4.31	◉ 6		Köln Hbf	5.41	5.47	EC	26	⁷¹	7.53	Mo - Fr	▬
6.02	IC 513	▣	Mainz Hbf	8.11	8.19	⊙ 8			8.46	Mo - Sa	05
6.11	RE 10002		Köln Hbf	6.42	6.54	IC	609	▣	8.55	täglich	01
6.28	ICE 823	¹¹							9.00	täglich	01
6.44	IR 2213	▣	Mainz Hbf	8.04	8.10	RB 13515			8.38	Mo - Fr	▬

Listen to questions and information about the three connections on the timetable. Then write the missing words into the gaps.

> um | **Intercity** | direkt | **umsteigen** | **Regional-Express** | S-Bahn

1. Wann fährt der _____ aus Düsseldorf ab?

2. Um **6.**02 Uhr. Man muss in Mainz umsteigen und die _____ nehmen.

3. Der _____ um **6.**11 Uhr fährt nach Köln.

4. Der ICE kommt _____ **9.**00 Uhr in Frankfurt an.

5. Man muss nicht _____ .

6. Die Verbindung ist _____ .

 CD 1 - TR. 52

3

The fastest way to Benrath (where the crocodile was seen) is by public transport. That's why Thomas, Aynur and Sylvia hurry to the main station. Now they are in the station hall studying the timetable and asking at the information desk which tickets they'll need.
Listen to the dialogue and look at the pictures. They will help you to get the general sense. Later we'll look for details.

4

 CD 1 – TR. 52

Let's look a little more closely at the dialogue for some details.
Listen to the dialogue again and decide if the statements below are true
(T) or false (F). In the appendix you'll find the tapescript.

	true	false
1. There isn't a direct connection to Benrath.	☐	☐
2. Thomas and his colleagues decide to take the S-Bahn.	☐	☐
3. The journey to Benrath will take six minutes.	☐	☐
4. Aynur is travelling with the same ticket as Sylvia and Thomas.	☐	☐
5. The tickets are available from a ticket machine.	☐	☐
6. The train leaves from Platform 15.	☐	☐

5

 CD 1 – TR. 53

 NICE TO KNOW

In the introductory dialogue, there were some very useful questions you'll
need when you're travelling by public transport.
Read and listen to the questions. What do they mean? Match the translation to the corresponding questions.

1. Wie spät ist es? ____ **A** *Where can we buy the ticket?*

2. Wann fährt der nächste Zug nach
Benrath? ____ **B** *How long will it take?*

____ **C** *What time is it?*

3. Müssen wir umsteigen? ____ **D** *Do we have to change trains?*

4. Um wie viel Uhr kommen
wir an? ____ **E** *Which platform does the train
leave from?*

5. Wie lange fahren wir? ____ **F** *What time will we arrive?*

6. Wo können wir das Ticket kaufen? ____ **G** *When's the next train to
Benrath?*

7. Auf welchem Gleis fährt
der Zug ab?

In Austria and in Sou-
thern Germany, you
may hear **Wann geht
der nächste Zug nach
Wien?**, even though
gehen, when used to
indicate movement,
normally means *to
walk.*

Practice makes perfect

NICE TO KNOW

Note that, using the example **10.15 Uhr**, the **Uhr** is written after the time, but in spoken German, you say: **zehn Uhr fünfzehn**.

6

1. If you want to know what time it is, you ask:
- **Wie spät** ist es? or **Wie viel Uhr** ist es? *(What time is it?)*
  and you answer: **Es ist** 10 **Uhr.** *(It's 10 o'clock.)*

2. If you want to know the time when someone will come or leave you, ask:
- **Um wie viel Uhr** kommst du? *(What time are you coming?)* and answer: **Um 10.15 Uhr.** *(At 10.15.)*
- **Wann** fährt der Zug nach Köln? *(When does the train to Cologne leave?)* and answer: **Um 10.23 Uhr.** *(At 10.23.)*

3. If you want to know how long the journey is, you ask:
- **Wie lange** fahren wir? *(How long will we travel for?)*
  and answer: Eine **Stunde** und 20 **Minuten.** *(One hour and 20 minutes.)*

Complete the sentences and write the missing words into the gaps.

> Minuten | spät | Uhr | um | lange | Stunde | wie viel

1. Um _____ Uhr kommen die Kollegen?

2. Wie _____ fährst du? – Nur 15 _____ .

3. Ich denke, Peter ist _____ 8 Uhr hier.

7

You already know the German words for some means of transport. Which means of transport do you see in the pictures? Listen and write the numbers into the gaps after the names. The first has been done for you.

1. die Straßenbahn 4, das Taxi _____ ,

2. die U-Bahn _____ , die S-Bahn _____ ,

3. der Bus _____ , der Zug _____

4. das Schiff _____ , das Flugzeug _____

Typical questions are:
- **Nehmen wir den Bus oder die Straßenbahn?**
(Shall we take the bus or tram?)
- **Fahren wir mit dem Bus oder mit der Straßenbahn?**
  (Shall we go by bus or tram?)
Masculine and neuter nouns use **mit dem**; feminine **mit der**.

8

 CD 1 – TR. 57

In the introductory dialogue you have the sentence:

Um wie viel Uhr **kommen** wir in Benrath **an**?

(What time do we arrive in Benrath?)

The infintive of the verb **ankommen** *(to arrive)* is written as one word. But to form a correct sentence e. g. in the present tense the prefix **an-** is separated from the main part of the verb **kommen** and placed at the end of the sentence:

Wir **kommen** um 8 Uhr **an**. *(We'll arrive at 8 o'clock.)*

Here are other examples. Note that the prefix is always stressed:

aussteigen *(to get off)*, **abfahren** *(to leave)*, **zurückkommen** *(to return)*

Fill in the gaps with the correct form of the verb.

aussteigen: Wir **(1)** _____ in Bilk **(2)** _____ .

zurückkommen: Wann **(3)** _____ du **(4)** _____?

abfahren: Wann **(5)** _____ der Bus **(6)** _____?

The separable prefixes you already know are: **ab-**, **an-**, **auf-**, a**us-**, **ein-**, **hin-**, **um-** and **zurück-**. Note that these little prefixes can change the meaning of a verb completely. Look at the word box for more examples.

hinfahren – *to go there (by means of transport)*

zurückfahren – *to go back*

hingehen – *to go there (on foot)*

zurückgehen – *to go back*

einsteigen – *to get on*

umsteigen – *to change (train, bus or tram)*

9

In this unit you have worked with a lot of words which have to do with **fahren**. Do you remember verbs and nouns which contain the stem -**fahr**-? Read the words on the left. Then match the corresponding translation. To memorize the words repeat them out loud and look at the word box.

 NICE TO KNOW

Abfahren and **zurückfahren** have a separable prefix:
Der Zug fährt um 10 Uhr ab.
Ich komme um 18 Uhr zurück.

1. die Fahrt   ___ A *departure*

2. die Abfahrt   ___ B *driver*

3. zurückfahren   ___ C *journey*

4. der Fahrplan   ___ D *return ticket*

5. der Fahrkartenschalter   ___ E *single ticket*

6. die Einzelfahrkarte   ___ F *ticket machine*

7. der Fahrer   ___ G *ticket office*

8. die Hin- und Rückfahrkarte   ___ H *timetable*

9. abfahren   ___ I *to leave*

10. der Fahrkartenautomat   ___ J *to return*

CD 1 - TR. 58

KÖNNEN

kann	können
kannst	könnt
kann	können

MÜSSEN

muss	müssen
musst	müsst
muss	müssen

WOLLEN

will	wollen
willst	wollt
will	wollen

° 10

Read and listen to these sentences with modal auxiliaries:

Was **kann** ich für Sie **tun**? *(What can I do for you?)*
Ich **muss** hier **aussteigen**. *(I have to get off here.)*
Wir **wollen** nach Benrath **fahren**. *(We want to go to Benrath.)*

Some rules:
1. The modals **können** *(to be able to, can)*, **müssen** *(to have to, must)*
   and **wollen** *(to want to)* are conjugated and they always go with
   another verb, which is always an infinitive.
2. Word order: The modal is in the usual verb position: The infinitve form
   of the second verb is at the very end.

Complete the sentences by writing the words into the gaps.
Look at the word box if you aren't sure about the forms.

> kann | müssen | wollt | kaufen | umsteigen

Wohin (1) _____ ihr fahren?

Wir (2) _____ in Köln (3) _____.

Wo (4) _____ ich Fahrkarten (5) _____?

The most important meanings are:
können: *possibility, ability or polite request.*
müssen: *necessity (obligation) or strong request.*
wollen: *willingness or intention.*

° 11

 § 10

Here you can practise the modals **können**, **müssen** and **wollen**. Rewrite
the sentences by using the modal verb in brackets.
Think of the correct form of the modal and the word order. In sentences
with modal auxiliaries, the verb in the infinitive form is at the very end.

1. Ich komme nicht. *(können)*
2. Peter nimmt den Bus. *(wollen)*
3. Sie fahren mit dem IC um 11 Uhr. *(können)*
4. Ich steige hier aus. *(müssen)*
5. Wohin fährst du? *(wollen)*

12

CD 1 - TR. 59

There are various ways of expressing that you want to buy a railway ticket at the ticket office. And, of course, there are different tickets, too.
Listen to the sentences and write the missing words into the gaps. Look at the word box if you need help with vocabulary.

eine Hin- und Rück-
fahrkarte –
a return ticket

eine Fahrkarte 2. Klas-
se (zweiter Klasse) –
second-class ticket

eine Fahrkarte 1. Klas-
se (erster Klasse) –
first-class ticket

1. Ich möchte eine Hin- und **(1)** _____ nach München.

2. Zwei Fahrkarten 2. **(2)** _____ nach Bonn, hin und

   (3) _____ .

hin und zurück –
return (ticket /s)

eine einfache Fahrt –
one way /(single) trip

3. Eine **(4)** _____ Fahrt nach Köln und einen

   IC-**(5)** _____ .

der IC-Zuschlag –
additional charge for Intercity trains

4. Drei Fahrkarten, bitte. Zwei **(6)** _____ und ein Kind.

zwei Erwachsene –
two adults

das Kind – *child*

> einfache | Erwachsene | Klasse | Rückfahrkarte | zurück | Zuschlag

When you are travelling by public transport (bus, tram, underground or S-Bahn) you can buy **eine Einzelfahrkarte** (*single journey ticket*) or **eine Mehrfahrtenkarte** (*multiple journey ticket*).

And finally: There are three different places where you can buy tickets: **am Fahrkartenschalter** (*at the ticket office*), **am Fahrkartenautomaten** (*at the ticket machine*), **beim Fahrer** (*from the driver*).

13

NICE TO KNOW

Tickets bought from the driver have already been cancelled. Tickets bought from machines or ticket offices usually have to be stamped at the cancelling machines inside the trains or in stations.

In these rows of letters, there are hidden sentences that you can use when buying tickets. Split the chains of letters so that the sentences are correct. After doing that repeat the sentences out loud.

1. ZweiFahrkartenhinundzurücknachKöln.

2. WokannichFahrkartenfürdieS-Bahnkaufen?

3. IchmöchteeineEinzelfahrkarte.

4. MussichdieFahrkarteentwerten?

5. IchbraucheeinenZuschlagfürdenICE.

6. EineeinfacheFahrtzweiterKlassenachBonn.

CD 1 – TR. 60

 NICE TO KNOW

The word **das Gleis** indicates the platform and also the rail track. Another very common word for *platform* is **der Bahnsteig**.

 14

Here are some useful questions you can ask when you are travelling by public transport:

1. Wo muss ich aussteigen? *(Where do I have to get off?)*
2. Ist die nächste Haltestelle „Benrath"? *(Is the next stop "Benrath?")*
3. Hält der Zug auch in Bilk? *(Does the train stop in Bilk?)*
4. Muss ich umsteigen? *(Do I have to change trains?)*
5. Auf welchem Gleis fährt der Zug nach Köln ab? *(Which platform does the train to Cologne leave from?)*
6. Brauche ich einen Zuschlag? *(Do I need to pay extra for this train?)*

 CD 1 – TR. 61

Listen to three answers and write the number of the question which fits each answer.

answer **(a)** question ____

answer **(b)** question ____

answer **(c)** question ____

15

Choose the correct word in each sentence.

1. Entschuldigung, ich *brauche / kann / muss* nicht kommen.
2. Wann fährt die S-Bahn nach Benrath *ab / an / hin*?
3. Eine Fahrkarte nach München, *einfach / Hinfahrt / hin* und zurück.
4. Wir müssen am Fahrkartenschalter *kaufen / fragen / entwerten*.
5. Der Intercity *geht / fährt / hält* nicht in Benrath.
6. Die Fahrt mit der U-Bahn dauert nur 12 *Minuten / Euro / Uhr*.

16

These sentences are mixed up. Put the words in the correct order. Then repeat the sentences aloud.

1. ab. | 16 | ICE nach München | Gleis | auf | Der | fährt
2. Peter | Uhr | Um | an. | kommt | wie | viel
3. zurück? | Fährst | 10 Uhr | du | um
4. nicht | Ich | fahren. | will | mit der Straßenbahn
5. Fahrkarten | kaufen? | können | Wo | wir
6. umsteigen? | Köln | Muss | in | ich

° 1

 CD 1 – TR. 62

What can you do in your leisure time? Look at the pictures and listen to what the activities are called in German. Then read them aloud.

1. schwim-
men
2. Musik hö-
ren
3. spazieren
gehen
4. fernsehen
5. in den Zir-
kus gehen

6. schlafen
7. ins Kino
gehen
8. Deutsch
lernen
9. joggen
10. Tennis
spielen

° 2

 CD 1 – TR. 63

Which situations do the pictures portray? Listen to the expressions and then match them to the corresponding picture.
You have probably noticed that the differences between the sentences depend on the modal verb used.
Translations of the sentences are in the word box.

**Er will nicht schwim-
men.** – *He doesn't
want to swim.*

**Er kann nicht
schwimmen** –
He can't swim.

**Er soll nicht schwim-
men.** –
He shouldn't swim.

**Er darf nicht schwim-
men.** – *He isn't allowed
to swim.*

**Er mag nicht schwim-
men.** –
*He doesn't like
swimming.*

_____ **A** Er will nicht schwimmen.

_____ **B** Er kann nicht schwimmen.

_____ **C** Er soll nicht schwimmen.

_____ **D** Er darf nicht schwimmen.

_____ **E** Er mag nicht schwimmen.

CD 1 - TR. 64

3

You already know that today Sylvia is going to Benrath with Aynur and Thomas to look for the crocodile. Today is Tuesday. Let's have a look at Sylvia's further plans for today and the next few days.

Listen to what Sylvia's doing today and during the rest of the week.

Did you understand all the sentences?

Here they are, together with some help with the vocabulary:

<u>Heute</u> fährt Sylvia nach Benrath. *(today)*

Heute <u>Abend</u> geht sie in den <u>Sportverein</u>. *(evening – sports club)*

Am Mittwoch geht sie vielleicht in den Zirkus.

Am Donnerstag muss sie Claudia <u>anrufen</u>. *(to call)*

Am Freitag muss sie nicht <u>arbeiten</u>. *(to work)*

Um <u>Viertel vor eins</u> spielt sie Tennis *(a quarter to 1 p.m.)*

Am Sonntag <u>geht</u> sie mit Dieter <u>spazieren</u>. *(to go for a walk)*

Am <u>Nachmittag</u> geht sie ins Café. *(afternoon)*

4 CD 1 – TR. 65

For more than two hours the team has been searching for the crocodile on the banks of the Rhine in Benrath. Now they are bored and are looking for Sylvia who wandered off to take some pictures. They are making suggestions about what to do next in order to keep up the newspaper story. Listen to the dialogue and look at the pictures. They will help you to understand the gist.

5 CD 1 – TR. 65

In the introductory dialogue, Thomas, Sylvia and Aynur made various suggestions about what to do next and where to go.
Let's look a little more closely at the expressions which introduce suggestions and how to react to them. Listen to the dialogue again. Write the expressions below into the right part of the table. Can you guess the meaning of the expressions?

1. Making suggestions	2. Reacting to suggestions

A Ich habe eine Idee.
B Einverstanden!
C Was haltet ihr davon?
D Kommst du mit?

E Gute Idee!
F Ich habe keine Zeit.
G Was meinst du?
H Ja, gerne.

Practice makes perfect

 CD 1 – TR. 66

° 6

If you want to know what someone is doing, you can ask:
- **Was machst du jetzt / heute / am** Sonntag / **am Wochenende / um** 15 **Uhr**? *(What are you doing now / today / on Sunday / at the weekend / at 3 p.m.?)*

... and answer:
- **Ich spiele** Tennis. *(I'm playing tennis.)* / **Ich sehe fern.** *(I'm watching TV.)* / **Ich gehe spazieren.** *(I'm going for a walk.)* / **Ich gehe in** den Sport-verein. *(I'm going to the sports club.)* / **Ich lerne** Deutsch. *(I'm learning German.)* / **Ich höre Musik.** *(I'm listening to music.)*

To answer the question **wohin?** *(where to?)* you use **in** + accusative:
- in den Sportverein, in den Zirkus
- in die Disco, in die Stadt
- ins Kino, ins Museum, ins Café (**in + das** becomes **ins**).

 CD 1 – TR. 67

Listen to a short conversation. Who is doing what? Write the right words into the gaps.

Karin geht in die **(1)** _____ .

Marco geht vielleicht ins **(2)** _____

und Doris geht in den **(3)** _____ .

° 7

Fill in the gaps with **in die**, **in den** or **ins**. The picture will help you to remember the rules about how to use the preposition **in**.

NICE TO KNOW

Wohin?

der Zirkus	in den Zirkus
die Disco	in die Disco
das Kino	ins Kino

1. Fahren wir zurück **(1)**_____ Büro?

2. Fährst du **(2)**_____ Bäckerstraße?

3. Gehen wir **(3)**_____ Museum oder **(4)**_____ Park?

4. Ich gehe heute nicht **(5)**_____ Schule.

5. Kommt Peter auch **(6)**_____ Café?

6. Ich fahre jetzt **(7)**_____ Hotel zurück.

CD 1 – TR. 68

§ 19

8

In these sentences personal pronouns with the accusative are used:

- Siehst du Peter? – Nein, ich sehe **ihn** nicht.
  (Can you see Peter? – No, I can't see him.)
- Ist der Kuchen für **dich**? – Ja, er ist für **mich**.
  (Is the cake for you? – Yes, it's for me.)

Look at the forms in bold script. They are new to you. The others are the same as the nominative personal pronouns.

	singular	**plural**
1st person	mich *(me)*	uns *(us)*
2nd person	dich *(you) (familiar form)* Sie *(polite form)*	euch *(you) (familiar form)* Sie *(polite form)*
3rd person	ihn, sie, es *(him, her, it)*	sie *(them)*

Choose the right pronoun and write it into the gap.

> sie | dich | euch | uns | mich | es

1. Anna, hier ist ein Anruf für _____!

2. Das Bier ist bitter. Ich trinke _____ nicht.

3. Sind die Karten für euch? – Ja, sie sind für _____.

9

The personal pronoun is missing in all sentences. Choose the correct one and write it into the gap.

> dich | mich | sie | ihn | uns | Sie | euch | es

1. Wo ist Anna? – Ich sehe _____ nicht.

2. Ist die Zeitung für dich? – Ja, sie ist für _____.

3. Wen soll ich fragen? Den Redakteur? – Ja, Sie können

_____ fragen.

4. Möchtest du _____ fotografieren? – Ja, ich

fotografiere euch.

5. Wollen Sie das Haus kaufen? – Nein, ich kaufe

_____ nicht.

Practice makes perfect

° 10

Sometimes there are several ways of telling the time in an informal way. For 10.40 Uhr you can say **zwanzig vor elf** or **zehn nach halb elf**.

What time is it? It's ... Listen and repeat.

These are the words you need to tell the time in an informal way:
• zehn **vor** zehn *(to)*
• fünf **nach** zwei *(past / after)*
• **Viertel** vor / nach zwei *(a quarter)*
• **! halb** neun *(half past eight!)*

 NICE TO KNOW

The words **morgens**, **vormittags** etc. are often used together with the time, expressed informally. You say e.g. **neun Uhr morgens** *(9 a.m.)* and **neun Uhr abends** *(9 p.m.)* to clarify what time you exactly mean.

° 11

Let's have a look at how to express the time of day:
• **Am Mittag** gehen wir ins Café. *(At around noon we are going to the café.)*
• Peter kommt **am Morgen**.   *(Peter is coming in the morning.)*

To answer the question **wann?** you use the preposition **am** before the time of day. The only exception is **in der Nacht** *(in the night)*.
You don't need a preposition with the adverbs **heute** *(today)*, **gestern** *(yesterday)*, **morgen** *(tomorrow)*:
• **Heute Nacht** fahre ich nach Italien. *(Tonight I'm going to Italy.)*

Listen and fill in the gaps in order to complete the cycle of a day from the morning until night.

_____, Vormittag, _____, Nachmittag, _____, Nacht

In German you can express whether an activity is done only once or regularly e.g. every morning, every noon etc. In the second case you say e.g. **morgens**, **vormittags**, **mittags** etc. So, you replace the capital letter with a lower case and add an **s** to the end of the word.

°12

Read the explanation of the German word which is hidden in the row of letters. Find the word and mark it.

1. The first working day of the week:
mkiudymontagdegij

2. German word for "Thursday":
geldonnerstagmanthleigk

3. "Wednesday" in German:
dopnermittwochigürsk

4. The German word for "weekend":
stewochenendefänngylam

5. The name of this day sounds very similar to the English:
penchöwifreitaghistulam

6. German word for "Saturday":
kortquesamstagbäynslky

7. On this day you normally don't work:
vürcmssonntagösengitalbont

8. "Tuesday" in German:
daanvopedienstagüfento

After you have marked the names of the weekdays and the German word for "weekend" look at the "Nice to know" box to get more information about their use.

 NICE TO KNOW

In Northern and Middle Germany, people use the word **Sonnabend** instead of **Samstag** (*Saturday*).

 NICE TO KNOW

To answer the question **wann?** you use **am**:
Ich komme am Montag. Am Wochenende fahre ich nach Köln.
If you want to say *every Monday, every Tuesday* etc. you say:
montags, dienstags etc.
Montags spiele ich Tennis.
Gender: **der Montag, der Dienstag, ... der Sonntag, das Wochenende**

°13

The following words are mixed up. Put the words into chronological order. For example:
Monday – Tuesday – Wednesday or 10 past 10 – a quarter past 10 etc.

1. Montag | Freitag | Sonntag | Mittwoch | Donnerstag | Dienstag | Samstag
2. sieben Uhr abends | elf Uhr vormittags | acht Uhr morgens
3. Abend | Morgen | Mittag | Nachmittag | Nacht | Vormittag
4. fünf nach zwei | halb drei | zwei Uhr | drei Uhr | Viertel nach zwei
5. Viertel vor vier | Viertel nach vier | halb fünf | halb vier | vier Uhr

CD 1 - TR. 71

DÜRFEN

darf	dürfen
darfst	dürft
darf	dürfen

MÖGEN

mag	mögen
magst	mögt
mag	mögen

SOLLEN

soll	sollen
sollst	sollt
soll	sollen

° 14

In German, there are six modal auxiliaries. The rules you already know for **können**, **müssen** and **wollen** (Unit 5) are also valid for **dürfen** (*to be allowed to, may*), **mögen** (*to like*) and **sollen** (*should, shall, to be supposed to*).
Read and listen to the examples:

Hier **darf** man nicht **weitergehen**. (*You're not allowed to go further here.*)
Ich **mag** nicht Fußball **spielen**. (*I don't like playing soccer.*)
Wo **sollen** wir das Krokodil **suchen**? (*Where should we look for the crocodile?*)

Look at the boxes on the left. Then write the correct form of the modals into the gaps. Use the words in the brackets.

1. Meine Mutter sagt, ich _____ keinen Alkohol trinken. (*sollen*)

2. Peter, du _____ keinen Kuchen essen! (*dürfen*)

3. Ich gehe ins Kino, aber Anna _____ nicht mitkommen. (*mögen*)

 10

 NICE TO KNOW

Mögen is often used alone: **Ich mag Bier.** (*I like beer.*). Together with a second verb it is especially used in negative and interrogative sentences.

° 15

Look at the pictures and read the sentences. Mark the statement which fits the situation in the picture.

1. ____ A Man muss nicht schwimmen.
____ B Man darf nicht schwimmen.
____ C Man mag nicht schwimmen.

2. ____ A Er kann arbeiten.
____ B Er will arbeiten.
____ C Er mag nicht arbeiten.

3. ____ A Birgit, du sollst kein Bier trinken.
____ B Birgit, du magst kein Bier trinken.
____ C Birgit, du kannst Bier trinken.

4. ____ A Ich muss einen Kuchen haben, und du?
____ B Ich will einen Kuchen haben, und du?
____ C Ich soll einen Kuchen haben, und du?

The most important meanings of the modals are:
dürfen - *permission*   **nicht mögen** - *dislike*
nicht dürfen - *ban, prohibition*   **müssen** - *necessity, request*
können - *possibility, ability, polite request*   **sollen** - *disposition, supposition*
mögen - *like*   **wollen** - *will, intention*

° **1**

Talking about hobbies and leisure-time activities is a good ice-breaker for people who don't know each other very well. Let's look at five small scenes. Listen and read to what people are asking and answering. Just listen to understand the general meaning. By focusing on the pictures it will be easy to guess what the hobby (**das Hobby**) is or what people are doing in their leisure time (**in der Freizeit**).

 CD 1 – TR. 72

 NICE TO KNOW

Die Fantastischen Vier is the name of a quite famous music group. The four musicians are from Stuttgart and were the first who made the German-speaking Hip Hop popular.

Was machst du in deiner Freizeit?

Hast du ein Hobby?

Ja, Computer und Internet.

Ich fahre gern Fahrrad.

Ich gehe oft ins Konzert. Und Sie?

Magst du Musik?

Gehen Sie oft ins Museum?

Ich auch. Ich gehe einmal in der Woche ins Konzert.

Ja, am liebsten höre ich „Die Fantastischen Vier".

Ja. Ich interessiere mich sehr für Kunst.

Listen in!

CD 1 - TR. 73

2

What do you celebrate? What do you give as a present? Who do you visit? Build up your vocabulary and learn some new words! Read and listen to the words given below and write them into the correct part of the table. After doing that repeat the words and try to memorize them.

1. What do you celebrate?	2. What do you give as apresent?	3. Who do you visit?
_____	_____	_____
_____	_____	_____
_____	_____	_____

A Freunde – *friends*

B eine Party – *a party*

C ein Kartenspiel – *a card game*

D ein Fahrrad – *a bike*

E deine Tante – *your aunt*

F ein Bilderbuch – *a picture book*

G eine CD – *a CD*

H meine Tochter – *my daughter*

CD 1 - TR. 74

3

Thomas, Sylvia and Aynur have finished their daily work at the office and are now ready to go home. Before leaving the office, they talk about what they are going to do that evening and about their hobbies in general. Sylvia has already mentioned that she's planning to go to the sports club and Aynur wants to know some details.

Just listen to the dialogue to get a feeling for the situation and don't worry about any words you don't know.

If you want to read the tapescript, look at the appendix.

4

CD 1 - TR. 74

Listen again to the dialogue and focus on the information about Thomas', Sylvia's and Aynur's hobbies and their activities this evening. Are the statements below true (T) or false (F)?

	true	false
1. Aynur likes cooking and listening to music.	☐	☐
2. Thomas' hobbies are sports like biking.	☐	☐
3. It's the birthday of Sylvia's aunt.	☐	☐
4. Thomas will have a party this evening.	☐	☐
5. Sylvia is going to Berlin to have some fun.	☐	☐
6. Aynur will meet a friend.	☐	☐

5

CD 1 - TR. 75

Let's take a closer look at some structures which are in the introductory dialogue. What can you ask if you want to know what someone is doing in their leisure time or if they have a hobby? How can you answer? Read and listen to the German questions, answers and phrases. Then match the correct translation to the corresponding sentence.

1. Was machst du in deiner Freizeit? ____

2. Hast du ein Hobby?

3. Gehst du regelmäßig in den Sport-verein?

4. Ich surfe gern im Internet.

5. Ich interessiere mich für Kunst und Kultur.

6. Meine Frau und ich besuchen oft Ausstellungen.

7. Am liebsten treffe ich Freunde. ____

8. Wir gehen zusammen aus, wir ko-chen oder wir hören Musik.

9. Ich wünsche euch viel Spaß!

A *We go out together, we cook or we listen to music.*

B *I like to surf the internet.*

C *Do you regularly go to the sports club?*

D *I wish you a lot of fun!*

E *My wife and I often go to ex-hibitions.*

F *Do you have a hobby?*

G *I'm interested in art and cul-ture.*

H *What do you do in your free time?*

I *Most of all I like meeting friends.*

 NICE TO KNOW

If you want to say *en-joy yourself!* it's very common to use **viel Spaß!** instead of the long phrase **Ich wünsche dir /euch viel Spaß!**

6

Read the following sample sentences:

- Was schenkst du **dem Vater**?
- Ich will **einer Kollegin** die Stadt zeigen.
- Sie bringt **mir** eine neue CD mit.

The marked words are in the dative case and answer questions with **wem?** *(to whom?)*.

 3

1. Dative singular:

gender	definite article	indefinite article	"kein"
masculine	**dem** Freund	ein**em** Freund	kein**em** Freund
neuter	**dem** Kind	ein**em** Kind	kein**em** Kind
feminine	**der** Tante	ein**er** Tante	kein**er** Tante

2. Dative plural:

 NICE TO KNOW

Be careful, the German dative case is not always reflected in the English translation.

gender	definite article	indefinite article	"kein"
all	**den** Freund**en**	Freund**en**	kein**en** Freund**en**
	den Kind**ern**	Kind**ern**	kein**en** Kind**ern**
	den Tant**en**	Tant**en**	kein**en** Tant**en**

All nouns end in **-n** except foreign words. These end in **-s**: **den** Kino**s**.

3. Dative personal pronouns:

	singular	plural
1st person	**mir** *(to me)*	**uns** *(to us)*
2nd person	**dir** *(to you)*	**euch** *(to you)*
3rd person	**ihm** *(to him)*, **ihr** *(to her)*, **ihm** *(to it)*	**ihnen** *(to them)*
polite form	**Ihnen** *(to you)*	**Ihnen** *(to you)*

7

NICE TO KNOW

The prepositions **mit** *(with)* and **nach** *(after)* govern the dative case.

Let's practise the dative case. Read the questions and complete the answers by filling in the correct dative article. In sentences 1 to 3 you need the indefinite article, 4 and 5 use the definite article.

1. Mit wem spielt Lisa? – Mit _____ Kind.

2. Wem schenkst du das Buch? – Ich schenke es _____ Freundin.

3. Mit wem spricht Peter? – Mit _____ Freund.

4. Wem schreibst du? – Ich schreibe _____ Kolleginnen.

5. Wann kommst du? – Nach _____ Sportverein.

8

What do you do in your free time? What's your hobby? Look at the pictures and listen to the answers. In the word box you can find translations of the German expressions.

 CD 1 – TR. 76

1. to surf the internet
2. to visit exhibitions
3. to meet friends
4. to cook
5. to go out
6. gymnastics
7. to go to concerts
8. to ride a bike
9. to play cards
10. to dance

1. im Internet surfen   **2.** Ausstellungen besuchen   **3.** Freunde treffen   **4.** kochen   **5.** ausgehen

6. Gymnastik   **7.** in Konzerte gehen   **8.** Fahrrad fahren   **9.** Karten spielen   **10.** tanzen

Now you know possible answers if someone asks you
- **Was machst du in deiner Freizeit? / Was machen Sie in Ihrer Freizeit?**
  (What do you do in your free time?) or
- **Was ist dein / Ihr Hobby?** *(What's your hobby?)*

 NICE TO KNOW

The verb **ausgehen** *(to go out)* is very common: **ich gehe aus** means that you'll leave your home to have some fun e.g. at a restaurant, a bar, a disco or a concert.

9

Let's talk a little bit about free time. Read and listen to the questions on the left. Which answer fits? Match it to the corresponding question.

1. Hast du ein Hobby?

2. Ich gehe gern in die Disco. Und Sie?

3. Was macht ihr in eurer Freizeit?

4. Magst du Tennis und Fußball?

5. Gehst du am Abend oft aus?

6. Besuchst du gern Ausstellungen?

___ A *Ich mag Discos nicht.*

___ B *Ja, drei oder vier Abende in der Woche.*

___ C *Ja, sehr gern. Ich mag Kunst.*

___ D *Ja, ich surfe regelmäßig im Internet.*

___ E *Nein, ich interessiere mich nicht für Sport.*

___ F *Wir fahren gern Fahrrad.*

 CD 1 – TR. 77

 NICE TO KNOW

Instead of **Fahrrad** *(bicycle)* you can also use the short form **Rad** *(bike)*, e.g. **ich fahre gern Rad.**

Practice makes perfect

° 10

In the introductory dialogue you have learned different ways of expressing how often someone does something. You can ask:

Wie oft gehst du ins Konzert? *(How often do you go to a concert?)*
Gehst du **regelmäßig** in den Sportverein? *(Do you regularly go to the sports club?)*

For your answer you can use one of the following adverbs:
Ich gehe **immer** *(always)*, **regelmäßig** *(regularly)*, **oft** *(often)*, **manchmal** *(sometimes)*, **selten** *(seldom)*, **nie** *(never)*, **einmal in der Woche** *(once a week)*, **zweimal am Tag** *(twice a day)* ins Café.

Let's practise the new words. Listen and fill in the missing words.

1. Ich gehe **(1)**_____ in der Woche ins Kino.

2. Samstags gehen wir **(2)**_____ in die Disco und

(3)_____ in ein Restaurant.

> Focus on the word order in the sentences of the exercise:
> In sentence 1 (normal word order) the adverb comes after the verb, in sentence 2 (inverted word order) it comes after the personal pronoun.

° 11

There are various ways of expressing likes or dislikes. You can use
• the expression **ich interessiere mich für** *(I'm interested in)* followed by an accusative,
• the word **gern** (translated by *I like* + verb) together with the verb that indicates an activity,
• **ich mag** *(I like)* followed by a noun.

For example, if you like – or don't like – music, you can say:

Ich interessiere mich für Musik. – Ich interessiere mich nicht für Musik.
Ich höre gern Musik. – Ich höre nicht gern Musik.
Ich mag Musik. – Ich mag Musik nicht.

Listen to three very short pieces about the activities below. Choose the tick if the person likes doing the activity, or a cross if they don't.

	✓	✗
1. Freunde treffen	☐	☐
2. Kunst	☐	☐
3. Kuchen essen	☐	☐

12

CD 1 – TR. 81

It's time to practise pronunciation. We'll focus on the letter **s** and how it changes its sound depending on the letters next to it.
Listen to how the letter **s** sounds in combination with other letters.

1. **sch**enken, Ge**sch**enk, wün**sch**en
2. **St**unde, Au**st**ellung
3. Spaß, **sp**ielen, Karten**sp**iel
4. **St**unde – Kun**st**
5. **Sp**iel – E**sp**resso
6. Das **Sp**iel ist fantastisch!

---

s + t and s + p:
s in front of **t** or **p** sounds like **sch**, but only at the beginning of the word or at the beginning of a syllable: **Sp**iel, Au**st**ellung.

In all other cases this letter combination sounds like **st** and **sp**: Kun**st**

13

CD 1 – TR. 82

 20

 NICE TO KNOW

There is only one little irregularity: the second **e** of **euer** (*your*) is dropped before adding an ending, e.g. **eure Mutter, mit euren Freunden**.

Every time you talk about belongings, you need possessive pronouns like *my, your, his*. First of all let's have a look at all possessive pronouns without their endings:

1st person	**mein** (*my*)	**unser** (*our*)
2nd person	**dein** (*your – familiar form*)	**euer** (*your -familiar form*)
	Ihr (*your – polite form*)	**Ihr** (*your – polite form*)
3rd person	**sein, ihr, sein** (*his, her, its*)	**ihr** (*their*)

To add the correct ending you have to look at the gender, the case and the number of the noun. Don't panic, you already know the endings! They are the same as those of **ein** and **kein**. So you have e. g. **das ist meine Tante** (*this is my aunt*) or **ich besuche seinen Vater** (*I visit his father*).

Listen to and write in the missing endings for the nominative (N), accusative (A) and dative (D) case.

N: mein Mann – mein____(1) Tante – mein Kind

A: sein____(2) Bruder – mein____(3) Mutter – ihr Haus

D: dein____(4) Freund – ihr____(5) Tante – unser____(6) Kind

The plural is easy: N + A: mein**e** Eltern, D: mein**en** Eltern.

CD 1 – TR. 83

NICE TO KNOW

Note that the words
die Eltern *(the pa-
rents)*, **die Großeltern**
(the grandparents) and
die Geschwister
(brothers and sisters)
are always used in the
plural form.

° 14

If you want to talk about the family you can start with the following
questions: **Hast du Geschwister?** *(Do you have any brothers and sisters?)*,
Wo leben deine Eltern? *(Where do your parents live?)* or **Wo lebt deine Familie?** *(Where does your family live?)*.

Listen to these German words to do with the family.

1. **die Großeltern** – *grandparents*	8. **der Sohn** – *son*
2. **die Großmutter** – *grandmother*	9. **die Geschwister** – *brothers*
3. **der Großvater** – *grandfather*	*and sisters*
4. **die Eltern** – *parents*	10. **die Schwester** – *sister*
5. **die Mutter** – *mother*	11. **der Bruder** – *brother*
6. **der Vater** – *father*	12. **die Tante** – *aunt*
7. **die Tochter** – *daughter*	13. **der Onkel** – *uncle*

15

Read the questions. Which of the four reactions fits? Mark the right
answers. Note that 2, 3 or even 4 answers could be correct.

1. Was machen Sie in Ihrer Freizeit?
   A ☐ Ich lese gern.
   B ☐ Nein, ich habe kein Hobby.
   C ☐ Ich gehe regelmäßig schwimmen.
   D ☐ Freunde treffen, Konzerte besuchen und Musik hören.

2. Tanzen Sie gern?
   A ☐ Nein, ich tanze nicht gern.
   B ☐ Oh ja, ich tanze sehr gern.
   C ☐ Ja, ich mag Familienfeste.
   D ☐ Ja, ich gehe sehr oft in Discos.

3. Wie oft macht ihr Sport?
   A ☐ Wir gehen oft in Ausstellungen.
   B ☐ Zweimal oder dreimal in der Woche.
   C ☐ Gymnastik mag ich nicht.
   D ☐ Nur manchmal.

4. Hast du Geschwister?
   A ☐ Ja, meine Familie lebt in Berlin.
   B ☐ Ja, zwei Brüder.
   C ☐ Nein, ich habe keine Geschwister.
   D ☐ Ja, eine Tante und einen Onkel.

CD 1 – TR. 84

1

It's Thomas' little daughter Lisa's birthday and she has received a card from her grandfather. Would you like to know what he has written? Listen to the single parts of the greeting card. Then write the missing words into the gaps.

1. _____ Lisa,

2. herzlichen _____ zum Geburtstag!

3. Ich wünsche dir viel Spaß _____ deiner Party

4. mit Mama und _____.

5. _____ von deinem Opa

6. PS: Es gibt eine _____ für dich!

Dear Lisa,

Happy birthday! I wish you a lot of fun at your party with mum and dad.

Kisses from your grandpa

PS: There will be a surprise for you!

 NICE TO KNOW

The ending **-chen** creates a diminutive. You can add it to many nouns, e.g. **der Kuss** (*kiss*) **– das Küsschen**. Nouns ending in **-chen** are always neuter.

Now repeat the sentences. Try to guess the meaning before reading the translation on the right.

2

 CD 1 – TR. 85

Which activities are shown in the pictures? Read the sentences below and write the letter of the correct one into the gap under the corresponding picture.
Don't worry about any new words. It's possible to guess the meaning with the help of the pictures.

1   2   3   4   5

____ **A** Sie singen ein Lied.

____ **B** Er gratuliert ihr zum Geburtstag.

____ **C** Die Mutter liest dem Kind ein Buch vor.

____ **D** Sie badet mit einem Schwimmtier.

____ **E** Sie packt ein Geschenk aus.

Listen in!

 CD 1 – TR. 86

○ 3

At the Kowalski's family home. It's Lisa's birthday. The Kowalskis always try to celebrate family birthdays all together. That's why Lisa is very impatient and can hardly wait to unwrap her gifts. Finally Thomas gets home from the office.

Listen to the dialogue and look at the pictures. Try to understand the general sense of the dialogue. Later we'll look for some details.

 CD 1 – TR. 87

○ 4

Listen again to the introductory dialogue. Then decide whether the words below appear in the dialogue or not. Choose the tick for "yes" or the cross for "no".

Most of the words below will be new to you. Look at the word box for the translation.

1. congratulations
2. to wish
3. funny
4. mum
5. to laugh
6. sweetheart
7. to congratulate
8. surprise
9. grandma
10. fun

	✓	✗		✓	✗
1. Glückwunsch	☐	☐	**6.** Schatz	☐	☐
2. wünschen	☐	☐	**7.** gratulieren	☐	☐
3. lustig	☐	☐	**8.** Überraschung	☐	☐
4. Mama	☐	☐	**9.** Oma	☐	☐
5. lachen	☐	☐	**10.** Spaß	☐	☐

CD 1 – TR. 88

5

Let's focus on the intonation of some very common expressions from the introductory dialogue.

Listen carefully to the intonation and emphasis of the expressions given below then try it yourself.

1. Da bist du ja endlich! *(You are here at last!)*

2. Das ist aber toll! *(That's really great!)*

3. Das ist wirklich lustig! *(That's really funny!)*

4. Das gibt es doch nicht! *(That can't be true!)*

6

Perhaps you have wondered how the little words **aber**, **denn**, **ja**, **doch** and **mal** are used in the introductory dialogue. There is a dictionary translation, but it has nothing to do with their meaning in sentences like:

• Wo ist **denn** Lisa? *(Where is Lisa?)*
• Das gibt es **doch** nicht! *(That can't be true!)*

These little words are used to emphazise a statement. They are called *particles* and without them a conversation sounds artificial, stiff or even harsh. Unfortunately, there isn't really a proper translation and for you it might be difficult to use them. So just be aware of these particles and only learn some easy and common phrases like the ones in the following task.

Listen and repeat. Then look at the translation.

1. Schau mal! *(Look!)*

2. Hör mal! *(Listen!)*

3. Das ist aber schön! *(That's very nice!)*

 NICE TO KNOW

Another meaning of **doch**: If you want to give a positive answer to a negated question you use **doch**, e.g. **Gehst du nicht ins Kino? – Doch!**

 CD 1 – TR. 89

Practice makes perfect

 CD 1 - TR. 91

7

For various occasions it's good to know some suitable phrases:
- **Viel Glück!** *(Good luck!)*
- **Ich wünsche dir viel Erfolg!** *(Good luck!)*
- **Ich wünsche Ihnen gute Besserung!** *(Get well soon!)*

To congratulate someone on his birthday or his wedding you can say:
- **Herzlichen Glückwunsch!** *(Congratulations!)*
- **Alles Gute zum Geburtstag! / Alles Gute zur Hochzeit!** *(Happy birthday! / Congratulations on your wedding!)*
- **Alles Liebe zu deinem Geburtstag!** *(Many happy returns!)*

Write the phrases next to the correct situations.

1. Your friend is getting married: _____

2. Someone is ill: _____

3. A friend applies for a new job: _____

> **Viel Erfolg!** | **Herzlichen Glückwunsch!** | **Gute Besserung!**

CD 1 - TR. 92

8

Listen to the phrases that are used to wish people well. Choose the correct translations and match them to the German.

1. Alles Gute zum Geburtstag!   ___ A *Congratulations!*

2. Viel Glück!   ___ B *Happy birthday!*

3. Ich wünsche dir alles Gute.   ___ C *Get well soon!*

4. Gute Besserung!   ___ D *With love from your mum.*

5. Herzlichen Glückwunsch!   ___ E *Kind regards.*

6. Alles Liebe von deiner Mama.   ___ F *I wish you all the best.*

7. Herzliche Grüße.   ___ G *Good luck!*

9

You already know a lot of prepositions which take the dative case.
The prepositions are: **aus** *(out, from)*, **bei** *(with, near, at)*, **mit** *(with)*, **nach** *(after, to)*, **seit** *(since, for)*, **von** *(from, by, of)*, **zu** *(to)*.

Bei, **von** and **zu** are usually contracted with the definite article:

bei + dem = **beim**, von + dem = **vom**
zu + dem = **zum**, zu + der = **zur**

Complete the sentences by choosing the right preposition.

1. Er fährt *aus / von / mit* dem Bus nach Köln.

2. Ich wohne *bei / aus / nach* meinen Eltern.

3. Alles Gute *zu / zum / zur* Geburtstag!

> Note that **in** *(in, into)* governs either the accusative or the dative case:
> **Wohin** gehst du? – Ich gehe **in** die Stadt, **ins** Kino. *(movement)*
> **Wo** bist du? – Ich bin **in** der Stadt, im Kino. *(position)*

10

Now practise the prepositions which take the dative.
Complete the sentences and write the missing words into the gaps.

1. Das ist ein Geschenk _____ meinem Freund.

2. Lisa badet _____ _____ Krokodil.

3. Herzlichen Glückwunsch _____ Hochzeit!

4. Die Familie kommt _____ _____ Türkei.

5. Ich wohne _____ _____ Mutter.

> zur | von | meiner | aus | mit | der | bei | einem

11

Let's build up your vocabulary by combining nouns and verbs.

1. eine Postkarte	lachen | spielen | schreiben
2. zum Geburtstag	gratulieren | bekommen | hören
3. einen Brief	baden | vorlesen | singen
4. ein Geschenk	feiern | auspacken | schreiben
5. viel Glück	wünschen | lesen | können
6. eine Geschichte	kommen | geben | erzählen

 NICE TO KNOW

The verbs **auspacken** (to unwrap) and **vorlesen** (to read s.th. to s.o.) have separable prefixes: **Ich packe das Geschenk aus und sie liest die Karte vor.**

CD 1 - TR. 93

° **12**

Here are some useful expression if you want to write a **Postkarte** *(post-card)* or a **Brief** *(letter)* to a friend or a close person.

You can start with:

Liebe Lisa *(Dear Lisa)* or **Lieber Kollege** *(Dear colleague)* or simply **Hallo**.

 NICE TO KNOW

In German letters, there is always a comma behind the form of address, e.g. **Hallo Thomas,** and the next line starts with a small letter.

At the end of a letter or a postcard you can use:

Herzliche Grüße *(Kind regards)*, **Viele Grüße** *(Best wishes)*, **Viele liebe Grüße** *(With lots of love)*, **Bis bald!** *(See you soon!)*, **Alles Liebe** *(With love)* or **Küsschen** *(Kisses)*.

Finally you add your name by writing e. g.

deine Oma, **dein Peter** *(your grandma, your Peter)* or **von (deiner) Oma**, **von (deinem) Peter** *(from (your) grandma, from (your) Peter)*.

Someone is reading you a postcard. Listen to it.

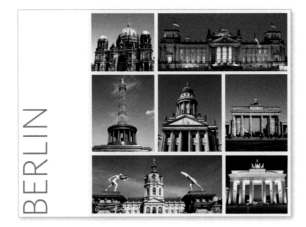

° **13**

Complete the letter by choosing the correct words.

> *Liebe* | *Lieber* | *Liebes* Peter, **(1)**
>
> ich wünsche *dir* | *dich* | *dein* alles Liebe zum Geburtstag. **(2)**
>
> Feierst du eine Party mit *einen* | *dem* | *deinen* Freunden? **(3)**
>
> Ich kann leider nicht *komme* | *kommen* | *kommt*, aber das **(4)**
>
> nächste Mal feiere ich *zu* | *von* | *mit* dir. **(5)**
>
> Bis bald! *Herzliche* | *Viel* | *Alles* Grüße **(6)**
>
> *dein* | *deines* | *deine* Maria **(7)**

14

With verbs like **schreiben** *(to write)*, **geben** *(to give)*, **erzählen** *(to tell)* and many more you can have a dative and an accusative component.

1. The dative object is placed in front of the accusative object if the accusative object is a noun:

   D – A Ich schreibe meiner Freundin einen Brief.
   (I'm writing a letter to my friend.)
   Ich schreibe ihr einen Brief. *(I'm writing a letter to her.)*

2. The word order changes if you replace the accusative object with a pronoun:

   A – D Ich schreibe ihn meiner Freundin. *(I'm writing it to my friend.)*
   Ich schreibe ihn ihr. *(I'm writing it to her.)*

3. If you want to add **zum Geburtstag** or another prepositional phrase, put it at the end of the sentence, e. g. **Ich schreibe ihr einen Brief zum Geburtstag.**

Write the words below into the right gap according to the word order rules. In the word box you'll find the translation.

> es | dir | eine Geschichte

1. Ich schenke _____ einen Computer.

2. Sie erzählt ihrer Tochter _____ .

3. Wir geben _____ ihm.

NICE TO KNOW

Negation: In a sentence with various complements, in general, **nicht** is placed behind the object and in front of a prepositional phrase, e.g. "Ich schenke ihm das Buch **nicht** zum Geburtstag."

I'll give a computer to you as a present.

She's telling a story to her daughter.

We'll give it to him.

15

Can you put the words given below into the right order and create a correct sentence? Don't forget to write a capital letter at the beginning and a full stop at the end.

1. einen Brief / ihr / ich / schreibe

   _____

2. wünscht / ihnen / sie / viel Glück

   _____

3. sie / Anna / dem Kind / schenkt

   _____

4. wir / es / ihm / erzählen

   _____

CD 1 - TR. 94

NICE TO KNOW

First names are often shortened by adding the suffix **-i**. So you'll hear names like **Susi** *(Susanne),* **Tommi** *(Thomas),* **Steffi** *(Stefanie)* or **Michi** *(Michael).*

° 16

In German, of course terms of endearment are common, especially when parents and grandparents are involved.

Listen to the missing word and fill in the gaps.

1. Mutter: _____ , Mami, Mutti

2. Vater: Papa, _____ , Vati

3. _____ : Oma, Omi

4. Großvater: _____ , Opi

Couples often say **Schatz** *(sweetheart)* or **Liebling** *(darling)* to each other. Sometimes names of animals are used. The diminutives **-chen** or **-i** of the words **Hase** *(bun),* **Maus** *(mouse)* and **Spatz** *(sparrow),* e. g.: **Hasi, mein Mäuschen, mein Spatz, Spatzi** are very common.

° 17

In German-speaking countries you'll hardly find families where more than three generations live under the same roof. Nowadays smaller families with one or perhaps two children are the norm. But there are various occasions, often with a religious background, when the generations all meet up. One of these occasions is a birthday party for a younger child (older children prefer parties with friends).

In Catholic families, not only children's birthdays, but also their **Namenstag** *(Saint's day)* are celebrated. There is often a family party when it's a grandparent's birthday, especially if it's their 60th, 70th or 80th, etc. Other typical family parties are **die Taufe** *(christening),* **die Verlobung** *(engagement),* which is celebrated less nowadays, and **die Hochzeit** *(wedding).* On the eve of a wedding, there is another kind of party celebrated with relatives and friends: **der Polterabend** *(eve-of-wedding ceremony),* at which crockery is smashed to bring good luck to the bride and groom.

1

In Units 5 – 8 you have learned a lot of expressions you can use in various situations. Let's have a look at a summary of the most important communication functions.

Here is a list. Match the corresponding sample sentences and repeat them.

1. *You can express your likes and dislikes.*

2. *You can make suggestions.*

3. *You can say how often you do something.*

4. *You can ask the time.*

5. *You can tell time.*

6. *You can say on what day you'll do something.*

7. *You can express your surprise.*

8. *You can congratulate someone.*

9. *You can ask what someone does in his leisure time.*

10. *You can buy tickets at the railway station.*

___ A Wie spät ist es?

___ B Ich möchte eine Fahrkarte zweiter Klasse nach Bonn.

___ C Es ist halb vier.

___ D Was machen Sie in Ihrer Freizeit?

___ E Ich mag Musik, aber ich gehe nicht gern in die Disco.

___ F Herzlichen Glückwünsch zum Geburtstag!

___ G Wollen wir heute Abend ins Kino gehen?

___ H Das gibt es doch nicht!

___ I Am Freitag besuche ich meine Freundin.

___ J Ich spiele dreimal in der Woche Fußball.

2

 15

The sentences on the birthday card to Mr. Holzmann are mixed up. Put each sentence into the correct position to get a correct postcard.

> Viele herzliche Grüße | ich wünsche Ihnen alles |
>
> PS: Sehe ich Sie am Montag im Büro? |
>
> Gute zum Geburtstag! | von Ihrer Kollegin Inge Munz
>
> Lieber Herr Holzmann,

_____

_____

_____

_____

_____

Communication

3

Do you remember what to say at the railway station or at a birthday party or during a conversation about free-time activities? Let's repeat some common phrases.

Look at the scenes shown in the pictures and listen. Then decide which sentence belongs to which picture. Put crosses in the boxes.

1. A ☐ Alles Gute zum Geburtstag!
   B ☐ Ich spiele gern Fußball.
   C ☐ Die Fahrkarte kostet 12 Euro 50.

2. A ☐ Machen Sie regelmäßig Gymnastik?
   B ☐ Sie lachen, singen und tanzen.
   C ☐ Wann fährt der Zug nach Bonn ab?

3. A ☐ Auf welchem Gleis kommt der ICE an?
   B ☐ Ich jogge dreimal in der Woche.
   C ☐ Ich möchte jetzt meine Geschenke auspacken.

4

Imagine you are meeting a German-speaking person who wants to know something about your family and what you like to do in your free time. What can you tell him? Answer the questions with your personal data, hobbies, likes and dislikes. Try to write complete sentences.

1. Haben Sie Geschwister?
2. Wo lebt Ihre Familie?
3. Wie feiern Sie Ihren Geburtstag? – Mit ......
4. Was sind Ihre Hobbies?
5. Machen Sie regelmäßig Sport?
6. Was machen Sie noch in Ihrer Freizeit?
7. Und am Wochenende?
8. Und was machen Sie nicht gern?

§ 20

° 5

What would Thomas say about these pictures?
Look at the pictures and complete the description from Thomas' point of view. Write the correct possessive pronoun (**mein, dein, sein, ihr, unser, euer**) and don't forget to choose the right ending. Remember that you have to use the same endings you would use with **ein** and **kein**. If you want to see again all endings look at the word box.

singular:
m.:mein (N),
    meinen (A),
    meinem (D)
f.: meine (N),
    meine (A),
    meiner (D)
n.: mein (N),
    mein (A),
    meinem (D)

plural:
    meine (N),
    meine (A),
    meinen (D)

1. Das ist _____ Frau Susanne.

2. Susanne, _____ Tochter und ich spielen Karten.

3. Das ist Lisa mit _____ Krokodil.

4. Hier sieht man Klaus und _____ Freundin.

° 6

In units 5 – 8 you have dealt with three groups of verbs which have special forms in the present tense. Read the rule for each group of verbs. Then complete the rules by filling in the missing words. In one case you are only looking for a single letter.
In the Nice to know box you'll find more information about rule 3.

§ 10, 24, 15

💡 NICE TO KNOW

Separable prefixes
and sample words:
ab-   abfahren
an-   ankommen
aus-   ausgehen
ein-   einsteigen
hin-   hingehen
um-   umsteigen
vor-   vorbereiten
zurück-   zurück-
           kommen

1. The present tense of the modal verbs **dürfen, (1)**_____ ,
    mögen, müssen, wollen and **sollen** is irregular, but fortunately the
    1st and 3rd person have the same form, e.g. **wollen**: "ich /er
    (2)_____ " and "wir /sie **wollen**".
2. With verbs whose stem ends in **t** you add the letter
    (3)_____ in the 2nd and 3rd person singular and the 2nd
    person plural, e.g. "du arbei**t**est, er **(4)**_____ , ihr arbei**t**et".
3. A lot of verbs have got separable prefixes, e.g. "Der Zug **fährt** um
    12 Uhr **(5)**_____ " or "Sie **liest** Lisa eine Geschichte
    (6)_____ ".

19, 21

° 7

Replace the accusative or dative complement in brackets with the corresponding personal pronoun. Write the pronoun into the gap.

1. Ich komme mit _____ (meinem Freund).

2. Sie schreibt _____ (ihren Eltern) zweimal in der Woche.

3. Das ist ein Geschenk für _____ (meinen Vater).

4. Er besucht _____ (seine Kinder) regelmäßig.

5. Hier ist ein Brief von _____ (Maria).

Just in case you are worried about mixing up the pronouns, here they are:

Personal pronouns

		accusative	dative
singular		mich	mir
		dich	dir
		ihn	ihm
		sie	ihr
		es	ihm
plural		uns	uns
		euch	euch
		sie	ihnen
polite form		Sie	Ihnen

° 8

Complete the sentences by choosing the correct preposition.

1. Ich wünsche dir alles Gute *für* | *zum* | *von* **Geburtstag!**

2. Das ist ein Geschenk *von* | *aus* | *zur* **meiner Oma.**

3. Er wohnt *seit* | *bei* | *in* **seinen Eltern.**

 10

° 9

Write the correct form of the modal verb given in brackets into the gap.

Er _____ heute leider nicht kommen. *(können)*

Wann _____ du nach Wien fahren? *(wollen)*

Kinder, ihr _____ hier nicht spielen! *(sollen)*

Ich _____ endlich bei meiner Oma anrufen. *(müssen)*

10

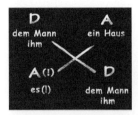 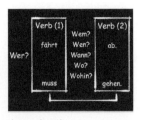

 NICE TO KNOW

"Normal word order" means that none of the elements in a sentence is emphazised.

In German, this is the normal word order:

subject – verb – complements.

The complements you already know are the dative, the accusative and the objects with a preposition (to indicate e.g. the location or direction):

subject	verb	dative	accusative	objects with prepositions
Er	zeigt	einem Freund	ein Museum	in Düsseldorf.

That's quite simple, but let's have a look at the following cases:
The word order changes if the accusative object is a pronoun.

subject	verb	dative	accusative (pronoun)	objects with prepositions
Er	zeigt	es	einem Freund	in Düsseldorf.

If you have got a verb with two parts (verbs with separable prefixes or modals + infinitive) the prefix and the infinitive are placed at the very end of the sentence:

subject	verb (1)	complements	verb (2)
Lisa	packt	ihre Geschenke nicht	aus.
Ich	muss	heute nach München	fahren.

If you want to negate a sentence that has an object with a preposition, place **nicht** in front of it:

Ich	muss	heute nicht nach München	fahren.

In the word box you'll find two tips for the position of time expressions like **um 13 Uhr**, **am Wochenende** or **am Abend**:

 NICE TO KNOW

1. In sentences with a complement of location (where?) or direction (where to? Where from?) it is placed in front of them:
   Ich fahre mit meiner Schwester am Montag nach Köln.

2. Often the time expression is placed at the beginning of the sentence (and the subject is directly behind the verb):
   Am Montag fahre ich mit meiner Schwester nach Köln.

Vocabulary

° 11

More members of the family:

der Cousin, die Cousine – *cousin*

der Neffe, die Nichte – *nephew, niece*

der Schwager, die Schwägerin - *brother-in-law, sister-in-law*

die Schwiegereltern – *parents-in-law*

der Schwiegervater, die Schwiegermutter – *father-in-law, mother-in-law*

der Schwiegersohn, die Schwiegertochter – *son-in-law, daughter-in-law*

die Enkelkinder – *grandchildren*

der Enkel, die Enkelin – *grandson, granddaughter*

Do you have a big family you want to talk about? Repeat the names of the members of the family and learn some new ones like **Schwiegermutter** *(mother-in-law)* or **Enkelin** *(granddaughter)*.
Look at the picture of the Kowalski family. Who is who? Read the sentences which describe the family constellation. Write the missing words into the gaps. Use the pictures to help you.
After doing that try to guess the meaning of the new words. Look at the word box to complete your knowledge about family vocabulary.

1. Oma Margarete hat zwei _____: Susanne und Verena.

2. Die _____ von Susanne Kowalski heißt Verena.

3. Verena ist die Schwägerin von _____ Kowalski.

4. Verena ist die _____ von Lisa. Lisa ist ihre Nichte.

5. Lisa ist die _____ von Oma Margarete.

6. Oma Margarete ist die _____ von Thomas.

> **Thomas | Tante | Töchter | Schwiegermutter | Schwester | Enkelin**

° 12

Write the words below in the right place.

1. Familienfest	2. Am Bahnhof	3. Hobby und Freizeit
_____	_____	_____
_____	_____	_____
_____	_____	_____

> **Abfahrt | Hochzeit | fernsehen | Ausstellungen besuchen | Oma |**
> **umsteigen | Herzlichen Glückwunsch! | Hin-und Rückfahrkarte**

Vocabulary

° 13

In the last four units you have learned many new words. It's time to repeat some of the most important ones.
Read the category and decide which of the four words <u>doesn't</u> fit.

1. Geburtstag
  A ☐ feiern
  B ☐ Glückwunsch
  C ☐ Geschenk
  D ☐ Hochzeit

2. Freizeit
  A ☐ arbeiten
  B ☐ Sport
  C ☐ fernsehen
  D ☐ Kartenspiel

3. Bahnhof
  A ☐ Überraschung
  B ☐ Gleis
  C ☐ Fahrschein
  D ☐ S-Bahn

4. Kultur
  A ☐ Ausstellung
  B ☐ Museum
  C ☐ Konzert
  D ☐ Fahrrad

5. Hobby
  A ☐ lesen
  B ☐ kochen
  C ☐ auspacken
  D ☐ tanzen

6. Fahrplan
  A ☐ Abfahrt
  B ☐ ausgehen
  C ☐ umsteigen
  D ☐ Verbindung

° 14

What are people doing in the pictures? Mark the correct answer.

1.
  A ☐ Sie fahren Fahrrad.
  B ☐ Sie nehmen die Straßenbahn.
  C ☐ Sie tanzen.

2.
  A ☐ Er sucht die Haltestelle.
  B ☐ Er steigt aus.
  C ☐ Er kauft Fahrkarten.

3.
  A ☐ Sie kochen zusammen.
  B ☐ Sie gehen aus.
  C ☐ Sie spielen gern.

Vocabulary

To ask the time you use:

Wie spät ist es? – *What time is it?*

Wann ... ? – *When ... ?*

Um wie viel Uhr ... ? – *At what time ... ?*

Wie oft ... ? – *How often ... ?*

 NICE TO KNOW

To tell the time you use:
um + time
am + day of the week
am + time of the day
(Exception: **in der Nacht**)

 NICE TO KNOW

Note that expressions composed of a day of the week and the time of the day are written in one word, e.g. **Dienstagmorgen** *(Tuesday morning)* or **Sonntagabend** *(Sunday evening)*.

° 15

Do you remember how to tell the time, the time of the day or the day of the week? Let's summarize all you know about asking or telling the time and the frequency.
Read and listen to the question. Then choose the correct answer.
Look at the word box to see the key words which you can use when asking the time.

1. Entschuldigung, wie spät ist es?
- A ☐ Es ist Viertel vor drei.
- B ☐ Am Nachmittag.
- C ☐ Um drei Uhr.

2. Wann fährt der nächste Zug nach Köln?
- A ☐ Ich fahre am Dienstagmorgen.
- B ☐ Er fährt manchmal nach Köln.
- C ☐ Um **13**.15 Uhr.

3. Wie oft machst du Sport?
- A ☐ Ich kann nicht.
- B ☐ Ich spiele montags immer Karten.
- C ☐ Nur einmal in der Woche.

4. Was meinst du, gehen wir am Wochenende in ein Konzert?
- A ☐ Ich besuche regelmäßig Konzerte.
- B ☐ Ich habe leider keine Zeit.
- C ☐ Manchmal.

5. Um wie viel Uhr triffst du deinen Freund?
- A ☐ Ich treffe ihn um fünf Uhr.
- B ☐ Mein Freund kommt morgen nicht.
- C ☐ Am Dienstag oder am Mittwoch.

6. Hast du morgen Abend Zeit?
- A ☐ Doch, ich besuche meine Eltern.
- B ☐ Ja, am Abend habe ich Zeit.
- C ☐ Nein, am Wochende fahre ich nie nach Berlin.

Ready for the next online test? Go for it! **www.pons.de/power**

CD 2 – TR. 01

°1

Let's have a look at some situations and subjects you'll find in this unit. Listen to what people are asking in the situations shown in the pictures. Then write the number of the corresponding picture next to the right answer. If you would like to read the questions look at the word box.

Wann hat Peter Geburtstag?

Was hast du in den letzten Tagen gemacht?

Hast du Haustiere?

Wo müssen wir aussteigen?

Wann habt ihr geheiratet?

____ A Ja, ich habe eine Katze und einen Hamster.

____ B Wir müssen an der 5. Haltestelle aussteigen.

____ C Wir haben 1998 geheiratet.

____ D Ich bin nach Wien gefahren.

____ E Er hat am 30. 6. Geburtstag.

°2

CD 2 – TR. 02

Listen to the pronunciation of some new words from this unit and write them in the corresponding space.
After doing that repeat the words of each category aloud in order to memorize them.

NICE TO KNOW

The number 1000 is called **(ein)tausend**. The **ein** is optional. To continue the counting is easy: you go on with **zweitausend**, **dreitausend** etc.

1. A person	2. Time and date	3. Marital status
_____	_____	_____
_____	_____	_____
_____	_____	_____

A der Monat – *month*
B geschieden – *divorced*
C gestern – *yesterday*
D verheiratet – *married*
E der Tierfreund – *animal lover*
F im Jahr 2002 – *in the year of 2002*
G am ersten Juni – *on June 1st*
H der Nachbar – *neighbour*

○ 3

How can you express activities which happened in the past? You need a new tense: the perfect tense.

Read these sentences which are written in the present tense, a tense you already know. Then look for the corresponding sentence in the perfect tense and match the two together.

At the moment it'll be enough just to see and recognize the forms of the perfect tense. Later you're going to learn the exact rules.

1. Sie liest.

2. Wir suchen das Krokodil.

3. Wir fahren nach Benrath.

4. Ich schreibe ihm.

5. Was machen Sie?

6. Was sagt sie?

7. Wir fragen die Leute.

____ **A** Was haben Sie gemacht?

____ **B** Sie hat gelesen.

____ **C** Wir haben die Leute gefragt.

____ **D** Wir haben das Krokodil gesucht.

____ **E** Was hat sie gesagt?

____ **F** Ich habe ihm geschrieben.

____ **G** Wir sind nach Benrath gefahren.

CD 2 - TR. 03

○ 4

It's June 4th: Thomas Kowalski is going into the office and he meets the secretary, Mrs. Schmidt, who is sitting at her desk. Because Thomas has been working a lot outside the office, the secretary is asking him what he's been doing. She's also giving him a message from a woman who read about the crocodile in the newspaper and who has got some new information. Listen to the conversation between Thomas and the secretary.

5

CD 2 – TR. 03

Listen again to the dialogue between Thomas and Mrs. Schmidt and look for some details.

Read the statements and decide if they are true (T) or false (F).

If you want to check your answers by reading the tapescript, look at the appendix.

	true	false
1. Thomas, Sylvia and Aynur went to Benrath on July 11th.	☐	☐
2. Mrs. Schmidt is very happy that the crocodile hasn't been found.	☐	☐
3. The day before there was a call for Thomas.	☐	☐
4. Oskar Greiner is the neighbour of Mrs. Schmidt.	☐	☐
5. Oskar Greiner has got a lot of exotic pets.	☐	☐
6. A crocodile is missing.	☐	☐
7. The secretary knows the address of Mr. Greiner by heart.	☐	☐
8. Thomas doesn't know the Neanderstraße.	☐	☐

6

CD 2 – TR. 04

Read and listen to the names of the months. Focus on the pronunciation and repeat them aloud.

1. Januar

2. Februar

3. März

4. April

5. Mai

6. Juni

7. Juli

8. August

9. September

10. Oktober

11. November

12. Dezember

NICE TO KNOW

The Austrians have another word for *January*: They use the word **Jänner**.

To answer the question beginning with **wann** *(when)* you have to use the preposition **im** in front of the name of the month, e.g. **Im Januar fahren wir in die Schweiz.** *(In January we'll go to Switzerland.)*

7

Ordinal numbers in the date:
1. am ersten
2. am zweiten
3. am dritten
4. vier**ten**
5. fünf**ten**
6. sechs**ten**
7. **siebten**
8. ach**ten**
9. neun**ten**

 CD 2 – TR. 05

10. zehn**ten**
11. elf**ten**
12. zwölf**ten**
13. dreizehn**ten**
...
19. neunzehn**ten**
20. zwanzig**sten**
21. einund-
    zwanzig**sten**
...
30. dreißig**sten** etc.

The **date** starts with the day followed by the month.
Am 21. Juli (einundzwanzig**sten**) habe ich Geburtstag.
(On July 21ˢᵗ it's my birthday.)
Am 21.7. (einundzwanzig**sten** Sieb**ten**) habe ich Geburtstag.

To express the date you'll need the ordinal numbers. They are formed by adding **-ten** to 1 to 19 and **-sten** to 20 and above.
Only a few numbers have got some irregularities. Look at the word box to see a systematic list.

Listen and write the missing dates into the gaps.

Am _____ fahren wir nach Wien, am 1. 9. weiter nach

Budapest und am _____ kommen wir zurück.

The year is placed at the end of the date:
Sie sind seit dem 7.7.2001 verheiratet.
(They are married since July 7 ᵗʰ, 2001.)
Ich bin am 13. April 1972 geboren.
(I was born on April 13ᵗʰ, 1972.)

Note: Years beginning with "1" are spoken this way: **19hundert72.**

 CD 2 – TR. 06

8

Listen and read. Which dates are people talking about? Mark the correct answer.

1. Wann habt ihr geheiratet?
   A ☐ 19. 8.
   B ☐ Im August 1987
   C ☐ Am 19. August

2. Wann ist dein Geburtstag?
   A ☐ 1. Dezember.
   B ☐ 12. September.
   C ☐ 11. Dezember.

3. Hast du Max in der letzten Zeit gesehen?
   A ☐ 8. 3.
   B ☐ 3. 8.
   C ☐ 13. 8.

4. Wann bist du geboren?
   A ☐ Am 5. 11. 1790.
   B ☐ Am 11. 4. 1917.
   C ☐ Am 11. 5. 1970.

 NICE TO KNOW

Note that there is no preposition in front of the year: **2001 sind wir nach England gefahren.** *(In 2001 we went to England.)* You can also say **im Jahr 2001** *(in the year of).*

9

The demonstrative pronoun **dieser**, **diese**, **dieses** *(this or that)* is used to indicate something or someone that is close by or has just been mentioned, e.g.:

Neanderstraße... Wo ist das? Kennen Sie diese Straße?
(Neander Street... Where is that? Do you know this street?)

The demonstrative pronoun is declined and has the following endings:

 § 6

	masculine	feminine	neuter	plural
nom.	dies**er** Mann	dies**e** Straße	dies**es** Haus	dies**e** Tiere
acc.	dies**en** Mann	dies**e** Straße	dies**es** Haus	dies**e** Tiere
dat.	dies**em** Mann	dies**er** Straße	dies**em** Haus	dies**en** Tieren

It's quite easy to learn these forms because the last letter is the same as the one of the corresponding definite article, e.g. de**r** – diese**r**.

Write the correct form of the demonstrative pronoun into the gap.

> diesen | dieser | diese | dieses

1. In _____ Stadt lebt meine Mutter.

2. Ich möchte _____ Buch kaufen. Was kostet es?

3. Oskar Greiner? Kennst du _____ Mann?

4. Ich mag _____ Leute nicht.

10

Look at the pictures and listen to what these animals are called in German. Then look at the word box for the spelling and the plural.

 CD 2 – TR. 06

If you want to start a conversation about pets you can simply ask:
Hast du Haustiere? *(Have you got pets?)* or **Haben Sie ein Haustier?**
(Have you got a pet?)

1. die Katze – Katzen
2. der Hund – Hunde
3. der Hamster – Hamster
4. der Vogel – Vögel
5. das Pferd – Pferde
6. die Maus – Mäuse
7. der Hase – Hasen
8. das Meer-schweinchen – Meerschweinchen
9. die Schildkröte – Schildkröten
10. der Goldfisch – Goldfische

Practice makes perfect

° 11

The perfect tense is a compound tense with the following parts:

> present tense of **haben** or **sein** + **past participle** of the verb
> • sie **hat** **gesagt** (she has said)
> • ich **bin** **gekommen** (I have come)

1. Haben or **sein**?
For most verbs **haben** is used to form the perfect. **Sein** is used for verbs that indicate motion: **kommen, gehen, fahren.**

2. The past participle of regular verbs has the structure:
• **ge-** unchanged present stem **-t** (gesucht ◄ suchen)

The following verbs are regular. Write the past participle into the gaps.

1. fragen _____

3. hören _____

2. kaufen _____

4. lernen _____

3. The past partciple of irregular verbs has the structure:
• **ge-** often a changed stem **-en** (gegangen ◄ gehen)
That means that they have to be memorized.

Past participle of
some irregular verbs:

gefahren ◄ fahren

gelesen ◄ lesen

geschrieben ◄
  schreiben

gesehen ◄ sehen

gesprochen ◄
  sprechen

getrunken ◄ trinken

! gewesen ◄ sein

° 12

Complete these four short dialogues by using the perfect tense of the verbs given in the box. Each verb should be used only once.
Write the forms of **haben** or **sein** and the past participle of the correct verb into the gaps.

hören *fahren* **machen** spielen kommen
lesen *ahren* **sein!** **lernen**

NICE TO KNOW

The perfect tense of the verb **sein** is an exception of the rules above. It takes "sein" as auxiliary verb: **ich bin gewesen** (I have been).

1. • Was habt ihr gestern **(1)**_____?

  • Wir **(2)**_____ Musik **(3)**_____.

2. • Hast du gestern Deutsch **(4)**_____?

  • Nein, ich **(5)**_____ ein Buch **(6)**_____.

3. • Wo sind Sie am Wochenende **(7)**_____?

  • Ich **(8)**_____ nach Köln **(9)**_____.

4. • Hast du mit Peter Karten **(10)**_____?

  • Nein, er **(11)**_____ leider nicht **(12)**_____.

CD 2 - TR. 08

 18

13

The perfect tense is the most important tense used to talk about the past in German. Especially in spoken language, it's used nearly all the time. Let's have a look at some typical questions:
• **Wo bist du gewesen?** *(Where have you been?)*
• **Was hast du gestern gemacht?** *(What did you do yesterday?)*
Note that the position of the past participle is at the end of the sentence.

If you want to specify the point of time in the past, you can use expressions like **gestern Morgen** *(yesterday morning)*, **vorgestern** *(the day before yesterday)*, **vor drei Tagen** *(three days ago)*, **in den letzten Tagen** *(in the last few days)*, **in letzter Zeit** *(recently)* or **(im) letzten Monat** *(last month)*.

Listen to the questions. Then write the correct answers.

 CD 2 - TR. 09

1. _____

2. _____

3. _____

> **Nein.** | **Vorgestern.** | **Ich habe gelesen.**

14

The words in each line are mixed up. Put them in chronological order. For example:
January – February – March or *one year ago – last weekend – yesterday.*

1. September | Mai | Juli | Juni | August

2. letztes Wochenende | gestern | vor einem Monat | vorgestern

3. verheiratet | geschieden | geboren

4. in den letzten Tagen | letzten Monat | im letzten Jahr | letzte Woche

5. am 5. März | am 3. 11. | am 11. 3. | am 9. 4. | am 15. April

 NICE TO KNOW

The months **Juni** *(June)* and **Juli** *(July)* sound similar. To distinguish them better you can often hear – especially on the phone – **Juno** and **Julei** instead of **Juni** and **Juli**.

Finishing up

wissen (to know)

It is used when talking about knowledge of facts – how something works, where something is etc.

Ich weiß es nicht.
(I don't know.)

kennen (to know)

It is used when talking about being acquainted or familiar with something or someone.

Ich kenne Wien nicht.
(I don't know Vienna.)

können (to know)

In this meaning it is used when talking about an individual ability that one has learned or acquired.

Ich kann kochen.
(I know how to cook.)

° 15

Do you already know the new words from this unit? Let's do an easy riddle.
Read the description. Which word is being looked for? You'll find it within the chain of letters. Mark it with a text marker!
By the way, the article of the missing noun is always **der**.

1. This man lives next door to you:
   wfghenachbargryü

2. The 3rd month of the year:
   bargeliumärztönigh

3. One word to express your regret:
   vafoteschadelrtennüpo

4. An animal that has wings:
   maufechvogelindeur

5. The irregular past participle of the verb **sein**:
   ismagewesenufering

6. A piece of paper to make notes:
   geäuzettelnichds

7. The German word for *divorced*:
   seltgeschiedenhufässe

° 16

The verbs **wissen**, **kennen** and **können** get often mixed up. That's a good reason to focus on the differences of their meaning.
First of all look at the word box and read the information about **wissen**, **kennen** and **können**.
Then complete the sentences by choosing the correct verb.

1. Peter *kann | weiß | kennt* Gitarre spielen.

2. Wo ist diese Straße? Ich *kann | kenne | weiß* es nicht.

3. Ich *weiß | kenne | kann* diesen Mann nicht.

4. Wie heißt der Fluss in München? *Kannst | Kennst | Weißt* du es?

5. Sie *kennt | kann | weiß* Deutsch, Englisch und Französisch!

6. *Wissen | Können | Kennen* Sie Bayern?

○1

CD 2 – TR. 10

Look at the picture. What do people say when they are asking for directions? Listen and read.

Wo ist bitte die Bushaltestelle?

der Kindergarten

Ich suche den Kindergarten.

Die Bushaltestelle liegt gegenüber dem Kiosk.

Die nächste Straße links.

Wie komme ich zur Post?

Gehen Sie an der Ampel rechts.

die Ampel

Tut mir leid. Ich bin nicht von hier.

---

die Bushaltestelle – *bus stop*
der Kindergarten – *kindergarten*
der Kiosk – *kiosk*
nächste / r / s – *next*

die Post – *post office*
die Ampel – *traffic light*
Tut mir leid. – *I'm sorry.*

Listen in!

 CD 2 - TR. 11

 NICE TO KNOW

The nine prepositions mentioned in this task take both the dative case (**Ich bin in der Stadt.**) and the accusative case (**Ich gehe in die Stadt.**).

 2

If you want to specify where something is or how to get somewhere, you'll need prepositions like *behind, between* or *over*.
Listen to a short description of the picture and write the right preposition into the gap.

$\S$ 21

| an | auf | hinter | in | neben | über | unter | vor | zwischen |

 CD 2 - TR. 12

 NICE TO KNOW

The preposition **ent-lang** *(along)* takes the accusative case and comes after the noun, e.g. **Ich gehe den Rhein entlang.** *(I'm going along the Rhine.)*

3

Let's have a look at some new words you'll need for getting around in town.
Read the expressions on the left and match them to the translations on the right. Then listen to the sample sentences.

1. entlang   ____ **A** *to walk*

2. die Kreuzung   ____ **B** *city map*

3. zu Fuß gehen   ____ **C** *opposite*

4. geradeaus   ____ **D** *along*

5. der Stadtplan   ____ **E** *far*

6. weit   ____ **F** *straight ahead*

7. gegenüber   ____ **G** *crossroad*

4

CD 2 - TR. 13

Thomas and his colleagues have heard about Mr. Greiner who is supposed to be missing one of his exotic pets – a good chance to continue the
newspaper's story about the crocodile. The man lives in Neander Street, a
small street without a bus stop. So, when Thomas, Sylvia and Aynur get
off bus No. 834 they still have to find the right street.
Listen to the dialogue and look at the pictures.

5

CD 2 - TR. 14

Listen to how to get to Neander Street and read the description of the
way.
The sentences in the English translation are mixed up. Match them into
the correct order.
Then repeat the German expressions line by line and compare them with
the translation.

1. Gehen Sie diese Straße entlang   ___ A *There turn right,*

2. immer geradeaus,   ___ B *That's Neander Street.*

3. am Kindergarten und an der   ___ C *Go along this street*
Schule vorbei
___ D *until you get to a crossroad.*
4. bis zur Kreuzung.
___ E *then again straight ahead.*
5. Dort gehen Sie nach rechts,
___ F *pass the kindergarten and the*
6. dann wieder geradeaus.   *school*

7. Dann die erste Straße links.   ___ G *Then the first street on the left.*

8. Das ist die Neanderstraße.   ___ H *always straight ahead,*

Practice makes perfect

1. baker's
2. pharmacy
3. book shop
4. kiosk
5. supermarket
6. florist's
7. travel agency
8. butcher's
9. drugstore
10. market

 NICE TO KNOW

To ask for a shop you can use the expression
Wo finde ich ...?
(*Where can I find ... ?*),
e. g. **Wo finde ich einen Kiosk?**

6

Which shops can you find in a town? Look at the pictures and listen. Then read the words aloud. In the word list to the left you find the translations.

1. die Bäckerei **2.** die Apotheke **3.** die Buch-handlung **4.** der Kiosk

5. der Super-markt **6.** der Blumen-laden **7.** das Reisebüro **8.** die Metzgerei

9. die Drogerie **10.** der Markt

7

Complete the sentences and write the missing words into the gaps.

1. In der _____ bekommt man Bücher.

2. Am _____ gibt es Zeitungen.

3. Peter bringt seine Briefe auf die _____ .

4. Sie geht ins _____ . Sie möchte in die Türkei fahren.

5. Schinken kauft man in der _____ .

6. In der _____ gibt es Kuchen und Torten.

> Bäckerei | Metzgerei | Kindergarten | Reisebüro | Apotheke | Kiosk
> Post | Blumenladen | Buchhandlung | Drogerie

8

CD 2 – TR. 16

 21

There is a group of prepositions that can take either the dative or the accusative case: **an** (at, on, to), **auf** (at, in, on), **hinter** (behind), **in** (in, into, to), **neben** (beside, next to), **über** (over), **unter** (under), **vor** (in front of) and **zwischen** (between).

 NICE TO KNOW

Offices or institutions like banks, post offices or schools take the preposition auf, e.g. **ich gehe auf die Bank** (... to the bank) or er arbeitet **auf der Post** (... at the post office).

The **dative** is used to indicate the position or location:
• **Wo** ist er? – Im Park. / Unter der Brücke. / Vor dem Kiosk.
  (Where is he? – In the park. / Under the bridge. / In front of the kiosk.)

The **accusative** is used to indicate a motion, direction or destination:
• **Wohin** geht er? – In den Park. / Unter die Brücke. / Vor den Kiosk. (Where is he going to? – Into the park. / Under the bridge. / In front of the kiosk.)

Write the correct article (dative or accusative) into the gaps.

1. Die Post liegt zwischen _____ Bahnhof und der Bank.

2. Ich gehe über _____ Brücke.

3. Auf _____ Straße spielt ein Kind.

Note that there are contractions with the following prepositions:
• in, an + dem ▶ **im**, **am**
• in, an, auf + das ▶ **ins**, **ans**, **aufs**

9

CD 2 – TR. 17

Listen to the expressions. Do they indicate a direction and a motion (**wohin?**) or a location (**wo?**). Write the expressions into the right box.

1. Wohin?	2. Wo?

A am Kiosk	E über die Kreuzung	I hinter dem Bahnhof
B auf die Post	F in die Straße	J neben dem Kino
C im Park	G auf den Platz	K unter die Brücke
D an der Ampel	H vor dem Hotel	

Practice makes perfect

 CD 2 – TR. 18

 NICE TO KNOW

The word **Weg** has different meanings: 1. **der Weg zum Zentrum** *(the way to the centre)*, 2. **der Weg durch den Park** *(the (foot)path through the park)*.

° 10

If you want to ask for directions you can use the following expressions:
- **Wie komme ich (von hier) zum Bahnhof / zur Neanderstraße / nach Benrath?** *(How do I get (from here) to the railway station / to Neander Street / to Benrath?)*
- **Ist das der Weg zum Bahnhof?** *(Is this the way to the railway station?)*
- **Ich suche den Bahnhof. Können Sie mir helfen?** *(I'm looking for the railway station. Can you help me?)*
- **Ist es weit? / Wie weit ist es?** *(Is it far? / How far is it?)*

You can give or receive the following answers:
- **Tut mir leid. Das weiß ich nicht.** *(I'm sorry. I don't know.)*
- **Ich bin nicht von hier.** *(I'm not from here.)*
- **Es ist ganz in der Nähe.** *(It's very near here.)*
- **Sie können zu Fuß gehen.** *(You can walk.)*
- **Es sind nur 10 Minuten zu Fuß.** *(There are only 10 minutes to walk.)*

 CD 2 – TR. 19

Listen to two short dialogues. Then repeat them aloud.
If you want to read the tapescript look at the appendix.

 CD 2 – TR. 20

 § 21

 NICE TO KNOW

The preposition **durch** *(through)* governs the accusative case, e.g. **Er geht durch den Park.**

° 11

Useful expressions for giving or receiving directions:
- **Gehen Sie / Fahren Sie ...** *(Go / Drive)*
- **... geradeaus / diese Straße entlang / Richtung Zentrum** *(straight ahead / along this street / in the direction of the centre)*
- **... die erste (Straße) links** *((take) the first (street) on the left)*
- **... an der Kreuzung / an der Ampel / an der Ecke rechts** *((Turn) right at the crossroads / at the traffic lights / at the corner)*
- **... über die Brücke / über die Straße / über den Platz** *(across the bridge / across the street / across the square)*
- **... durch den Park / durch die Fußgängerzone** *(through the park / through the pedestrian area)*
- **... bis zur Kreuzung / bis zum Bahnhof** *(until you get to the crossroads / until you get to the railway station)*

Look at the picture. How do you get to the post office? Choose the right words.

1. Gehen Sie geradeaus bis zur *Post | Kreuzung | Richtung.*

2. Dort gehen Sie *links | geradeaus | rechts,*

3. dann *die erste links | über die Ampel | entlang.*

Dann sehen Sie schon die Post.

12

For giving commands or making requests the imperative form of the verb is used. The rules are easy: the verb is at the beginning of the sentence and the forms of the imperative are derived from the present tense:

- **du**-form: **Geh geradeaus!** *(Go straight ahead!)*
  You have to drop the ending **-st** and the personal pronoun **du**.
  Some verbs add the ending **-e** as you can see in the word box.
- **ihr**-form: **Geht geradeaus!** *(Go straight ahead!)*
  You just have to drop the personal pronoun **ihr**.
- **Sie**-form: **Gehen Sie geradeaus!** *(Go straight ahead!)*
  This form just inverts the pronoun and verb.

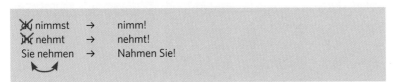

du nimmst → nimm!
ihr nehmt → nehmt!
Sie nehmen → Nahmen Sie!

Write the imperative form of the verbs in brackets into the gaps.

1. _____ Sie mir bitte das Buch, Frau Maier! *(geben)*

2. Peter, _____ nicht so spät! *(kommen)*

3. Tom und Stefanie, _____ mal! *(schauen)*

The only irregular form of the imperative is **sein**:
- **Sei / Seid / Seien Sie pünktlich!** *(Be punctual!)*

13

Fill in the gaps with the imperative form of the verbs given in brackets. Some of the verbs have separable prefixes or a change of the stem vowel.

1. Tina, _____ uns bitte die Zeitung! *(bringen)*

2. Peter und Susi, _____ mal! *(kommen)*

3. Du suchst den Park? Also, _____ geradeaus, dann rechts. *(gehen)*

4. Hast du das Buch? _____ es mir doch bitte! *(geben)*

5. Herr Manz, _____ Sie hier rechts _____ . *(abbiegen)*

6. Mama, _____ mir bitte eine Geschichte _____ ! *(vorlesen)*

 CD 2 – TR. 21

 7

Verbs ending in **-igen**, **-den** or **-ten** form the 2nd person singular of the imperative by adding an **-e**:

entschuldigen ▸ entschuldige!
(to excuse)

reden ▸ rede!
(to talk)

warten ▸ warte!
(to wait)

Verbs with special imperative forms:

fahren ▸ fahr!
(to go, to drive)

lesen ▸ lies!
(to read)

haben ▸ hab!
(to have)

 NICE TO KNOW

There is often an exclamation mark after the imperative form in order to emphazise the command or the request.

Finishing up

°14

With these few words it's possible to describe nearly any route. Also look at the Nice to know boxes to get more information about the use of **gegenüber** and **vorbeigehen**.

1. rechts   **2.** links   **3.** geradeaus   **4.** gegenüber   **5.** die Ampel

6. die Kreuzung   **7.** die Ecke   **8.** die Fußgängerzone   **9.** vorbeigehen   **10.** abbiegen

°15

Listen to the directions to one of the buildings or shops shown on the map. Write the name of the destination (the building) into the gap.

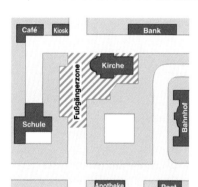

1. Route 1: Von der Schule
zu / zur / zum

_____ .

2. Route 2: Vom Bahnhof
zu / zur / zum

_____ .

Bank | Post | Bahnhof | Apotheke | Schule | Kirche |
Café | Kiosk

°1

 CD 2 – TR. 24

What have people done today? Listen and write the sentences under the
right pictures.
Then try to guess the meaning of the new words with the help of the
pictures.
If you want to see the present tense of the new verbs look at the word box.

1   2   3   4   5

A Ich habe gefrühstückt.
B Ich bin aufgestanden.
C Ich habe eingekauft.
D Ich bin ins Bett gegangen.
E Ich habe geduscht.

Every day's acitivities:

Ich dusche. *– I take a
shower.*

Ich frühstücke. *–
I have breakfast.*

Ich gehe ins Bett. *–
I go to bed.*

Ich kaufe ein. *–
I do the shopping.*

Ich stehe auf. *–
I get up.*

°2

In this exercise you'll learn some new words that will be part of the introductory dialogue on page 108.
Read the expressions below. Write them into the right box. Repeat the
words aloud.

1. Eating	2. Living	3. Colours
_____	_____	_____
_____	_____	_____
_____	_____	_____
_____		

 NICE TO KNOW

The German word
das Lokal is used in a
general sense to indi-
cate a place where
you can eat and drink
without specifying
whether it is a pub, a
bar or a restaurant.

A bunt *(colourful)*
B in der Altstadt *(in the old town
    centre)*
C ruhig gelegen *(quietly situated)*
D das Frühstück *(breakfast)*
E grün *(green)*
F ein kleines Lokal *(a small pub)*

G zentral *(central)*
H zum Abendessen einladen
    (to invite for dinner)
I blau *(blue)*
J ich habe Hunger *(I'm hungry)*
K zu Hause *(at home)*

CD 2 – TR. 25

3

At noon Thomas, Sylvia and Aynur arrive in Neander Street where they want to meet Mr. Greiner whose crocodile is supposed to have disappeared. Mr. Greiner hasn't arrived yet and Thomas and his colleagues are filling time by talking about the houses in the street, about what they have done today and other interesting things.
Listen to the dialogue and look at the pictures. They'll help you to understand the general sense.

CD 2 – TR. 25

4

In the introductory dialogue you heard Thomas, Sylvia and Aynur talking about various topics. Now we are going to look for more details.
Read the questions below. What would Aynur, Sylvia and Thomas answer? Yes or no?
Listen to the dialogue again and answer the questions for each person by marking the tick for "yes" and the cross for "no".
Check your answers by reading the tapescript in the appendix

	1. Aynur ✓	1. Aynur ✗	2. Sylvia ✓	2. Sylvia ✗	3. Thomas ✓	3. Thomas ✗
1. Who likes the house of Mr. Greiner?	☐	☐	☐	☐	☐	☐
2. Who has been in the old part of Düsseldorf today?	☐	☐	☐	☐	☐	☐
3. Who is invited to a dinner?	☐	☐	☐	☐	☐	☐
4. Who is quite impatient because he/she is hungry?	☐	☐	☐	☐	☐	☐
5. Who is going to have lunch at a greek restaurant?	☐	☐	☐	☐	☐	☐

5

 CD 2 – TR. 26

Listen to what the activities shown in the pictures are called.

 NICE TO KNOW

The word **zu** in **zu Mittag /zu Abend essen** can be dropped: **Ich esse Mittag.** (*I have lunch.*), **Hast du schon Abend gegessen?** (*Have you already had dinner?*).

Which of the activities do you normally do first? What do you do next? Here is an example for the course of a day. In the word box you find the translation.

I get up, I have a shower, I have breakfast. Then I take the children to school and I go to work. I have lunch, I do the shopping, I come home and I have dinner. Then I go to bed.

Ich stehe auf, ich dusche, ich frühstücke. Dann bringe ich die Kinder zur Schule und gehe zur Arbeit. Ich esse zu Mittag, ich kaufe ein, ich komme nach Hause und esse zu Abend. Dann gehe ich ins Bett.

6

 CD 2 – TR. 27

Here are some useful expressions to describe the location of a house or flat:
- **Das Haus / Die Wohnung / Die Straße ist ruhig ◀▶ laut gelegen.**
  (*The house / The flat / The street is a quiet ◀▶ noisy area.*)
- **Die Wohnung liegt nah am Zentrum ◀▶ weit vom Zentrum.**
  (*The flat is near the centre ◀▶ far from the centre.*)
- **Ich wohne zentral ◀▶ außerhalb.**
  (*I live in the town centre ◀▶ out of town.*)
- **Ich wohne im Erdgeschoss ◀▶ im ersten Stock.**
  (*I live on the ground floor ◀▶ on the first floor.*)
- **Ich wohne in einem Haus mit ◀▶ ohne Garten / Balkon / Terrasse.**
  (*I live in a house with ◀▶ without garden / balcony / terrace.*)
- **Ich lebe in der Stadt ◀▶ auf dem Land.**
  (*I live in town ◀▶ in the country.*)

Listen to how and where people live. Mark the tick if the word describes the living condition correctly and the cross if it doesn't.

	✓	✗
1. auf dem Land	☐	☐
2. zentral	☐	☐
3. laut	☐	☐

Practice makes perfect

 CD 2 - TR. 29

 NICE TO KNOW

The verb **gefallen** *(to like)* governs the dative case: **Das Haus gefällt mir /dem Mann.** Often, you'll find the dative object in the 1st position: **Mir / Dem Mann gefällt das Haus.**

° **7**

The following structures are used to express likes or dislikes.

- Ich **finde** das Haus von Herrn Greiner **(nicht) schön.**
  (I (don't) think Mr. Greiner's house is beautiful.)
- Ich **finde** es **zu klein** und **zu bunt**. *(I think it's too small and too colourful.)*
- Das Haus von Herrn Greiner **gefällt** mir (nicht).
  (I (don't) like Mr. Greiner's house.)
- Bunte Häuser **gefallen** uns (nicht). *(We (don't) like colourful houses.)*

The corresponding questions are:

- **Wie findest du** das Haus? **Wie finden Sie** das Haus?
  (How do you like the house?)
- **Gefällt dir / Ihnen** das Haus? **Gefallen dir / Ihnen** diese Häuser?
  (Do you like the house / these houses?)
- **Wie gefällt dir / Ihnen** das Haus? *(How do you like this house?)*
- **Welches Haus gefällt dir / Ihnen?** *(Which house do you like?)*

 CD 2 - TR. 30

 NICE TO KNOW

The declination of **welch-** is the same as **dies-** (unit 9)

Nominative:
welcher Mann?
welche Frau?
welches Haus?
welche Männer /
Frauen /Häuser?

Accusative:
welchen Mann?
welche Frau?
welches Haus?
welche Männer /
Frauen /Häuser?

Dative:
welchem Mann?
welcher Frau?
welchem Haus?
welchen Männern /
Frauen /Häusern?

° **8**

Listen to the questions. What could people answer? Choose the right answer and match it to the corresponding question.

1. Hat deine Wohnung einen Balkon?

2. Gefällt dir das Haus von Familie Kramer?

3. Ich finde die Musik zu laut. Und du?

4. Ist Ihre Wohnung zentral gelegen?

5. Wie finden Sie dieses Lokal?

6. Welche Farben gefallen dir?

7. In welchem Stock wohnst du?

____ A Du hast Recht! Sie ist wirklich laut!

____ B Ja, sie liegt ganz in der Nähe vom Zentrum.

____ C Nein, aber eine Terrasse und einen Garten.

____ D Ich wohne im zweiten Stock.

____ E Mir gefallen Grün und Blau.

____ F Es gefällt mir nicht. Es ist zu klein und es liegt nicht zentral.

____ G Ich finde es gut. Man kann hier sehr gut essen.

9

 16

As you already know the perfect tense is formed with the present tense of **haben** or **sein** and the past participle of the verb beginning with **ge-** and ending with **-t / -en**. And what about the following examples?
• Ich **bin** auf**ge**stand**en**. *(I have gotten up.)*
• Ich **habe** es vergess**en**. *(I have forgotten it.)*
• Ich **habe** heute viel fotografier**t**. *(I have taken a lot of pictures today.)*

Here are the rules:

1. The past participle of regular and irregular **verbs with separable prefixes** is formed like this:
  • Prefix + **ge-** + unchanged present stem + **-t**
    (aus**ge**packt ◀ aus|packen)
  • Prefix + **ge-**+ changed stem + (often) **-en**
    (auf**ge**stand**en** ◀ auf|stehen)

2. The past participle of **verbs beginning with be-, ent-, er-, ver-** doesn't have a **ge-** at the beginning:
  • unchanged present stem + **-t** (erzähl**t** ◀ erzählen)
  • changed stem + (often) **-en** (verstehen ◀ verstanden)

3. The past participle of verbs which end in **-ieren** always has the structure:
  • unchanged present stem + **-t** (fotografier**t** ◀ fotografieren)

 NICE TO KNOW

Remember that verbs that indicate a motion or a change of condition take **sein** as an auxiliary verb, e.g. **ich bin ausgestiegen** *(I got off)*, **ich bin losgegangen** *(I have set off)*.

10

 18

 CD 2 - TR. 31

Read and listen to the sentences. Which verbs are used? Write the infinitive form of each verb into the gap, e. g. **Ich habe Fotos gemacht. ▶ machen.**

1. Ich habe einen Kaffee **bestellt**. _____

2. An welcher Universität haben Sie **studiert**? _____

3. Hast du schon die Geschenke **ausgepackt**? _____

4. Wir sind in Köln **umgestiegen**. _____

5. Gestern Abend bin ich mit Christiane **ausgegangen**.

_____

6. Mein Freund hat mich zum Mittagessen **eingeladen**.

_____

7. Peter ist heute schon um 5 Uhr **aufgestanden**. _____

Practice makes perfect

CD 2 – TR. 32

° **11**

Read and listen to the names of the colours. Repeat them aloud.

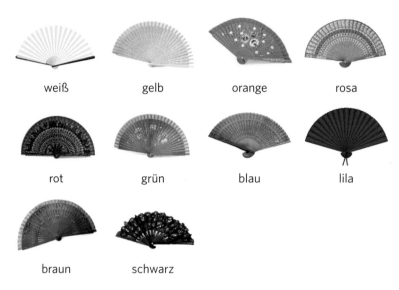

weiß	gelb	orange	rosa
rot	grün	blau	lila
braun	schwarz		

You'll get more **Farben** *(colours)* by adding the words **hell** *(light)* or **dunkel** *(dark)*, e. g. **hellblau** *(light blue)*. Also remember the word **bunt** *(colourful)*.

When colours are used as nouns, they are always neuter: **das Gelb** *(the yellow colour)*. The article is often dropped, e.g. **Ich mag Rot.** *(I like red.)*.

° **12**

Look at the picture. Which colours can you see? Fill in the name of the colour for each element given below.

1. Die Tür ist _____ .

2. Die Fenster sind _____ .

3. Die Katze ist _____ .

4. Der Weg ist _____

5. Der Balkon ist _____ .

6. Das Geschenk ist _____ .

7. Die Vögel sind _____ .

13

Focus on the adjective **grün** in the following sentences:
Die Tür ist grün. *(The door is green.)*
Das ist eine grüne Tür. *(That's a green door.)*
a) If the adjective is part of the predicate (**sein** + adjective) it is used without an ending.
b) If the adjective describes or modifies a noun it has an ending.
These are the endings for the nominative case:

der lange Weg –
the long way

die gute Idee –
the good idea

das blaue Haus –
the blue house

die ruhigen Straßen
– the quiet streets

 1

1. Definite article + adjective + noun:

singular	definite article	adjective	noun
masculine	der	lang**e**	Weg
feminine	die	gut**e**	Idee
neuter	das	blau**e**	Haus
plural	die	ruhig**en**	Straßen

2. Indefinite article + adjective + noun:

singular	indefinite article	adjective	noun
masculine	ein	lang**er**	Weg
feminine	eine	gut**e**	Idee
neuter	ein	blau**es**	Haus
plural		ruhig**e**	Straßen

Write the correct form of the adjective in brackets into the gap.

1. Die _____ Straße heißt Neanderstraße. *(klein)*

2. An der Ecke liegt ein _____ Café. *(italienisch)*

3. Mir gefallen _____ Farben. *(hell)*

4. Das ist aber ein _____ Tee! *(bitter)*

14

Complete the sentences by choosing the correct word.
Make sure that the endings of the missing word fit the gender and the numerus of the noun or that the missing word is in the right case.

1. Welche Farben *gefallen* | *gefällst* | *gefällt* Ihnen?
2. Das ist aber ein *schön* | *schöner* | *schönes* Geschenk!
3. Die *großes* | *große* | *groß* Wohnung von Peter finde ich toll.
4. *Welchen* | *Welches* | *Welche* Buch liest du?
5. *Mir* | *Ich* | *Mich* gefällt die Arbeit im Büro.
6. Das ist eine wirklich *lustig* | *lustige* | *lustiger* Geschichte!

°15

Match the opposites, e.g. *old – new, not yet – already*.
Then repeat each pair of words aloud.

1. schwarz	___ **A** auf dem Land
2. in der Stadt	___ **B** dunkel
3. nah am Zentrum	___ **C** ins Bett gehen
4. hell	___ **D** nach Hause kommen
5. aufstehen	___ **E** ruhig
6. spät	___ **F** schon
7. zur Arbeit gehen	___ **G** weiß
8. laut	___ **H** weit vom Zentrum
9. noch nicht	___ **I** früh

CD 2 – TR. 34

NICE TO KNOW

Don't mix up the spelling of das **Mittagessen** *(lunch)* and **Mittag essen** *(to have lunch)*. By the way, in Austria **mittagessen** *(to have lunch)* is written as one word with a small letter.

°16

Listen to some important expressions to do with meal times.

Das Frühstück *(breakfast)*, **das Mittagessen** *(lunch)* and **das Abendessen** *(dinner)* are the main meals in the German-speaking countries. By the way, in Switzerland they use the word **Zmorge** *(breakfast)* instead of **Frühstück**. It is normal to eat one warm meal a day. Lunch is traditionally the warm meal. A typical **Essen** *(meal)* will consist of a single main course: meat, vegetables or salad, usually with rice, pasta or potatoes.

And dinner? You'll often have just bread, e.g. dark bread with sliced meat or cheese. But if you're invited to a dinner in a German family, you won't only have sandwiches, but a warm meal, too!

Between the main meal times there are other opportunities to eat and drink, for example the coffee and cake tradition in the afternoon. As a second breakfast or a snack in the afternoon there is another meal called

die Brotzeit *(snack)* in Germany and **die Jause** *(snack)* in Austria. There you normally eat a sandwich and maybe drink a beer.

1

What an untidy room! Look at the picture and listen to what people are looking for or where they want to put things.
Can you guess the meaning of the pieces of furniture people are talking about?

 CD 2 – TR. 35

§ 21

> **Wohin hängst du die Jacken?**

> **Ich hänge sie an die Garderobe.**

> **Wohin stelle ich die Lampe?**

> **Stell sie auf den Tisch!**

> **Wo sind die Bücher?**

> **Sie liegen auf der Heizung.**

> **Wohin legen wir die Fotos?**

> **Wir legen sie ins Regal.**

Have you noticed that the German language uses different words for "to put"? Look at the word box for more information.

stellen – *to put something in a vertical position*	**hängen** – *to put something in a hanging position, to hang sth. up*
legen – *to put something in a horizontal position*	

Listen in!

 CD 2 - TR. 36

 NICE TO KNOW

Instead of das **Bade-zimmer** (bathroom) you can also use the short version **das Bad** (bathroom).

2

Let's have a look at the inside of a house. Which rooms and what furniture can you find there?
Listen to what the names of rooms (**Zimmer**) and the pieces of furniture (**Möbel**) are called in German. Write the words into the right spaces.
Then repeat the words aloud and try to learn their meaning.

1. Zimmer   2. Möbel

_____   _____

_____   _____

_____   _____

_____   _____

A die Küche – *kitchen*	**F** das Regal – *shelf*
B das Badezimmer – *bathroom*	**G** der Flur – *corridor*
C der Schrank – *cupboard*	**H** der Stuhl – *chair*
D das Wohnzimmer – *living-room*	**I** das Arbeitszimmer – *study*
E die Couch – *sofa*	**J** der Teppich – *carpet*

3

a. In Australia, there are parrots.

b. Snakes are sometimes poisonous.

c. The terrarium with the snakes is above the radiator.

d. He's stroking the turtle.

e. The parrot is sitting in a cage.

Look at the pictures. Then read the sentences and match them to the corresponding pictures.
This exercise will be easier if you just focus on the words you already know or guess their meaning with the help of the picture. In the word box you will find the exact meaning of the sentences.

1.   _____ **A** In Australien gibt es Papageien.

2.   _____ **B** Schlangen sind manchmal giftig.

3.   _____ **C** Das Terrarium mit den Schlangen steht über der Heizung.

4.   _____ **D** Er streichelt die Schildkröte.

5.   _____ **E** Der Papagei sitzt in einem Käfig.

4

 CD 2 - TR. 37

In Mr. Greiner's flat: Thomas, Sylvia and Aynur have already introduced
themselves and now they want to know more about the pets in the flat.
Oskar Greiner is an expert in exotic animals and pleased that someone is
interested in his hobby and so he is immediately willing to show the
rooms where the pets are.
Listen to the dialogue and look at the pictures.

 CD 2 - TR. 37

5

Let's look at the introductory dialogue in more detail.
Listen again to the dialogue. Then read the statements below and decide
whether they are true (T) or false (F).

	true	false
1. Die Garderobe ist im Wohnzimmer.	☐	☐
2. Die Terrarien sind im Wohnzimmer.	☐	☐
3. Die Schildkröten stehen über der Heizung.	☐	☐
4. Die Schlangen sind nicht gefährlich.	☐	☐
5. Aynur möchte die Schlangen nicht streicheln.	☐	☐
6. Die Papageien sind im Wohnzimmer.	☐	☐
7. Die Fotos von Australien hängen in der Küche.	☐	☐
8. Das Krokodil ist im Badezimmer.	☐	☐

Do you still have any doubts about any of the contents of the dialogue?
In the appendix you can find the translation.

CD 2 – TR. 38

 NICE TO KNOW

Instead of **das Zimmer** *(room)* **der Raum** *(room, space)* is also used which is the more general word of the two. It is often used for rooms where you don't live, e.g. the cellar.

 CD 2 – TR. 39

6

Let's have a look at the names of rooms.

The first group is easy to learn because all words are neuter and composed of **Zimmer** *(room)*:

das **Arbeitszimmer** *(study)*, das **Badezimmer** *(bathroom)*, das **Esszimmer** *(dining-room)*, das **Kinderzimmer** *(children's room)*, das **Schlafzimmer** *(bedroom)*, das **Wohnzimmer** *(living-room)*.

The other rooms are called:

die **Küche** *(kitchen)*, der **Flur** *(corridor)*, der **Keller** *(cellar)*, die **Toilette** *(toilet)*, das **Bad** *(bathroom)* as a short form of **Badezimmer**.

Listen to the description of the rooms and enter their names into the gaps.

1. _____   3. _____

2. _____   4. _____

 CD 2 – TR. 40

Singular and plural:

1. der Stuhl, Stühle

2. das Sofa, Sofas die Couch, Couchs

3. der Sessel, Sessel

4. der Tisch, Tische

5. der Schrank, Schränke

6. das Regal, Regale

7. das Bett, Betten

8. der Teppich, Teppiche die Lampe, Lampen

9. die Garderobe, Garderoben der Spiegel, Spiegel

10. die Kommode, Kommoden

7

The word for *furniture* is mostly used in the plural: **die Möbel** *(furniture)*. A single piece of furniture is **das Möbelstück** *(piece of furniture)* rather than **das Möbel**.

Look at the pictures and listen to the names of the furniture. The names and their plural forms are in the word box.

8

 CD 2 - TR. 41

 21

Compare the following sentences:

Wo? (Location, position)	**Wohin?** (Movement, direction)
Die Lampe **steht** im Regal. *(The lamp is (standing) on the shelf.)*	Er **stellt** die Lampe ins Regal. *(He puts the lamp onto the shelf.)*
Das Buch **liegt** auf dem Sofa. *(The book is (lying) on the sofa.)*	Er **legt** das Buch aufs Sofa. *(He puts the book on the sofa.)*
Das Kind **sitzt** auf dem Stuhl. *(The child is (sitting) on the chair.)*	Er **setzt** das Kind auf den Stuhl. *(He sits the child on the chair.)*
Das Foto **hängt** an der Wand. *(The picture is (hanging) on the wall.)*	Er **hängt** das Foto an die Wand. *(He hangs the picture on the wall.)*

All these verbs are used with the prepositions you have learnt in unit 10:
an, auf, hinter, in, neben, über, unter, vor and **zwischen**.

> You have to use the **dative** case if the verb indicates a fixed position and the **accusative** case if the verb indicates movement.

Write the correct word into the gaps.

> sitzt | setzt | legt | liegt | stellt

1. Er _____ die Jacke über den Stuhl.

2. Der Papagei _____ im Käfig.

3. Die Zeitung _____ zwischen den Büchern.

The perfect tense of the verbs:
The verbs that indicate movement have a regular past participle:
er hat **gestellt** ◀ stellen *(to put into a vertical position)*
er hat **gelegt** ◀ legen *(to put into a horizontal position)*
er hat **gesetzt** ◀ setzen *(to sit down)*
er hat **gehängt** ◀ hängen *(to put into a hanging position)*

The verbs that indicate a fixed position have an irregular past participle:
er hat | ist **gestanden** ◀ stehen *(to stand)*
er hat | ist **gelegen** ◀ liegen *(to lie)*
er hat | ist **gesessen** ◀ sitzen *(to sit)*
er hat | ist **gehangen** ◀ hängen *(to hang)*

Haben is used in Northern Germany, **sein** in Southern Germany and in Austria.

Practice makes perfect

9

What is where? Look at the picture. Complete the sentences and write the missing prepositions into the gaps.

1. Das Sofa steht _____ Wand.

2. Der Spiegel hängt _____ Kommode.

3. Die Heizung ist _____ Tür.

4. Die Zeitungen liegen _____ Tisch.

5. Der Teppich liegt _____ Tisch.

6. Peter sitzt _____ Sessel und liest.

7. Die Lampe steht _____ Ecke,

8. _____ Sessel.

> unter dem | im | an der | am | hinter dem | über der
> in der | neben der | auf der | auf dem | vor der

 CD 2 - TR. 42

10

Listen to the questions. Answer the questions with the help of the information from the picture.
Write complete sentences , e. g. **Ich setze das Kind auf den Stuhl.** or **Ich setze es auf den Stuhl.** Don't forget the capital letter at the beginning of the sentence and the full stop at the end.

1. _____

2. _____

3. _____

11

To describe the position of a piece of furniture you can use the expressions:

Es ist | steht | liegt | hängt … (*It is | stands | lies | hangs …*)
… auf dem Fußboden (*on the floor*), **an der Decke** (*from the ceiling*), **an der Wand** (*on the wall*), **in der Mitte** (*in the middle*), **in der Ecke** (*in the corner*), **oben ◀▶ unten** (*at the top ◀▶ at the bottom*), **vorne ◀▶ hinten** (*in the front ◀ ▶ at the back*).

NICE TO KNOW

Note that **liegen** can have the meaning *to lie* and *to be situated*, e.g. **Birk liegt im Süden.**

 21

Look at the picture on the right and complete the description by filling in the missing words.

Das Bett steht rechts an der **(1)**_____. In der

(2)_____ liegt ein Teppich. Das Zimmer hat ein Fenster. Es ist

(3)_____.

If you move house, furnish your flat or tidy up your room you can ask and answer:

Wohin stellen | legen | hängen wir … ? (*Where do we put … ?*)
… auf den Fußboden (*on the floor*), **an die Wand** (*on the wall*), **in die Mitte** (*in the middle*), **neben das Sofa** (*next to the sofa*), **auf den Tisch** (*on the table*) etc.

12

Here are some useful expressions to talk about living conditions:
- **Wir besitzen eine Eigentumswohnung.**
  (*We own a flat.*)
- **Wir wohnen in einem Einfamilienhaus | in einer 3-Zimmer-Wohnung.**
  (*We live in a detached house | in a flat with three rooms.*)
- **Wie viele Räume | Quadratmeter hat die Wohnung?**
  (*How many rooms | square meters does the flat have?*)
- **Ich lebe in einer Wohngemeinschaft | in einer WG.**
  (*I live in a shared flat | house*)
- **Ich habe ein möbliertes Zimmer im Studentenwohnheim.**
  (*I have a furnished room in a student accomodation.*)
- **Ich wohne zur Miete | in einer Mietwohnung.**
  (*I'm renting a flat | living in a rented flat.*)
- **Wie hoch ist die Miete | die Kaltmiete | die Warmmiete?**
  (*How much is the rent | the rent without additional costs | the rent including additional costs?*)
- **Die Miete ist 400 Euro ohne Nebenkosten.**
  (*The rent is 400 Euros without additional costs.*)

 CD 2 - TR. 43

 NICE TO KNOW

Instead of **300 Euro Kaltmiete/Warmmiete** (*300 Euros rent without/including additional costs*) you can also say **300 Euro kalt/warm**. By the way, the literal meaning of *warm* is **warm**.

CD 2 - TR. 44

NICE TO KNOW

Singular m., f., n.
Nominative:
der, die das
Accusative:
den, die, das
Dative: dem, der, dem

Plural
Nominative: die
Accusative: die
Dative: denen

° 13

Der, **die**, **das** etc are forms of the definite article.
But what do they mean in the following sentences?
Wo ist der Papagei? – **Der** ist in seinem Käfig.
(Where is the parrot? – It is in his cage.)
Kennst du seine Freundin? – Nein, **die** kenne ich nicht.
(Do you know his girlfriend? – No, I don't know her.)
Wie findest du den Schrank? – **Den** finde ich hässlich.
(Do you like the cupboard? – I think it's ugly.)

> Wo ist der Papagei?
> - Der ist dort.

> The marked words are demonstrative pronouns that refer to something mentioned before. They are used to avoid the repitition of the noun. The demonstrative pronoun comes before the verb and is emphasized.

Listen to the intonation of the sentences above. Then try it yourself and read the sentences aloud.
Look at the word box to see the forms of the demonstrative pronoun.

° 14

Let's have a look at some new words from this unit. It's worth learning them because they are very common.
Read the description and mark the missing word within the word snake.

1. The opposite of **unten** (at the bottom):
VOSRTENOBENUNGHEL

2. Another word for **Zimmer**: WOHASDERAUMYCH

3. Rent in German: CARMOMMIETELOTRER

4. The opposite of **hinten** (behind): TIRECKWVORNESCHLÄMM

5. To stroke in German: KINREGKLESTREICHELNLAG

6. A flat, which belongs to someone:
WERHBEIGENTUMSWOHNUNGTIG

7. Mr. Greiner's profession: FOLEHRERTOMIN

8. What do you have to pay apart from the rent?
QUETNEBENKOSTENIENEN

1

CD 2 – TR. 45

In Units 9 – 12 you have learnt a lot of expressions you can use in various situations. Here you have a list with sentences which describe these situations. Match the corresponding sample sentences and repeat them.

1. *asking for directions*

2. *giving directions*

3. *expressing your likes and dislikes*

4. *expressing regret*

5. *talking about the past*

6. *saying your date and place of birth*

7. *talking about your day*

8. *expressing the exact position of something*

9. *talking about your fl at or house*

10. *giving commands*

____ **A** Ich bin am 14. 12. 1974 in München geboren.

____ **B** Der Spiegel hängt über dem Sofa zwischen den Fotos.

____ **C** Wir wohnen in einer Mietwohnung nah am Zentrum.

____ **D** Tut mir leid. Ich bin nicht von hier.

____ **E** Gib mir bitte sofort das Buch!

____ **F** Wie komme ich von hier zum Bahnhof?

____ **G** Gestern habe ich Petra getroffen.

____ **H** Sie gehen bis zur Kreuzung und dann rechts.

____ **I** Mir gefallen helle Farben, aber Rosa finde ich nicht schön.

____ **J** Um 6 Uhr stehe ich auf, dann dusche und frühstücke ich.

2

What can you write about yourself, your flat and your likes and dislikes? Write your personal answers. Try to write complete sentences.
In the appendix you find a proposal of how the answers could look like.

1. Wann ist Ihr Geburtstag?

2. In welchem Jahr sind Sie geboren?

3. Sind Sie verheiratet? Seit wann?

4. Haben Sie Haustiere? Welche?

5. Wie viele Zimmer hat Ihre Wohnung (oder Ihr Haus)?

6. Wie ist Ihre Wohnung (oder Ihr Haus) gelegen?

7. Welche Farben gefallen Ihnen?

8. Was haben Sie heute gemacht?

9. Und was haben Sie heute nicht gemacht?

○ 3

Look at the pictures. Which sentence fits? Match the sentence to the picture.

1.

_____ **A** Biegen Sie rechts ab.

2.

_____ **B** Fahren Sie bis zur zweiten Kreuzung.

3.

_____ **C** Gehen Sie durch die Fußgängerzone.

4.

_____ **D** Gehen Sie geradeaus.

 CD 2 - TR. 46

○ 4

Read and listen to the questions. Then read three possible reactions. Only one of them is correct. Which one?

1. Gefällt Ihnen Düsseldorf?
- **A** ☐ Ja, Düsseldorf liegt am Rhein.
- **B** ☐ Ja, die Stadt gefällt mir gut.
- **C** ☐ Ja, ich wohne in der Nähe.

2. Wohin stellen wir den Tisch?
- **A** ☐ Er liegt oben im Regal.
- **B** ☐ Ja, im Esszimmer ist ein großer Tisch.
- **C** ☐ Wir stellen ihn in die Mitte auf den Teppich.

3. Wohnst du im Studentenwohnheim?
- **A** ☐ Nein, in einer Eigentumswohnung.
- **B** ☐ Ja, diese Zimmer finde ich schön.
- **C** ☐ Nein, die Straße ist zentral gelegen.

Grammar

5

 18

The perfect tense is the most important past tense in the German language. It is composed of **haben** or **sein** (for verbs that indicate motion or a change of condition) and the past participle of the verb. Let's repeat the rules of how to form the past participle.

Read the rules of how to form the past participle and complete the sample sentences by writing the corresponding infinitive or past participle into the gaps.

1. ge- ... -t for regular verbs: ich habe _____ .

2. ge- ... -en for irregular verbs: ich bin _____ .

3. prefix -ge- ... -t / -en for verbs with separable prefixes: ich habe

_____ .

4. -t / -en for verbs beginning with *be-, ent-, er-, ver-*: ich habe _____ .

5. -t for verbs ending in *-ieren*: ich habe _____ .

6. Exceptions are the verbs _____ ▶ ich bin **gewesen**,

_____ ▶ ich habe **gedacht** and _____ ▶ ich habe **gebracht**.

> eingekauft | bringen | studiert | gegangen | erzählt |
> getanzt | sein denken

> **NICE TO KNOW**
>
> Remember the word order: The past participle is always placed at the end of the sentence: **Ich bin gestern ins Kino gegangen.**

6

18, 15

Write sentences in the perfect tense. Use the words given below, e.g.
Mein Vater: mich anrufen ▶ Mein Vater hat mich angerufen.
Start your sentence with a capital letter and don't forget the full stop at the end.

1. Wir: eine Ausstellung in Köln besuchen

_____

2. Peter: viel Bier trinken

_____

3. Ich: gestern sieben Briefe schreiben

_____

4. Er: schon um 5 Uhr wegfahren

_____

5. Sie: die Kinder in die Schule bringen

_____

Grammar

 § 19, 1

° **7**

A young couple has moved house and they are looking for new and modern furniture. Now they are in front of a shop-window and are talking about the furniture.

Complete the text with the help of the picture and write the correct forms of **welch-**, **dies-** and the adjectives into the gaps:

1. • Schau mal! Wie findest du _____ Lampe?

2. • _____ Lampe? Die blaue rechts an der Wand?

3. • Nein, die _____ Lampe links oben.

4. • Die ist toll! Und wie gefällt dir der _____ Tisch?

5. • Nein, ein _____ Tisch ist langweilig!

6. • Und wie gefällt dir _____ Sofa?

7. • _____ ? Das _____ Sofa vor dem Schrank? Das ist zu klein!

> Welcher | Welche | Welches | dieser | diese | dieses | rote
> rote | weiße | weißer | gelbes | gelbe

 CD 2 - TR. 47

§ 7

Sie-form:
kommen Sie!

ihr-form: **kommt!**

du-form: **komm!**

Exceptions:

fahren ▶ **fahr!**,

lesen ▶ **lies!**,

haben ▶ **hab!**

verbs ending in
-igen, **-den** or **-ten**:
the **du-form** of the
imperative gets an **-e**.

The imperative of
sein is irregular:
seien Sie!, **seid!**, **sei!**

° **8**

The imperative is used to give an instruction or to make a request. Depending on the intonation and the use of little words like **bitte**, **mal** and **doch** the instruction can vary in its directness.

Read and listen to the sentences. Repeat the sentences and focus on the word order and the intonation.

Next replace the imperative with the form indicated in brackets, e. g. replace **Kommen Sie** (▶ **du**) with **Komm**. Write the missing forms into the gaps.

1. Legen Sie bitte die Briefe auf den Tisch. (▶ du)   _____

2. Geht doch noch nicht! (▶ du)   _____

3. Bring mir doch mal meine Jacke! (▶ Sie)   _____

4. Warten Sie mal, ich komme mit! (▶ du)   _____

5. Entschuldigen Sie bitte, wo ist der Bahnhof? (▶ du)   _____

6. Gib mir sofort die Fotos zurück! (▶ ihr)   _____

7. Sei bitte pünktlich! (▶ Sie)   _____

Grammar

° 9

 CD 2 – TR. 48

 21

You already know a lot of prepositions and it's time to revise them systematically. A good way of learning them is to look for the case they govern. Is it the accusative case, the dative case or even both?
Listen to the sample sentence for each preposition. Write the preposition to the right category.
Of course you know more than the 12 prepositions given below. There are some more in the word box.

 NICE TO KNOW

Remember that the position of **entlang** (along) is behind the noun: **die Straße entlang** (along the street).

1. prepositions with accusative	2. prepositions with dative	3. prepositions with accusative and dative
_____	_____	_____
_____	_____	_____
_____	_____	_____
_____	_____	_____

> an | auf | durch | entlang | gegenüber | hinter |
> nach | ohne | seit | über | vor | zu

Other prepositions with accusative:

bis, für, gegen, um

The preposition **gegen** (against, about) is new:

Ich spiele gegen Peter. (I'm playing against Peter.)

Es ist gegen 3 Uhr. (It's about 3 o'clock.)

> Prepositions with accusative and dative: Remember that the **accusative** case is used to indicate **movement**: Ich stelle das Sofa neben die Tür. (I put the sofa next to the door.) and the **dative** case to indicate a **fixed position**: Das Sofa steht neben der Tür. (The sofa is (standing) next to the door.)

Other prepositions with dative:

aus, bei, mit, von

Other prepositions with accusative and dative:

in, neben, unter, zwischen

° 10

Complete the short descriptions of the pictures and fill in the gaps with the missing preposition, e. g. **Sie hängt über dem Tisch.**

1. Die Jacke hängt _____ der Garderobe.

2. Die Lampe steht _____ dem Tisch.

3. Die Katze liegt _____ dem Bett.

Vocabulary

° 11

In Units 9 – 12 you have learnt a lot of words from various topics.
In this task you can repeat the most common ones. Read the category
and the four possible answers. Mark the expression which doesn't fit.

1. Tiere:
  A ☐ die Schlange
  B ☐ die Katze
  C ☐ der Käfig
  D ☐ der Hund

2. Hier kann man etwas kaufen:
  A ☐ Im Kindergarten.
  B ☐ In der Bäckerei.
  C ☐ In der Apotheke.
  D ☐ Am Kiosk.

3. Möbel:
  A ☐ der Tisch
  B ☐ die Kommode
  C ☐ der Sessel
  D ☐ die Ampel

4. Farben:
  A ☐ grün
  B ☐ warm
  C ☐ gelb
  D ☐ braun

5. Hier kann man wohnen:
  A ☐ In einer Metzgerei.
  B ☐ Im Studentenwohnheim.
  C ☐ In einer Eigentums-
     wohnung.
  D ☐ In einer Mietwohnung.

6. Zimmer:
  A ☐ die Küche
  B ☐ das Bad
  C ☐ die Miete
  D ☐ der Flur

7. Wie komme ich zum Bahnhof?
  A ☐ Gehen Sie geradeaus.
  B ☐ Gehen Sie nach Hause.
  C ☐ Gehen Sie an der Ecke
     rechts.
  D ☐ Gehen Sie bis zur
     Kreuzung.

8. Wo liegen die Zeitungen?
  A ☐ Im Regal.
  B ☐ Auf dem Schrank.
  C ☐ Unter dem Tisch.
  D ☐ Vor einer Woche.

° 12

Put the words in a logical, chronological order.

1. das Abendessen | das Mittagessen | das Frühstück

2. ins Bett gehen | zu Hause frühstücken | im Büro arbeiten |

   nach Hause kommen

3. im letzten Jahr | morgen | gestern | heute | vor einer Woche

4. April | Februar | Januar | Mai | Juni | März | Juli

5. am 6. 11. | am 11. 6. | am Tag vor Weihnachten | am 3. September

13

What have the people in the pictures done today? Mark the correct answer.

1.
   A ☐ Sie hat geduscht.
   B ☐ Sie ist ausgegangen.
   C ☐ Sie hat gefrühstückt.

2.
   A ☐ Er ist nach Hause gekommen.
   B ☐ Er ist aufgestanden.
   C ☐ Er hat zu Mittag gegessen.

3.
   A ☐ Ich bin zur Arbeit gegangen.
   B ☐ Ich bin ins Bett gegangen.
   C ☐ Ich habe das Essen vorbereitet.

14

Which of the four expressions doesn't tell a time or a date?

1. A ☐ im Januar
  B ☐ im Bad
  C ☐ im März
  D ☐ im August

2. A ☐ im 3. Stock
  B ☐ am 12. 5.
  C ☐ im Juni 2002
  D ☐ am 3. Oktober

3. A ☐ gestern
  B ☐ im letzten Jahr
  C ☐ vor einer Woche
  D ☐ in der Nähe

15

Read the sentences and replace the marked word with its opposite, e. g.
Das Haus ist **alt ◀▶ neu**.

1. Gehen Sie an der Ampel **rechts**. _____

2. Die Wohnung ist **ruhig** gelegen. _____

3. Ist es **nah**? Können wir zu Fuß gehen? _____

4. Die Zeitung liegt **unten** im Regal. _____

Vocabulary

NICE TO KNOW

If someone is knocking on your door you can say **herein!** *(come in!)*. It's a short form of the verb **hereinkommen** *(to come in)*.

° **16**

Let's have a look at six questions that are often used in private conversations.

Read the questions and mark the correct answers. Note that two, three or even four answers could be correct.

1. Wann ist dein Geburtstag?
 A ☐ Ich weiß es nicht.
 B ☐ Ich habe am 18. 7. Geburtstag.
 C ☐ Am 3. November.
 D ☐ Herzlichen Glückwunsch!

2. Was hast du gestern gemacht?
 A ☐ Ich habe viel gearbeitet.
 B ☐ Ich esse mit den Kollegen zu Mittag.
 C ☐ Ich bin in die Altstadt gefahren.
 D ☐ Ich frühstücke immer im Büro.

3. Wo wohnen Sie?
 A ☐ Ganz in der Nähe vom Zentrum.
 B ☐ In einem Haus auf dem Land.
 C ☐ Kommen Sie herein!
 D ☐ Im 4. Stock.

4. Sind Sie verheiratet?
 A ☐ Ja, ich bin 1972 geboren.
 B ☐ Nein, am 4. Februar.
 C ☐ Ja, seit zwei Jahren.
 D ☐ Nein, ich bin geschieden.

5. Wie gefällt dir die Stadt?
 A ☐ Ich finde sie toll.
 B ☐ Sie gefällt mir sehr gut.
 C ☐ Ja, ich wohne im Zentrum.
 D ☐ Sehr gut. Ich lebe gern hier.

6. Haben Sie ein Haustier?
 A ☐ Ja, ich kenne viele Tiere.
 B ☐ Ja, ich habe einen Hund.
 C ☐ Nein, ich mag Tiere nicht.
 D ☐ Nein, meine Wohnung ist zu klein.

The third online test is waiting for you at **www.pons.de/power**

1

What's the weather like? That's a very common topic and now you are going to learn a few new words you can use to talk about the weather. Listen, then write the names of the seasons and the short descriptions into the gaps. Repeat the phrases aloud.

> **A** Frühling | **B** Sommer | **C** Herbst | **D** Winter | **E** Die Sonne scheint. |
> **F** Es schneit. | **G** Es regnet. | **H** Das Wetter ändert sich.

1. _____   2. _____

_____   _____

3. _____   4. _____

_____   _____

The gender of the four seasons is masculine: **der Frühling** (spring), **der Sommer** (summer) etc. The seasons are often used with the preposition **im: im Winter** (in winter).

Listen in!

CD 2 - TR. 50

NICE TO KNOW

Wenn introduces a subordinate clause and has the meanings *if* and *when*.
Ich komme mit dem Auto, wenn es nicht schneit. *(I'm coming by car if it isn't snowing.)*
Er liest immer die Zeitung, wenn er Kaffee trinkt. *(He always reads the newspaper, when he is drinking coffee.)*

CD 2 - TR. 51

abholen – *to pick up*

bleiben – *to remain, to stay*

passen – *to suit*

passt es euch? – *does it suit you?*

der Sekt – *sparkling wine*

Oberkassel – *This is the name of a district of Düsseldorf. There are beautiful large meadows at the Rhine.*

2

Listen and then match the two halves of the sentences.
You have probably noticed the word **wenn** in each sentence.
Can you guess the meaning of this short but important word? Look at the word box for some information.

1. Wir machen ein Picknick,   ___ **A** wenn sie Zeit hat.

2. Sie besucht ihre Eltern am Wochenende,   ___ **B** wenn er nicht arbeiten muss.

     ___ **C** wenn ihr sie sehen wollt.

3. Ich bringe einen Kuchen mit,   ___ **D** wenn das Wetter schön ist.

4. Wir gehen nicht spazieren,   ___ **E** wenn wir uns am Samstag

5. Er freut sich,   treffen.

6. Ich zeige euch meine Fotos,   ___ **F** wenn es regnet.

3

Imagine a couple of friends planning to have a picnic on the meadows next to the Rhine. You are now going to have a look at various ideas of what has to be planned or thought of.
Read the sentences below and match them to the right picture. Don't worry about the new words. The pictures will help you to guess their meaning. There is more information in the word box.

___ **A** Ich bringe eine Flasche Sekt mit.

___ **B** Ich hole Peter ab.

___ **C** Passt es euch um 3 Uhr?

___ **D** Hoffentlich bleibt das Wetter schön!

___ **E** Wir treffen uns an der Brücke nach Oberkassel.

° 4

 CD 2 - TR. 52

Thomas' wife Susanne is calling the office. She wants to arrange an invitation because she would like to meet Thomas' colleagues Sylvia and Aynur. She and Thomas are making plans when and where they should meet. After the conversation Thomas suggests the picnic to his colleagues. Listen to the dialogue and look at the picture.

° 5

 CD 2 - TR. 52

Let's have a look at some details from the introductory dialogue. Listen again to the dialogue. Read the questions and decide which of the answers is correct. Look at the word box for the translation of the questions.

1. Warum will Susanne ein Picknick machen?
- A ☐ Sie isst gerne Kuchen.
- B ☐ Sie kennt Sylvia und Aynur noch nicht.
- C ☐ Sie will mit ihrer Familie feiern.

2. Was macht Lisa? Kommt sie mit?
- A ☐ Sie bleibt zu Hause.
- B ☐ Sie kommt mit.
- C ☐ Sie kann nicht mitkommen.

3. Wann ist das Picknick?
- A ☐ Am Nachmittag.
- B ☐ Am Abend.
- C ☐ Am Sonntag.

4. Was sagt das Radio?
- A ☐ Es regnet.
- B ☐ Es schneit.
- C ☐ Die Sonne scheint.

5. Wo treffen sie sich?
- A ☐ Im Biergarten.
- B ☐ In der Wohnung von Thomas.
- C ☐ An einer Brücke.

6. Wer bereitet das Picknick vor?
- A ☐ Susanne.
- B ☐ Sylvia und Aynur.
- C ☐ Thomas und Lisa.

1. Why does Susanne want to have a picnic?

2. What does Lisa do? Is she coming along, too?

3. When is the picnic?

4. What does the radio say?

5. Where do they meet?

6. Who is preparing the picnic?

Practice makes perfect

CD 2 – TR. 53

6

Read and listen to the words describing the weather.

1. die Tempera- **2.** der Nebel **3.** die Wolke **4.** der Himmel
tur

5. die Sonne **6.** der Regen **7.** der Wind **8.** der Schnee

CD 2 – TR. 54

The weather report often uses very short sentences by adding directions, e. g.: Das Wetter in Deutschland: Im Süden und Osten blauer Himmel und Sonne, im Norden Wind, im Westen Regen. *(The weather in Germany: In the South and East blue sky and sun, in the North wind, in the West rain.)*

7

CD 2 – TR. 55

Wie ist das Wetter? *(What is the weather like?)* is the main question if you want to talk about the weather. Let's have a look at possible answers:

 NICE TO KNOW

When talking about the temperature the word **Grad** *(degree)* is always used in the singular. That's why you can also say: **Es ist 20 Grad.** *(It's 20 degrees.)*

- **Es regnet.** *(It's raining.)* **Es schneit.** *(It's snowing.)* **Die Sonne scheint.** *(The sun is shining.)*
- **Das Wetter ändert sich.** *(The weather is changing.)*
- **Das Wetter bleibt schön / schlecht.** *(The weather is going to stay fine / bad.)*
- **Es ist sonnig / windig / neblig / kalt / heiß.** *(It's sunny / windy / foggy / cold / hot.)*
- **Es ist regnerisch / bewölkt / wechselhaft.** *(It's rainy / cloudy / changeable.)*
- **Herrliches Wetter heute!** *(Wonderful weather today!)* ◄► **Furchtbares Wetter heute!** *(Terrible weather today!)*

If you want to know the temperature you can ask and answer:
- **Wie hoch ist die Temperatur?** *(What's the temperature?)*
- **Es sind 25 Grad.** *(It's 25 degrees.)* **Es sind minus 3 Grad.** *(It's 3 degrees below freezing.)*

CD 2 – TR. 56

25

8

The conjunction **wenn** (**1.** *if, in case,* **2.** *when*) introduces a subordinate clause with a conditional or a temporal meaning:

• Wir bleiben zu Hause, **wenn** es am Wochenende regnet.
  (We'll stay at home, if it rains at the weekend.)
• Er liest die Zeitung, **wenn** er frühstückt.
  (He always reads the newspaper, when he has his breakfast.)

You have probably noticed the new word order: The conjugated verb is always at the end of the subordinate clause. This rule is also valid if the verb has two parts, e. g.:

• Wir gehen spazieren, wenn das Wetter **schön ist**.
  (We'll go for a walk if the weather is fine.)
• Ich frühstücke, wenn ich **geduscht habe**.
  (I have breakfast when I've had a shower.)
• Er freut sich, wenn er nicht **arbeiten muss**.
  (He's glad when he doesn't have to work.)

Put the **wenn**-sentences into the right order. After doing that repeat the sentences aloud.

1. Wir machen ein Picknick, | scheint. | die Sonne | wenn

_____

2. Ich gehe aus, | ich | habe. | gegessen | wenn

_____

3. Er kommt um 12 Uhr an, | ist. | pünktlich | wenn | der Zug

_____

9

Connect the two sentences by using the conjunction **wenn**. In the word box are two sample sentences.
Watch out for the word order and don't forget to put a comma in front of the clause starting with **wenn**.

1. Er freut sich. Er bekommt Geschenke.
2. Ich komme gern. Ich habe Zeit.
3. Bring ihm das Buch mit. Du siehst ihn morgen.
4. Wir gehen spazieren. Das Wetter bleibt schön.
5. Sie geht in die Disco. Sie will ihre Freunde treffen.

Er freut sich nicht. Er muss arbeiten.

▶ Er freut sich nicht, wenn er arbeiten muss.

Wir gehen in den Biergarten. Es regnet am Abend nicht.

▶ Wir gehen in den Biergarten, wenn es am Abend nicht regnet.

Practice makes perfect

CD 2 – TR. 57

NICE TO KNOW

The expression **es geht (nicht)** (that is / isn't all right) or the emphazised version **das geht (nicht)** also have another meaning. You can use it to express that something functions or not it works / it doesn't work.

° 10

To arrange the place and time of an official meeting or a private date you can use the following phrases:

- **Haben Sie am Samstag (schon) etwas vor?**
  (Do you have anything (already) planned for Saturday?)
- **Was hast du heute Abend vor?** (What have you planned for this evening?)
- **Wann und wo treffen wir uns (mit Frau Müller)?**
  (When and where do we meet (Mrs. Müller)?)
- **Wann passt es Ihnen | dir?** (What time would suit you?)
- **Passt es Ihnen | dir um 3 Uhr?** (Would it suit you at 3 o'clock?)
- **Können Sie | Kannst du am 11. März?** (Can you do it on March 11ᵗʰ?)
- **Geht es morgen?** (Is tomorrow all right?)

To express that you already have other plans you can use the same structures as in the exercise below.

CD 2 – TR. 58

Listen to the answers and fill in the gaps.

1. Das _____ mir leider nicht.

2. Nein, es _____ leider nicht.

3. Tut mir leid, ich _____ nicht.

CD 2 – TR. 59

° 11

What can you say if you want to invite someone out or if you are invited out?

- **Ich möchte dich zu einem Picknick | zum Abendessen einladen.**
  (I'd like to invite you to a picnic | to dinner.)
- **Ich bedanke mich herzlich für die Einladung.**
  (Thank you very much for the invitation.)

What do you have to think of? Here are a few common questions and answers:

- **Holst du mich ab?** (Will you pick me up?)
  Können Sie mich abholen? (Can you pick me up?)
- **Ja, ich kann dich um 7 am Bahnhof abholen.**
  (I can pick you up at the railway station at 7 p.m.)
- **Soll ich etwas mitbringen?** (Shall I bring something along?)
- **Nein, das ist nicht nötig.** (No, that's not necessary.)

By the way, like in many other countries, it is common to bring a small gift for the host. Typical gifts are:
eine Flasche Sekt (a bottle of sparkling wine), **Blumen** (flowers), **Schokolade** (chocolate), **Pralinen** (pralinee)

12

CD 2 – TR. 60

Compare the following two sentences:
- **Ich ändere mich.** *(I'll change myself.)* – Infinitive: sich ändern
- **Ich ändere etwas.** *(I'll change something.)* – Infinitive: ändern

The first sentence has a reflexive verb, the second hasn't.

The sign for the infinitive of a reflexive verb is the pronoun **sich** *(oneself)*. The reflexive pronoun refers back to the subject and is identical with it. The forms are:

Singular:	ich ändere mich, du änderst dich, er /sie /es ändert sich
Plural:	wir ändern uns, ihr ändert euch, sie ändern sich
Polite form:	Sie ändern sich

Write reflexive pronouns into the gaps.

1. Interessierst du _____ für Kunst?

2. Wir freuen _____ auf euren Besuch.

3. Treffen Sie _____ heute mit Frau Müller?

The **perfect tense** of reflexive verbs is always formed by using the auxiliary verb haben: **ich habe mich geändert, du hast dich geändert** etc.

Watch out if the German verb takes a preposition or not:

sich freuen – *to be pleased /glad*

sich freuen über – *to be pleased about*

sich freuen auf – *to look forward to*

sich treffen mit – *to meet*

treffen (not reflexive!) – *to meet*

 NICE TO KNOW

The forms of the 1st and 2nd person are identical with the accusative pronoun. Only the polite form and the 3rd person have the **sich**. It's easy, isn't it?

13

Fill the gaps. Write reflexive pronouns and the present tense of the verbs given in brackets.

 23

1. Ich (1)_____ (2)_____ sehr über das Geschenk.
   (sich freuen)

2. Sylvia und Aynur (3)_____ (4)_____ für die Einladung. *(sich bedanken)*

3. Wir (5)_____ (6)_____ heute mit den Kollegen.
   (sich treffen)

4. Das Wetter (7)_____ (8)_____ . Schade! *(sich ändern)*

5. (9)_____ du (10)_____ schon auf die Party?
   (sich freuen)

° 14

Let's have a look at the new words from this unit. What is shown in the pictures? Mark the right word.

1.
   A ☐ Blumen
   B ☐ Pralinen
   C ☐ Sekt

2.
   A ☐ der Norden
   B ☐ die Schokolade
   C ☐ die Temperatur

3.
   A ☐ das Grad
   B ☐ der Schnee
   C ☐ der Herbst

4.
   A ☐ der Osten
   B ☐ der Frühling
   C ☐ der Besuch

° 15

Scrambled sentences! Put the words into the right position in order to get correct statements, questions and subordinate clauses.
Then repeat each sentence and focus on the position of the conjugated verb.

1. über deinen Besuch | habe | gefreut. | mich | Ich
2. am Wochenende, | Was | wir | machen | es regnet? | wenn
3. dir | das Buch, | Ich | gebe | wenn | ich | habe. | es | gelesen
4. interessiert. | für Kunst | Er | hat | nie | sich
5. im Norden? | es | bei euch | Schneit
6. gelernt. | seine Freunde | hat | kennen | Sie | endlich
7. mir | Es | passt | gut, | wenn | am Freitag | treffen. | wir | uns

Remember the word order.

> Main clauses:
> Subject – **conjugated verb** – complements.
> Interrogative pronoun – **conjugated verb** – subject – complements?
> **Conjugated verb** – subject – complements?
> Subordinate clauses:
> ..., conjunction – subject – complements – **conjugated verb**

1

CD 2 - TR. 61

Look at the picture. What can you buy in a supermarket? What do people talk about? Listen and read.
In the word box below you can also read the translations of the sentences.

2. Was darf es sein?

3. 200 Gramm Käse am Stück, bitte.

8. Die Tomaten sind aber billig!

9. Aber ich mag lieber Gurken.

7. die Tasche

1. die Verkäuferin

6. Oh ja! Der ist lecker!

4. der Einkaufskorb

5. Schmeckt der Käse?

---

2. *What can I get you?*
3. *200 grams of cheese in one piece, please.*
5. *Do you like the taste of this cheese?*

6. *Oh yes! It's delicious!*
8. *The tomatoes are really cheap!*
9. *But I prefer cucumbers.*

Listen in!

CD 2 - TR. 62

NICE TO KNOW

Adjectives from the exercise and their forms are used to compare something:
billig – billig**er** *(cheaper)*
groß – größ**er** *(bigger)*
klein – klein**er** *(smaller)*
warm – am wärm**sten** *(warmest)*
gefährlich – **am** gefährlich**sten** *(most dangerous)*

§ 1

2

Look at the pictures. Read and listen to the questions. Write the correct answers into the gaps. It's not very difficult to guess the meaning of the sentences. On the left there is more information about the new structures.

1. Was ist billiger?

_____

2. Welches Haus ist größer?

Das gelbe oder das hellblaue?

_____

3. Wer ist kleiner?

Hans oder Martin?

_____

4. Wo ist es am wärmsten?

_____

5. Welches Tier ist am gefährlichsten?

_____

A Hans ist kleiner.

B Das Krokodil ist am gefährlichsten.

C Das Mineralwasser ist billiger.

D In Köln ist es am wärmsten.

E Das gelbe Haus ist größer.

○ 3

 CD 2 – TR. 63

Read the names of the food and their translation in the word box.
Read and listen to the names of the food below. Where can you buy
them? Write the words into the right box.
After doing that repeat the words aloud.

die Salami – *salami*

frisches Obst –
fresh fruit

vier Brötchen –
four rolls

der Salat – *lettuce*

1. Bäckerei	2. Markt	3. Metzgerei
_____	_____	_____
_____	_____	_____
_____	_____	_____

drei Scheiben Schin-
ken – *three slices of
ham*

das Gemüse –
vegetables

die Bratwurst –
frying sausage

das Brot – *bread*

> **die Salami | frisches Obst | vier Brötchen | der Salat |
> drei Scheiben Schinken | das Gemüse | die Bratwurst | das Brot**

○ 4

 CD 2 – TR. 64

 NICE TO KNOW

It's Friday and Susanne Kowalski is planning the picnic. She has already
decided what to prepare and now she's going to do the shopping. Her
husband Thomas wants to know what they are going to have for the picnic and whether Susanne needs some help.
Listen to the dialogue and look at the picture. Then read the tapescript in
the appendix and listen again to the dialogue.

Der Salat has two
meanings: *lettuce* and
salad as in **Obstsalat**
(*fruit salad*). To avoid
misunderstandings
you can use the word
Kopfsalat (*lettuce*).

Practice makes perfect

○ **5**

Let's have a look at some details from the introductory dialogue.
Answer the questions below. Note that two, three or even four answers
are possible.
Then check your understanding by reading the translation of the whole
dialogue in the appendix.

1. Was macht Susanne morgen?
  A ☐ Sie kauft Getränke.
  B ☐ Sie geht in die Bäckerei.
  C ☐ Sie kauft Brötchen.
  D ☐ Sie geht in den Super-
     markt.

2. Was macht oder sagt Thomas?
  A ☐ Er geht mit Lisa einkaufen.
  B ☐ Er möchte Susanne helfen.
  C ☐ Er kauft die Getränke.
  D ☐ Er möchte Brötchen
     zum Picknick.

3. Was kauft Susanne in der Metzgerei?
  A ☐ Sie kauft 400 Gramm Salami.
  B ☐ Sie kauft die Salami am Stück.
  C ☐ Sie kauft zehn Bratwürste.
  D ☐ Sie kauft auch Schinken.

 CD 2 - TR. 65

○ **6**

Read and listen to the names of the food. On the left you can also see the
article and the singular form.

die Kartoffel
die Apfelsine
die Nudel
das Ei
die Zwiebel
die Banane
die Birne
der Apfel
die Karotte
die Bohne

1. Kartoffeln **2.** Apfel-   **3.** Nudeln **4.** Eier **5.** Zwiebeln
              sinen

6. Bananen **7.** Birnen **8.** Äpfel **9.** Karotten **10.** Bohnen

> Note that the following **Lebensmittel** *(food)* are only used in the singular: **der
> Reis** *(rice)*, **das Fleisch** *(meat)*, **das Obst** *(fruit)*, **das Gemüse** *(vegetables)*.

7

CD 2 – TR. 66

If you want to buy food it's good to know some measures and weights.
Here are the most common ones:
der Liter *(liter)*, **der halbe Liter** *(half liter)*,
das Gramm *(gram)*, **das Pfund** *(pound)*, **das Kilo / Kilogramm** *(kilogram)*,
das Stück *(piece)*; don't mix it up with **am Stück** *(in one piece)*.

These words are used in the singular even if you buy more than one
piece or more than one liter. In the word box are also the most important
abbreviations.

What do the following abbreviations stand for? Listen and complete the
gaps with the missing words.

1. 5 kg Kartoffeln = fünf _____ Kartoffeln.

2. 2 St. Gurken = zwei _____ Gurken.

3. ½ l Milch = ein halber _____ Milch.

You could also buy:
drei Scheiben Käse *(three slices of cheese)*, **zwei Flaschen Bier** *(two bottles
of beer)*, **vier Dosen Cola** *(four tins of coke)*, **zwei Tüten Chips** *(two bags
of crisps)*, **zwei Packungen Reis** *(two packets of rice)*.

The following abbre-
viations are often
used on price-tags:

l	= Liter
Ltr.	= Liter
g	= Gramm
kg	= Kilo /Kilo-gramm
St.	= Stück
Fl.	= Flasche
Pckg.	= Packung

 NICE TO KNOW

In Austria a further
weight is used: **das
Deka** or das **Deka-
gramm** *(10 grams)*.

8

Look at Mrs. Müller's shopping list. What's she going to buy? Complete
the text by writing the missing words into the gaps.
Remember that the weights are used in the singular form.

Zuerst geht Frau Müller in den Supermarkt. Dort kauft sie einen

(1)_____ Milch, 5 **(2)**_____ Kartoffeln
und 300 **(3)**_____ Käse. Sie besorgt auch zwei
Packungen **(4)**_____ und eine **(5)**_____
Chips. Dann geht sie zum **(6)**_____ und kauft
zwei **(7)**_____ Kuchen und ein **(8)**_____
Brot.

Supermarkt

1 l Milch
5 kg Kartoffeln
300 g Käse
2 x Nudeln
1 x Chips

Bäcker

2 St. Kuchen
1 kg dunkles Brot

CD 2 - TR. 67

9

Let's have a look at some typical questions you could be asked in a super-market and their possible answers:

- **Was darf es sein?** *(What can I get you?)*
- **Ich hätte gern 400 Gramm Salami / 1 Pfund Käse.**
  (I'd like 400 grams of Salami / one pound of cheese.)
- **Am Stück oder geschnitten?** *(In one piece or sliced?)*
- **Geschnitten. Ganz dünne Scheiben, bitte.** *(Sliced. Very thin slices, please.)*
- **Darf es auch etwas mehr ◀▶ weniger sein?**
  (Would a little bit more ◀▶ less be OK?)
- **Ja, gerne. / Nein, ich brauche genau 400 Gramm.**
  (Yes, please. / No, I need exactly 400 grams.)
- **Darf es sonst noch etwas sein?** *(Would you like anything else?)*
- **Danke, das ist alles.** *(Thank you, that's all.)*

CD 2 - TR. 68

Listen to the questions and write the answers.

1. _____

2. _____

3. _____

> 4 Bratwürste. | Ja. | Am Stück.

CD 2 - TR. 69

10

If you want to talk about the quality or the price of food you can use the following expressions:

- **Ist das Brot frisch?** *(Is the bread fresh?)*
  Ist das Brot von heute? *(Is the bread from today?)*
- **Das Toastbrot ist hart.** *(The toast is hard.)*
- **Frisches Obst ist gesund.** *(Fresh fruit is healthy.)*
- **Schneiden Sie die Salami bitte ganz dünn.**
  (Slice the salami very thin, please.)
- **Die Tomaten sind im Angebot.** *(The tomatoes are on offer.)*
  Sie sind sehr billig! *(They are very cheap!)*
- **Was kostet ein Kilo Bohnen?** *(How much is one kilogram of beans?)*
  Wie viel kosten die Bohnen? *(How much are the beans?)*
- **Die Bohnen kosten 2 Euro das Kilo / pro Kilo.**
  (The beans cost 2 Euros per kilogram.)

° 11

Comparison of adjectives and adverbs

1. Regular forms:

klein	kleiner	**am kleinsten**
laut	lauter	**am lautesten**
alt	**älter**	**am ältesten**

- The comparative is formed by adding the ending **-er**.
- The superlative is formed with **am** and the ending **-sten** or **-esten** for adjectives ending in **-d**, **-t**, **-s**, **-ß**, **-sch** and **-z**.
- One-syllable adjectives often change the vowel into an 'Umlaut'.

2. Some forms are irregular and have to be learned by heart:

gut	**besser**	**am besten**
viel	**mehr**	**am meisten**

Look at the word box for more examples.

Complete the series and write the missing forms into the gaps.

1. hell – heller – _____

2. jung – _____ – am jüngsten

3. kalt – _____ – am kältesten

° 12

If you want to compare two unequal qualities you have to use the comparative form and **als** (than):

- Ich bin **älter als** meine Schwester. (I'm older than my sister.)
- Brötchen schmecken **besser als** Brot. (Rolls taste better than bread.)
- Frisches Gemüse ist **gesünder als** Gemüse aus der Dose.
  (Fresh vegetables are healthier than vegetables from a tin.)
- Im Garten ist es **schöner als** auf dem Balkon.
  (It's nicer in the garden than on the balcony.)

Complete the sentences by filling in the comparative form and **als**.

1. Bier ist _____ Wein.

2. In Köln ist es _____ in Berlin.

3. Ich trinke Kaffee _____ Tee.

Sidebar:

1. Regular forms with umlauts

warm (warm) – wärmer – am wärmsten

lang (long) – länger – am längsten

kurz (short) – kürzer – am kürzesten

Adjectives in -el or -er drop the e in the comparative form.

dunkel (dark) – dunkler – am dunkelsten

teuer (expensive) – teurer – am teuersten

2. Irregular forms

groß (big) – größer – am größten

hoch (high) – höher – am höchsten

nah (near) – näher – am nächsten

! gern (to like) – lieber (to prefer) – am liebsten (to like best of all)

 CD 2 – TR. 70

 NICE TO KNOW

Be careful when comparing gern: **ich trinke gern Wein** (I like drinking wine), **er trinkt lieber Cola** (he prefers coke), **sie trinkt am liebsten Bier** (she likes beer best of all).

 CD 2 – TR. 71

Finishing up

° **13**

Read the description and mark the missing word.

1. The opposite of **billig**: V R T G E R T E U E R M U R C K S

2. Which word means "the same to you"?
I N T Ä G T G L E I C H F A L L S B E G R T Z

3. If you go shopping you can use a shopping bag or a ...
B E N Z E I N K A U F S K O R B L Ö G E R

4. The German word for "healthy": G E N Ü S S G E S U N D S I N G D

5. The infinitive form of the past participle **geschnitten** (*sliced*):
F O R S C H N E I D E N G R Ü S D U

° **14**

Complete the sentences by choosing the right expression.

1. Ich finde, Orangen schmecken _____ als Äpfel.
   A ☐ nicht   B ☐ schlecht   C ☐ besser

2. Ich esse _____ Käse zum Frühstück.
   A ☐ am liebsten   B ☐ lieber als   C ☐ gut

3. Wir kaufen immer im Supermarkt ein. Dort ist es _____.
   A ☐ weniger   B ☐ am billigsten   C ☐ sehr teuer

° **15**

The names for food in the German-speaking countries vary a lot. Let's have a look at some examples. "Carrots" have a lot of different names e. g. **Karotten**, which is used in some German regions and in Austria. Other names for "carrots" are for example: **Möhren** in Middle Germany or **Gelberüben** in Southern Germany.

Also "potatoes", "oranges" and "rolls" have different names: **Kartoffeln** (*potatoes*) and **Brötchen** (*rolls*) are used in in the North and in the Middle of Germany. **Erdäpfel** (*potatoes*) and **Semmeln** (*rolls*) are used in Southern Germany and in Austria. The other very common word for **Orangen** is **Apfelsinen** (*oranges*).

And what about Switzerland? There, people say **Erdäpfel**, **Weggli** and **Orangen** (*potatoes, rolls, oranges*).

Then there are words which are only used in Austria. If you'd like to buy "ein Kilo Tomaten und einen Blumenkohl" (*a kilogram of tomatoes and a cauliflower*) you would say: **Ich möchte ein Kilo Paradeiser und einen Karfiol.**

1

Look at the picture. How have people changed? Read and listen to what the situation was 8 years ago compared to now.

Can you guess the meaning of the sentences with the help of the pictures? In the word box you get more information about a new tense.

 CD 2 – TR. 72

 NICE TO KNOW

The following forms of **sein** and **haben** are forms of the past tense:
er **war** – he was
wir **waren** – we were
sie **hatte** – she had
ich **hatte** – I had

vor 8 Jahren

1. Er war Student.

3. Wir waren gute Schüler.

7. Ich hatte noch keinen Computer.

5. Sie hatte viele Freunde.

jetzt

2. Jetzt ist er Arzt.

4. Jetzt sind wir Geschäftsleute.

8. Jetzt habe ich einen Computerladen.

6. Jetzt hat sie keine Freunde.

Listen in!

° 2

What are the people in the pictures doing? Write the sentences below to the corresponding picture.
Repeat the sentences and focus on the verbs. What is the exact meaning? Look at the word box for help.

holen – *to get, to fetch*

malen – *to paint*

probieren – *to try*

anbieten (ich biete an) – *to offer*

wegwerfen (ich werfe weg) – *to throw away*

1. _____

2. _____

3. _____

4. _____

5. _____

A Er bietet Kuchen an.
B Der Künstler malt ein Bild.

C Die Männer holen den Abfall.
D Sie probiert den Wein.
E Er wirft die Flasche weg.

° 3

Which questions would you ask a child? Listen to some typical questions and match the correct translation to the corresponding question. Repeat the questions aloud and focus on the intonation.

1. Was ist dein Traumberuf?

2. Was möchtest du einmal werden?

3. Sind deine Eltern sehr streng?

4. Macht dir die Schule Spaß?

5. In welche Klasse gehst du?

6. Möchtest du Eis zum Nachtisch?

____ A *In which year at school are you?*

____ B *Do you like ice-cream for dessert?*

____ C *What's your dream job?*

____ D *Do you enjoy school?*

____ E *Are your parents very strict?*

____ F *What would you like to be when you grow up?*

4

Thomas, Susanne, their daughter Lisa and their guests Sylvia and Aynur are sitting on the meadows close to the river Rhine having a picnic. Susanne is making friends with Thomas' colleagues. The atmosphere is very good, only Lisa is a bit shy. Now the picnic is nearly over. Listen to what they were talking about during the picnic.

5

Listen again to the introductory dialogue and focus on the professions and personal characteristics that are mentioned.
Decide whether the words given below appear in the dialogue or not.
Mark the tick for "yes" and the cross for "no".
The professions and characteristics listed below are new in this unit. Look at the right margin for the translation.

Jobs:

die Ärztin – *female doctor*

die Geschäftsfrau – *business woman*

die Künstlerin – *female artist*

die Malerin – *female painter*

die Sportlerin – *sportswoman*

Characteristics:

freundlich – *kind*

hungrig – *hungry*

nett – *nice*

satt – *full (after having eaten enough)*

schüchtern – *shy*

1. Künstlerin ✓ ✗   **2.** Malerin ✓ ✗

3. Sportlerin ✓ ✗   **4.** Ärztin ✓ ✗

5. Geschäftsfrau ✓ ✗   **6.** schüchtern ✓ ✗

7. nett ✓ ✗

8. freundlich ✓ ✗   **9.** satt ✓ ✗

10. hungrig ✓ ✗

Practice makes perfect

 CD 2 - TR. 76

6

Let's have a look at some useful expressions for a private invitation. In the role of the **Gastgeber** *(host)* you could say:
- **Was kann ich Ihnen anbieten?** *(What can I offer you?)*
- **Darf ich Ihnen noch etwas anbieten?** *(May I offer you anything else?)*
- **Möchten Sie noch etwas Nachtisch / Kaffee / Obstsalat?**
  (Would you like more dessert / coffee / fruit salad?)
- **Bitte bedienen Sie sich.** *(Please help yourself.)*

Of course, you can use the same expressions in the du-form.

As the **Gast** *(guest)* you can use the following phrases:
- **Ich hätte gern ein Glas Mineralwasser.**
  (I'd like to have a glass of mineral water.)
- **Ich nehme gern noch etwas / noch eine kleine Portion.**
  (I like another bit / another small portion.)
- **Danke, ich bin satt.** *(Thank you, I'm full.)*
- **Das war sehr lecker.** *(That was very delicious.)*
  Das war wirklich ausgezeichnet. *(That was really excellent.)*

Male and female job titles:

der Sportler,
   die Sportlerin

der Zahnarzt,
   die Zahnärztin

der Automecha-
   niker, die Auto-
   mechanikerin

der Landwirt,
   die Landwirtin

der Geschäfts-
   mann, die Ge-
   schäftsfrau

 CD 2 - TR. 77

der Lehrer,
   die Lehrerin

der Sänger,
   die Sängerin

der Schreiner,
   die Schreinerin

der Kranken-
   pfleger, die Kran-
   kenschwester

der Frisör / Friseur,
   die Frisörin /
   Friseurin.

Both spellings are used. The pronunciation remains the same. Also, the older female form **die Friseuse** is in use, too.

7

Listen to what the jobs illustrated in the pictures are called. Look at the word box to read both the male and the female job titles.

Sportlerin   Zahnarzt   Automecha-   Landwirt   Geschäfts-
                        niker   mann

Lehrerin   Sängerin   Schreiner   Kranken-   Frisör
                                  schwester

If you want to know someone's profession you can ask:
- **Was sind Sie von Beruf? / Was machst du beruflich?**
  (What's your profession?).
- **Ich bin Künstler.** *(I'm an artist.)*
  Ich arbeite als Künstler. *(I work as an artist.)*

CD 2 – TR. 78

8

To describe somebody's appearance you can use the words:
- **hübsch** *(pretty)*, **attraktiv** *(attractive)*, **sportlich** *(sporty)*
- **schlank ◀▶ mollig** *(slim ◀▶ plump)*

To describe someone's character you can use:
- **nett** *(nice)*, **freundlich** *(friendly)*, **sympathisch** *(pleasant)*, **höflich** *(polite)*
- **schüchtern ◀▶ selbstbewusst** *(shy ◀▶ self-confident)*
- **fleißig ◀▶ faul** *(diligent ◀▶ lazy)*

Do you miss the opposite of some of the adjectives? It's easy to form them as you can see in the following exercise.

Listen and write the missing words into the gaps.
The translation is in the word box.

1. Das ist aber eine _____ Person!

2. Du bist _____, wenn du zu spät kommst.

3. Er ist mir _____.

> unhöflich | unsympathisch | unfreundliche

The prefix **un-** is also used with **unsportlich** *(unathletic)* and **unattraktiv** *(unattractive)*.

9

What's the opposite? Write the missing word into the gap.

1. freundlich _____

2. hungrig _____

3. fleißig _____

4. unhöflich _____

5. selbstbewusst _____

6. mollig _____

7. sympathisch _____

NICE TO KNOW

You can use words like **nett** or **attraktiv** also to characterize things or situations, e.g. **eine nette Geschichte** *(a nice story)*, **das Angebot ist attraktiv** *(the offer is attractive)*.

CD 2 – TR. 79

That's a really unfriendly person!

You are impolite if you arrive too late.

I don't like him.

○ 10

In the introductory dialogue forms like **ich war** *(I was)* and **du hattest** *(you had)* are used. These are forms of the past tense of **haben** and **sein**. Let's have a look at the paradigm.

	haben	sein
ich	hatte	**war**
du	hattest	**war**st
er, sie, es	hatte	**war**
wir	hatten	**war**en
ihr	hattet	**war**t
sie	hatten	**war**en
Sie	hatten	**war**en

It's not difficult to memorize these forms. All you need is the stem of the past form and then, usually, just add the normal endings.

CD 2 - TR. 80

NICE TO KNOW

Note that the use of the German past tense doesn't automatically correspond with the simple past tense in English or in your native language.

○ 11

When do you have to use the past tense?

> The good news is that only the past tense of a few verbs like **haben** and **sein** and the modals (see unit 16) are really used **in the spoken language**. To talk about the past the perfect tense is much more common.

Nevertheless, let's have a look at some examples in which you do use the past tense:

- **Als Kind war ich oft allein.** *(As a child I was often on my own.)*
- **Meine Großeltern hatten sehr strenge Lehrer.** *(My grandparents had very strict teachers.)*
- **Hatten Sie 1964 schon ein Auto?** *(Did you already have a car in 1964?)*
- **Früher hatte er einen Traumberuf. Er war Arzt.** *(He used to have a dream job. He was a doctor.)*

Fill in the gaps with the past tense of **haben** and **sein**.

 17

1. Als Kind _____ ich viele Haustiere.

2. Früher _____ wir oft in der Schweiz.

3. 1980 _____ er viel Erfolg mit seiner Musik.

In written German you'll find the past tense a lot, if the story starts and ends in the past. The typical beginning of a fairy-tale is:
Es war einmal ... *(Once upon a time ...)*

12

Complete the sentences and write the correct past tense form into the gaps. Then repeat the sentences aloud.

NICE TO KNOW

In Southern Germany and in Austria the perfect tense is often used instead of the past tense, e.g. **Wo bist du gewesen?** instead of **Wo warst du?** (*Where have you been?*).

> war | warst | wart | waren | hatte | hatten

1. 1998 _____ ich zum ersten Mal in Rom.

2. Frau Schulze, _____ Sie früher Haustiere?

3. Peter, wo _____ du am Wochenende?

4. Warum _____ ihr nicht im Sportverein?

5. Gestern _____ ich keine Zeit für das Picknick.

6. Franz und Tina _____ letzte Woche in Berlin.

13

CD 2 – TR. 81

Listen to what Mrs. Kramer and Mr. Kolb are telling you about their childhood.
Then answer the questions by marking the tick for "yes" and the cross for "no". Do this for both people.
Then answer the questions as they relate to you.

	Frau Kramer yes	no	Herr Kolb yes	no	Myself yes	no
1. Waren Sie als Kind schüchtern?	☐	☐	☐	☐	☐	☐
2. Sind Sie gern in die Schule gegangen?	☐	☐	☐	☐	☐	☐
3. Waren Sie ein guter Schüler / eine gute Schülerin?	☐	☐	☐	☐	☐	☐
4. Hatten Sie einen Traumberuf?	☐	☐	☐	☐	☐	☐
5. Hatten Sie viele Freunde?	☐	☐	☐	☐	☐	☐
6. Haben Sie früher Fußball gespielt?	☐	☐	☐	☐	☐	☐

CD 2 – TR. 82

NICE TO KNOW

There is a slight difference between **Abfall** and **Müll**. **Abfall** is used more for organic waste and **Müll** is all kind of waste that is collected and transported in containers.

14

Here are some useful phrases to do with environmental awareness in German-speaking countries:

• **Sind das Pfandflaschen?** *(Are these refundable bottles?)*
• **Gibt es auf die Flaschen Pfand?** *(Is there a deposit on the bottles?)*
• **Kann ich das (einfach) wegwerfen?** *(Can I (just) throw that away?)*
• **Sortiert ihr den Müll?** *(Do you sort the waste?)*
• **Wohin kann ich die Flaschen / das Papier / die Verpackungen bringen?**
  (Where can I take the bottles / the paper / the packagings?)

And where can you put the waste? Here are some possibilities:
• **Wirf es in den Abfalleimer / in die Mülltonne / in den Container!**
  (Throw it into the rubbish bin / into the dustbin / into the container!)
• **Bring die Flaschen in den Supermarkt zurück.**
  (Take the bottles back to the supermarket.)

You get 15 cents deposit per bottle.

Don't throw the bottle away. It's a refundable bottle.

We sort paper, glass and plastic.

Complete the sentences by choosing the correct word. The translation is on the left.

1. Man bekommt 15 Cent *Müll / Pfand / Papier* pro Flasche.

2. Wirf die Flasche nicht *zurück / ab / weg*! Es ist eine Pfandflasche.

3. Wir *sortieren / werfen / kommen* Papier, Glas und Plastik.

15

Recycling is taken very seriously in all German-speaking countries and environmental protection has a long tradition. Already little children as the one in the introductory dialogue are sensitized to an enviromentally waste recovery. Packaging materials that have **der grüne Punkt** *(a green dot on the packaging)* are placed in special recycling bins or bags. Non-refundable bottles and glasses are collected in separate containers for white, green and brown glass. Paper and cardboard are also collected and disposed of separately. And what about organic waste? People who live in the country-side usually have a compost heap. However, some towns provide bins especially for organic waste. Otherwise you have to put the organic waste in a bin for **der Restmüll** *(waste that cannot be recycled)*.

When shopping, people usually take a bag or basket with them in order to avoid superfluous waste like plastic bags. Talking about superfluous waste, you can leave packaging materials behind in the shop where you bought a product. The shopkeeper is obliged to take back packaging.

° 1

The carnival is one of the biggest events in many German-speaking countries. What is this event all about?

Look at the pictures and hear the description. Then write the expression you heard into the gap. To make sure you understand the meanings of the words look at the words in the right margin..

colorful floats

children in costumes

a parade through the town

funny masks

big and crazy figures

1. _____ **2.** _____ **3.** _____

 NICE TO KNOW

Das Kostüm has two meanings:
1. the costume you wear at the carnival and
2. a (dress) suit for women.

4. _____ **5.** _____

A lustige Masken   C große und verrückte Figuren
B Kinder in Kostümen   D bunte Festwagen
                             E ein Umzug durch die Stadt

° 2

 CD 2 – TR. 84

Who could that shadow in the picture be? What do you think? Listen to six different ideas and write the missing word into the gap.

After doing that repeat the sentences aloud and try to guess the meaning. Check your understanding with the help of the information in the word box.

New structures:

aussehen wie –
to look like

so groß wie –
as tall as

ich vermute, dass –
I suppose that

┌───┐
│   **so** | **vermute** | **kann** | **sieht nicht aus** | **Clown** | **wie**   │
└───┘

1. Wer _____ das sein?

2. Vielleicht ist es ein _____ .

3. Die Person _____ wie eine Frau.

4. Ich _____ , dass es ein Mann ist.

5. Die Person ist _____ groß

_____ Peter.

 NICE TO KNOW

The word **dass** (*that*) introduces a subordinate clause.

Listen in!

3

Read the sentences and match them with the corresponding German translation. This task isn't difficult if you focus on the words you already know.

After doing that try to memorize the new words. It's worth knowing them because they are common.

In the Nice to know box below you can read some information about the grammar used in these sentences.

 NICE TO KNOW

The past participle of **verstehen** (to understand) is irregular: **ich habe verstanden** (I have understood).

1. I'm sorry, I don't understand the question.

2. To whom does this bag belong?

3. Yesterday he had to work for ten hours.

4. We couldn't attend the party.

5. Have you already planned your wedding ceremony?

6. The clubs build figures for the carnival.

7. I wasn't in Bonn, because I didn't have time.

A *Wir konnten nicht an der Party teilnehmen.*

B *Tut mir leid, ich verstehe die Frage nicht.*

C *Ich war nicht in Bonn, weil ich keine Zeit hatte.*

D *Die Vereine bauen Figuren für den Karneval.*

E *Wem gehört diese Tasche?*

F *Gestern musste er zehn Stunden arbeiten.*

G *Plant ihr schon eure Hochzeit?*

 NICE TO KNOW

Grammar explanations:
1. The word **weil** (because) introduces a subordinate clause.
2. There are two new past tense forms:
   wir konnten – we could
   er musste – he had to
3. The verb **gehören** (to belong to) governs the dative case:
   die Tasche gehört mir – the bag belongs to me
4. The verb **teilnehmen** (to attend) has got a separable prefix and is often followed by the preposition an:
   ich nehme am Karneval teil – I attend the carnival

4

After the picnic the Kowalskis, Sylvia and Aynur are on their way back to the car. The way is along the Rhine. Lisa, who is walking in front of the others, suddenly spots something swimming close to the bank of the Rhine. Everybody starts to wonder what this might be.
Listen to the dialogue at least twice. The first time just listen and look at the pictures. After doing that look at the appendix to read the tapescript and listen again.

CD 2 - TR. 86

5

Let's have a look at some details from the introductory dialogue. Listen again to the dialogue.
Read the sentences and decide whether they are true or false. Mark the tick for "yes" and the cross for "no".
Look at the word box for the translation of the dialogue.

CD 2 - TR. 86

	✓	✗
1. Das Krokodil sieht aus wie das Schwimmtier von Lisa.	☐	☐
2. Das Krokodil ist aus Papier und Plastik.	☐	☐
3. Sylvia geht oft ins Theater.	☐	☐
4. Das Krokodil ist vielleicht eine Figur für den Karneval.	☐	☐
5. Man bereitet den Karneval das ganze Jahr vor.	☐	☐
6. Sylvia kennt den Karneval in Düsseldorf nicht.	☐	☐
7. Thomas war im Februar in Wien.	☐	☐

6

What do people do during the carnival?

Practice makes perfect

 CD 2 - TR. 87

 NICE TO KNOW

Apart from *to wear* the verb **tragen** has another important meaning. It also means *to carry*, e.g. **ich trage die Tasche** (*I carry the bag*).

 23

- Die Leute **verkleiden sich**. (*People dress up.*)
- Sie **tragen** Verkleidungen. (*They wear fancy dress.*)
- Sie **ziehen** verrückte Kostüme **an**. (*They put on crazy costumes.*)
- Die Kinder **haben sich** als Clowns **verkleidet**.
  (*The children are dressed up as clowns.*)

In daily life you wouldn't dress up but you would do the following:
- Ich **ziehe mich an**. (*I get dressed.*)
- Sie **zieht sich** dreimal am Tag **um**.
  (*She changes her clothes three times a day.*)
- Er **zieht sich aus** und geht ins Bett. (*He undresses and goes to bed.*)

Complete the sentences by choosing the correct verb.

1. Willst du die Jacke nicht *tragen / verkleiden / ausziehen*?
Es ist sehr warm.

2. Ich stehe um 6 Uhr auf, dusche und ziehe mich *aus / an / um*.

Have you noticed that two of the new verbs have a reflexive and a non-reflexive variant? The verbs are:
- **sich anziehen** (*to get dressed*) and **anziehen** (*to put sth. on*)
- **sich ausziehen** (*to undress*) and **ausziehen** (*to take sth. off*)

7

 CD 2 - TR. 88

 NICE TO KNOW

Note that the plural of **das Material** is irregular, e.g. **Welche Materialien magst du?** (*Which materials do you like?*).

If you want to know the material something is made of you can ask:
Aus welchem Material ist das? (*Which material is this made of?*)

The answer has the structure "**aus** + name of the material":
Aus Papier. Aus Plastik. Aus Glas. (*Of paper. Of plastic. Of glass.*)

Other materials are:
das Holz (*wood*), **der Stein** (*stone*), **das Leder** (*leather*),
das Metall (*metal*), **das Gold** (*gold*), **das Silber** (*silver*),
der Stoff (*cloth*), **der Kunststoff** (*plastic*), **das Styropor** (*polystyrene*).

If you want to be sure that something is real you can ask:
Ist das echtes Gold / Silber / Leder? (*Is that real gold / silver / leather?*)

8

Read the expressions and write them into the right category.

1. Materialien   2. Karneval

_____   _____

_____   _____

_____   _____

_____   _____

_____   _____

NICE TO KNOW

If you are very surprised or astonished about something you can use the word **verrückt** (*crazy*) in expressions like **verrückt!** or **das ist ja verrückt!**

A echtes Leder
B der Kunststoff
C der Festwagen
D das Holz
E ich verkleide mich

F der Stein
G Gold und Silber
H eine Maske tragen
I verrückte Figuren
J ein großer Umzug

9

Do you remember? Only the past tense of a small number of verbs such as **haben**, **sein** and the modals are really used in the spoken language, e. g.:

 CD 2 - TR. 89

 17

• **Ich musste nach Wien fahren.** (*I had to go to Vienna.*)
• **Er konnte nicht am Karneval teilnehmen.** (*He couldn't attend the carnival.*)
• **Als Kind wollte sie Zahnärztin werden.**
  (*As a child she wanted to become a dentist.*)

The past tense forms of **müssen**, **können** and **wollen** are regular. Write the paradigm of the past tense of **wollen** in the table.

	müssen	können	wollen
ich	musste	konnte	_____
du	musstest	konntest	_____
er, sie, es	musste	konnte	_____
wir	mussten	konnten	_____
ihr	musstet	konntet	_____
sie	mussten	konnten	_____
Sie	mussten	konnten	_____

10

To ask for a reason you can use **warum?** (*why?*)

Practice makes perfect

 CD 2 – TR. 90

- **Warum** kommst du nicht ins Restaurant mit?
  (Why don't you come along to the restaurant?)

To give a reason you can use a subordinate clause starting with **weil** *(because)*.

- **Weil** ich keine Zeit habe. *(Because I don't have any time.)*
- **Weil** ich keine Lust habe. *(Because I don't feel like it.)*
- **Weil** Peter mich schon zum Abendessen eingeladen hat.
  (Because Peter has already invited me for dinner.)
- Ich kann nicht mitkommen, **weil** ich arbeiten muss.
  (I cannot come along, because I have to work.)

> Whether a main clause is used or not, the word order in the subordinate clause with **weil** always remains the same: the conjugated verb has to be placed at the end.

° 11

§ 25

Look at the picture and answer the question. Mark the answers that correspond to the picture. Note that two, three or even four answers could be correct and that the number of the questions corresponds to the numbers on the picture.

1. Warum seid ihr nicht spazieren gegangen?
- A ☐ Weil wir ein Picknick gemacht haben.
- B ☐ Weil es geregnet hat.
- C ☐ Weil das Wetter schlecht war.
- D ☐ Weil wir viel Spaß hatten.

2. Warum haben Sie kein Auto?
- A ☐ Weil ich lieber Fahrrad fahre.
- B ☐ Weil ich kein Auto brauche.
- C ☐ Weil ich nicht viel Geld habe.
- D ☐ Weil ein Auto sehr teuer ist.

3. Warum warst du nicht in der Disco?
- A ☐ Weil ich zu Hause bleiben wollte.
- B ☐ Weil ich tanzen wollte.
- C ☐ Weil ich lieber schlafen wollte.
- D ☐ Weil ich noch arbeiten musste.

° 12

In the introductory dialogue you can find sentences like:

CD 2 - TR. 91

- Ich vermute, **dass** das Krokodil dem Theater gehört.
  (I suppose that the crocodile belongs to the theatre.)
- Kann es sein, **dass** ihr genau dieses Krokodil sucht?
  (Could it be that you are looking exactly for this crocodile?)

In these sample sentences the conjunction **dass** *(that)* introduces a subordinate clause, where a thought or supposition is reported. To express a supposition you can use the following verbs:

- **denken** *(to think)*, **meinen** *(to think / to mean)*, **glauben** *(to believe)*, **vermuten** *(to suppose)*, **es kann sein** *(it can be)*

Apart from these expressions there are many other verbs which are often followed by a **dass**-sentence, e. g.:

- **erzählen** *(to tell)*, **schreiben** *(to write)*, **berichten** *(to report)* etc.
- Sie hat mir erzählt, **dass** sie einen neuen Freund hat.
  (She told me that she's got a new boyfriend.)

Complete the sentences and put the words into the right position.

1. Es kann sein, dass / verkleidet / sie sich / hat. / als Clown

2. Wir vermuten, dass / ist. / schon nach Hause / er / gegangen

13

To express that two items are the same you can use the following structures:
so / genauso + adjective / adverb + **wie** *(as ... as / just ... as)*
Maria ist **genauso** alt **wie** du. *(Maria is as old as you are.)*
Ich komme **so** bald **wie** möglich. *(I'll come as soon as possible.)*

Also the following structure is used to compare something:
aussehen + **wie** + nominative of a noun / pronoun *(to look like)*

Watch out for the word order. There are two possibilities:
Das Ding im Rhein **sieht aus wie** ein Krokodil.
(The thing in the Rhine looks like a crocodile.)
Das Ding im Rhein **sieht wie** ein Krokodil **aus**.
(The thing in the Rhine looks like a crocodile.)

Put the words into the right order.

1. mein Freund / aus. / wie / siehst / Du

2. aus / Das Tier / eine kleine Schlange. / sieht / wie

 CD 2 - TR. 92

 NICE TO KNOW

The verb **aussehen** *(to look like)* is also used to describe the appearance of somebody, e.g.: **Er sieht gut aus.** *(He looks good.)*

° 14

Let's practice the new vocabulary by combining verbs and nouns.
Read the question and decide which of the answers doesn't fit. Mark the wrong answer.

1. Was können Sie anziehen?
- A ☐ eine Jacke
- B ☐ eine Maske
- C ☐ einen Festwagen
- D ☐ ein Kostüm

2. Was können Sie planen?
- A ☐ eine Fahrt nach Wien
- B ☐ die Hochzeit
- C ☐ ein Wochenende
- D ☐ ein Stück Styropor

3. Was können Sie verstehen?
- A ☐ eine Sprache
- B ☐ eine Frage
- C ☐ ein Buch
- D ☐ einen Stein

4. Was können Sie bauen?
- A ☐ eine Unterbrechung
- B ☐ eine Figur
- C ☐ ein Haus
- D ☐ eine Straße

CD 2 - TR. 93

NICE TO KNOW

If you cannot believe something someone is telling you, you can ask **echt?** (really?).

° 15

Read and listen to the questions. What are the correct answers? Match them to the corresponding questions.

1. Aus welchem Material ist der Tisch?

2. Ist das echtes Leder?

3. Verkleidest du dich für den Umzug morgen?

4. Warum fahren Sie nicht mit dem Bus?

5. Was hat Maria erzählt?

6. Wie sieht der neue Freund von Petra aus?

7. Wem gehören diese verrückten Figuren?

8. Was wolltest du früher einmal werden?

____ **A** Ja, es ist echt.

____ **B** Sie gehören meinem Vater.

____ **C** Ja, ich verkleide mich als Clown.

____ **D** Er ist aus Holz und Metall.

____ **E** Ich wollte Automechaniker werden.

____ **F** Sie hat erzählt, dass sie im Juli heiratet.

____ **G** Er sieht sehr gut aus. Er ist ein attraktiver Mann!

____ **H** Weil ich lieber zu Fuß gehe.

1

CD 2 - TR. 94

In Units 13 – 16 you have learnt various expressions you can use in different situations. Match the description to the corresponding sample sentences and repeat them.

1. *You can talk about the weather.*

2. *You can say what you used to do in the past.*

3. *You can compare qualities.*

4. *You can do the shopping in a food store.*

5. *You can ask for someone's profession.*

6. *You can offer something during a meal.*

7. *You can ask for the reason.*

8. *You can give the reason.*

9. *You can make an arrangement.*

10. *You can make suppositions.*

_____ A Was machen Sie beruflich?

_____ B Frisches Obst ist gesünder als Obst aus der Dose.

_____ C Passt es Ihnen am Montag, um 15 Uhr?

_____ D Ich komme nicht mit, weil ich keine Lust habe.

_____ E Ich vermute, dass diese Tasche Maria gehört.

_____ F Es regnet und es ist windig.

_____ G Ich hätte gern 200 Gramm Salami am Stück.

_____ H Warum warst du nicht auf der Party?

_____ I Darf ich Ihnen noch etwas Nachtisch anbieten?

_____ J Früher war ich schüchtern und hatte wenig Freunde.

2

What can you tell somebody about your profession, your childhood, your likes and your native country? Write down your personal answers. Try to form complete sentences.
In the appendix you find a proposal of what to answer.

1. Was wollten Sie als Kind werden?
2. Und was sind Sie heute von Beruf?
3. Wie waren Sie als Schüler/Schülerin?
4. Warum lernen Sie Deutsch?
5. Was ist gesundes Essen? Was meinen Sie?
6. Wie ist das Wetter heute?
7. Feiern Sie zu Hause Karneval? Erzählen Sie!
8. Was bringt man in Ihrem Land zu einer Einladung mit?

3

There are different ways of expressing the same thing. Always read the first sentence in the examples below and decide which of the other three sentences has a similar meaning.

1. Er arbeitet als Lehrer.
  A ☐ Er ist Lehrer von Beruf.
  B ☐ Er möchte später Lehrer werden.
  C ☐ Sein Vater ist Lehrer.

2. Gehört dir die Jacke?
  A ☐ Was kostet die Jacke?
  B ☐ Warum ziehst du die Jacke aus?
  C ☐ Ist das deine Jacke?

3. Cola ist nicht so billig wie Bier.
  A ☐ Bier ist am teuersten.
  B ☐ Cola ist teurer als Bier.
  C ☐ Cola ist am billigsten.

4. Kannst du um 3 Uhr?
  A ☐ Gehst du um 3 Uhr nach Hause?
  B ☐ Bist du pünktlich?
  C ☐ Passt es dir um 3 Uhr?

5. Sie trägt ein Kostüm und eine Maske.
  A ☐ Sie sieht sehr schlecht aus.
  B ☐ Sie hat sich verkleidet.
  C ☐ Sie ist sympathisch.

6. Äpfel schmecken lecker.
  A ☐ Ich esse sehr gern Äpfel.
  B ☐ Ich mag keine Äpfel.
  C ☐ Äpfel sind gesund.

4

Complete the sentences to make comparisons.

> als | am | wie | lieber | größten | hoch

1. Das Haus ist so (1)_____ (2)_____ der Turm.

2. Peter ist (3)_____ (4)_____ .

3. Ich esse frisches Gemüse (5)_____ (6)_____ Gemüse aus der Dose.

Grammar

CD 2 - TR. 95

§ 23

5

Do you remember forms of reflexive verbs like **ich bedanke mich, du ziehst dich um** etc.?
Listen to the sample sentence. Then write the missing words into the gaps in order to complete the paradigm.

1. ich _____ mich an

2. du freust _____

3. er, sie, es ändert _____

4. wir _____ _____

5. ihr duzt _____

6. sie _____ _____

7. Sie _____ _____

8. ich _____ mich angezogen.

After doing that repeat the forms aloud and read the rules.

Reflexive verbs:
The marker for the infinitive is the pronoun **sich**:
• **sich umziehen** (to change one's clothes)

Forms of reflexive pronouns:
They are identical with the accusative pronouns apart from the 3rd person and the polite form. In these cases the pronoun is **sich**.
• **Er zieht sich dreimal am Tag um.**

Perfect tense:
The reflexive verbs always take **haben** as an auxiliary verb.
• **Er hat sich dreimal am Tag umgezogen.**

 NICE TO KNOW

A = accusative case,
D = dative case

abholen von + D
danke /vielen Dank
  für + A
einladen zu + D
sich bedanken für
  + A
! sich freuen auf +A
  (to look forward to)
! sich freuen über
  + A (to be pleased
  about)
sich interessieren
  für +A
sich treffen mit + D
teilnehmen an +D
vorbeigehen an + D
warten auf + A
Zeit haben für + A

6

Many verbs are used with a particular preposition, e. g. **sich interessieren für**. Listen to the sentences and fill in the gap with the missing preposition.
In the word box you can find a list of verbs with prepositions you have already learnt. Repeat them!

1. Hast du Zeit _____ ein Picknick am Rhein?

2. Ich warte schon 20 Minuten _____ den Bus.

3. Darf ich dich _____ Abendessen einladen?

4. Wir freuen uns schon jetzt _____ den Sommer.

5. Wir freuen uns _____ deinen Erfolg.

6. Nimmst du _____ Karneval teil?

7. Können Sie mich bitte _____ Bahnhof abholen?

8. Wir bedanken uns _____ die Einladung.

 CD 2 - TR. 96

 NICE TO KNOW

There aren't any rules about which verb takes which preposition. So you have to learn them by heart.

17

° 7

Do you remember? Only the past tense of a few verbs like **haben** and **sein** and of the modal verbs are used in the spoken language. Read the sentences and replace the present tense form with the corresponding past tense form. Write the form into the gap.

1. Meine Eltern **sind** sehr streng. _____

2. Müssen Sie wirklich nach Wien fahren? _____

3. Anna **will** Malerin werden. _____

4. Meine erste Freundin **kann** sehr gut tanzen. _____

5. Wir **haben** viel Spaß in der Schule. _____

6. Das Essen **ist** ausgezeichnet! _____

 CD 2 - TR. 97

⑤ 1

🔅 **NICE TO KNOW**

The word **früher** has two meanings:
1. *earlier*, e.g. **ich komme früher** and
2. *in the past*, e.g. **früher war ich sehr dick.**

° 8

In the last few units you have learnt how to compare two items. Complete the sentences and write the correct word into the gaps.
On the left there is summary of the comparison of adjectives.

1. • Wie alt ist Hans? Ist er so _____ wie Peter?

2. • Nein, Peter ist _____ als Hans.

3. • Welche Stadt finden Sie _____ ? Paris oder London?

4. • Paris, aber Rom finde ich am _____ .

5. • Ich mag Tomaten _____ als Gurken. Und du?

6. • Ich finde, Gurken schmecken _____ als Tomaten.

7. • Kannst du schon _____ als 20 Uhr kommen?

8. • Ich komme so _____ wie möglich.

groß - größer - am größten
klein - kleiner - am kleinsten
! viel - mehr - am meisten

A ist so groß wie B.
C ist größer als A und B.
D ist am größten.

A schön	**B** schöner	**C** schönsten
D gern	**E** lieber	**F** liebsten
G alt	**H** älter	**I** ältesten
J gut	**K** besser	**L** besten
M früh	**N** früher	**O** frühsten

9

Subordinate clauses are easy to recognize: they start with a conjunction and have a special word order.

CD 2 - TR. 98

25

NICE TO KNOW

Watch out for the spelling of verbs with separable prefixes like **zurückkommen**. In the subordinate clause they have to be written as one word.

- Conjunction **weil** *(because)*
  Wir können nicht kommen, **weil** wir arbeiten müssen.
  (We cannot come because we have to work.)
  Function: **weil** is used to give the reason for something. To ask for the reason you use **warum?** *(why?)*.

- Conjunction **wenn** *(if, when)*
  a) Wir gehen spazieren, **wenn** es nicht regnet.
     (We go for a walk if it isn't raining.)
  b) Er hört immer Musik, **wenn** er Bilder malt.
     (He always listens to music when he is painting pictures.)
  Function: **wenn** has two meanings: a) conditional and b) temporal.

- Conjunction **dass** *(that)*
  Die Zeitung berichtet, **dass** ein Kind das Krokodil gefunden hat.
  (The newspaper's reporting that a child has found the crocodile.)
  Function: **dass** is used to report a thought, a speech, a supposition or an opinion etc. of yourself or of somebody else. The exact function depends on the meaning of the main clause, e. g.:

  Ich vermute, **dass** ...   *(I suppose that ...)*   ▶ supposition,
  Es ist besser, **dass** ...   *(It's better that ...)*   ▶ opinion,
  Es ist schade, **dass** ...   *(It's a pity that ...)*   ▶ regret etc.

The conjugated verb has to be placed at the end of the sentence. Compare:

main clause	▶ subordinate clause
Es regnet nicht.	▶ ..., dass es nicht **regnet**.
Er ist gekommen.	▶ ..., wenn er gekommen **ist**.
Ich musste gehen.	▶ ..., weil ich gehen **musste**.
Ich komme bald zurück.	▶ ..., weil ich bald **zurückkomme**.

Vocabulary

° 10

Connect the two sentences by using the conjunction in brackets. Watch out for the word order in the subordinate clause and don't forget to write a comma after the main clause (**Ich freue mich, wenn ...**).

1. Ich freue mich. Du kommst mit. *(wenn)*
2. Er schreibt ihr. Er hat ein Auto gekauft. *(dass)*
3. Er kommt zu spät. Er muss sich noch umziehen. *(weil)*
4. Es ist schade. Er nimmt nicht teil. *(dass)*
5. Wir essen nur frisches Obst. Das ist gesünder. *(weil)*
6. Sie hört Musik. Sie arbeitet zu Hause. *(wenn)*

° 11

Three words fit the category, one doesn't. Mark the word which doesn't fit.

1. Gutes Wetter:
   - A ☐ 25 Grad
   - B ☐ sonnig
   - C ☐ Gold
   - D ☐ warm

2. Materialien:
   - A ☐ Ei
   - B ☐ Holz
   - C ☐ Stein
   - D ☐ Metall

3. Eigenschaften von Personen:
   - A ☐ freundlich
   - B ☐ neblig
   - C ☐ fleißig
   - D ☐ sympathisch

4. Obst:
   - A ☐ Bananen
   - B ☐ Apfelsinen
   - C ☐ Nudeln
   - D ☐ Birnen

5. Berufe von Frauen:
   - A ☐ Kollegin
   - B ☐ Krankenschwester
   - C ☐ Frisörin
   - D ☐ Ärztin

6. Schlechtes Wetter:
   - A ☐ es regnet
   - B ☐ sehr windig
   - C ☐ Nebel
   - D ☐ ausgezeichnet

7. Berufe von Männern:
   - A ☐ Landwirt
   - B ☐ Gast
   - C ☐ Schreiner
   - D ☐ Automechaniker

8. Gemüse:
   - A ☐ Figuren
   - B ☐ Blumenkohl
   - C ☐ Kartoffeln
   - D ☐ Tomaten

Vocabulary

° **12**

Write the words below into the right category.

1. Materials	2. Packagings	3. Food
_____	_____	_____
_____	_____	_____
_____	_____	_____

> **A** das Holz | **B** das Brot | **C** die Kartoffeln | **D** die Tüte |
> **E** der Kunststoff | **F** die Dose | **G** die Packung | **H** das Gemüse

° **13**

Which kind of packaging fits with which food? Mark the right answer.

1. Eine Dose
- A ☐ Salami
- B ☐ Bier
- C ☐ Zwiebeln

2. Eine dicke Scheibe
- A ☐ Käse
- B ☐ Orangen
- C ☐ Pralinen

3. Zwei Packungen
- A ☐ Reis
- B ☐ Cola
- C ☐ Brot

4. Eine Tüte
- A ☐ Bratwurst
- B ☐ Chips
- C ☐ Obstsalat

5. 200 Gramm
- A ☐ Milch
- B ☐ Kopfsalat
- C ☐ Wurst

6. Vier Stück
- A ☐ Sahne
- B ☐ Gurken
- C ☐ Nudeln

7. Ein halber Liter
- A ☐ Bohnen
- B ☐ Milch
- C ☐ Brötchen

8. 5 kg
- A ☐ Kartoffeln
- B ☐ Rotwein
- C ☐ Eier

° **14**

What's the name of the job described? Decide whether you need the male or the female name of the job title.

1. Er malt Bilder und er mag Farben. Er ist _____ .

2. Sie arbeitet in einer Schule. Sie ist _____ .

3. Bei ihm kann man Brot, Brötchen und Kuchen kaufen.

Er ist _____ .

Vocabulary

° **15**

What is the activity called shown in the picture? Mark the right answer.

1.
A □ Sie probiert den Müll.
B □ Sie sucht den Müll.
C □ Sie wirft den Müll weg.

2.
A □ Sie kauft Sekt ein.
B □ Sie bietet Sekt an.
C □ Sie trinkt Sekt.

3.
A □ Er zieht sich an.
B □ Er bedient sich.
C □ Er freut sich.

° **16**

Which of the four expressions doesn't fit the category? Mark the odd one.

1. Weather:
A □ Papier
B □ Wind
C □ Schnee
D □ Regen

2. Seasons:
A □ Frühling
B □ Herbst
C □ Sommer
D □ Temperatur

3. What's the weather like?
A □ Es regnet.
B □ Die Sonne scheint.
C □ Es ist wichtig.
D □ Es ist neblig.

You're almost there!
Go to **www.pons.de/power** to complete the last online test.

APPENDIX

1

 1 ADJECTIVES

1. Adjectives don't have an ending when they are used with the verb **sein** (to be).
Die Tür ist **grün**. – The door is green.
Die Häuser sind **alt**. – The houses are old.
2. Adjectives have an ending when they describe or modify a noun.
Die **grüne** Tür ist schön.
The green door is nice.
Die **alten** Häuser in Bonn.
The old houses in Bonn.

Declination

The ending of the adjective depends on the case and the gender of the noun and whether you use the definite article **der** or the indefinite article **ein**.

Definite article + adjective (nominative case)

Singular

Masculine	Feminine	Neuter
der alt**e** Turm	die alt**e** Tür	das alt**e** Haus

Plural – *all gender*: die alt**en** Tische

Indefinite article + adjective (nominative case)

Singular

Masculine	Feminine	Neuter
ein alt**er** Turm	eine alt**e** Tür	ein alt**es** Haus

Plural – *all gender*: alt**e** Tische

Note: The adjectives **teuer** and **dunkel** drop the **e** when they are declined:
der **teure** Tisch – *the expensive table*
ein **dunkler** Turm – *a dark tower*

 2 ADVERBS

Characteristics

The main characteristic of an adverb (= word that modifies the meaning of the verb) is that it isn't declined.

Adverbs of place:
hier (here), dort (there), **oben** (up, upstairs, at/on the top), **unten** (down, downstairs, at the bottom), **rechts** (right), **links** (left)

Adverbs of time:
heute (today), **morgen** (tomorrow), **gestern** (yesterday), **jetzt** (now)

Adverbs of frequency:
immer (always), **nie** (never), **zweimal** (twice), **montags** (every Monday)

Adverbs of modality:
gern (like to), **auch** (also), **nur** (only, just)

Except for **gern**, none of the adverbs above can be compared.
Ich trinke **gern** Bier, mein Freund trinkt **lieber** Wein. Er mag **am liebsten** Rotwein.
I like drinking beer, my boyfriend prefers drinking wine. He likes red wine best of all.

Many adjectives can be used as adverbs. The forms are identical, also in the comparative and superlative:
Sabine kocht sehr **gut**.
Sabine cooks very well.
Sprich bitte **langsamer**!
Please speak more slowly!

Word order

In general, the adverb is placed behind the verb and in front of other elements like (a) prepositional phrases, (b) the word **nicht** or (c) an infinitive:
(a) Wir gehen **oft** ins Kino.
   We often go to the cinema.
(b) Ich komme **morgen** nicht.
   I don't come tomorrow.
(c) Du musst **rechts** abbiegen.
   You have to turn right.

Adverbs of time often come first. The verb always remains in the 2nd position followed by the subject:

Morgen arbeite ich nicht.
I'm not working tommorow.
Gestern war ich in Bonn.
I was in Bonn yesterday.

3 ARTICLE - DEFINITE

In German, there are three articles for **the**: **der**, **die** and **das**. The article indicates the gender, the case and the number of the noun.

Declination

Singular	Masculine	Feminine	Neuter
Nom.	**der** Hund	**die** Katze	**das** Pferd
Acc.	**den** Hund	**die** Katze	**das** Pferd
Dat.	**dem** Hund	**der** Katze	**dem** Pferd

Plural	All Gender
Nom.	**die** Tiere
Acc.	**die** Tiere
Dat.	**den** Tieren

Use

You use the definite article when it is clear from the context which thing or person you mean:
Der Garten liegt hinter **dem** Haus.
The garden is behind the house.
Ich muss **den** Chef fragen.
I have to ask the boss.

The definite article is also used when you are thinking of one particular thing or person:
Hast du **die** Zeitung gesehen?
Did you see the newspaper?
Ich kenne **den** Freund von Maria nicht.
I don't know the boyfriend of Maria.

Without article

You don't use an article in the following cases:

1. Proper names:
Das ist **Herr Kowalski**. Seine Tochter heißt **Lisa**.
This is Mr. Kowalski. His daughter's name is Lisa.

2. Countries and towns:
Deutschland ist schön, oder?
Germany is beautiful, isn't it?
Wie gefällt dir **München**?
How do you like Munich?

But: Some countries are always used with the definite article: **die Schweiz** *(Switzerland)*, **die Türkei** *(Turkey)*.

3. Nationalities:
Sylvia ist **Österreicherin**. – *Sylvia is Austrian.*
Ich bin **Italiener**. – *I'm Italian.*

4. Job titles:
Er arbeitet als **Arzt**.
He works as a doctor.
Meine Mutter ist **Lehrerin**.
My mother is a teacher.

5. Uncountable nouns:
Ich kaufe **Reis**, **Milch** und **Zucker**.
I'm buying rice, milk and sugar.

6. Expressions with **haben**, **spielen**, **hören** and **machen**:
Ich habe Zeit. – *I have time.*
Er spielt Gitarre. – *He plays the guitar.*
Sie hört gern Musik.– *She likes listening to music.*
Das macht Spaß. – *That's fun.*

4 ARTICLE - INDEFINITE

The forms of the indefinite article depend on the gender, the case and the number of the corresponding noun.

Grammar overview

§ 4 – 7

Declination

Singular	Masculine	Feminine	Neuter
Nom.	**ein** Hund	**eine** Katze	**ein** Pferd
Acc.	**einen** Hund	**eine** Katze	**ein** Pferd
Dat.	**einem** Hund	**einer** Katze	**einem** Pferd

Note: The indefinite article has no plural forms.

Use

You use the indefinite article when it's the first time you talk about something or someone and when the noun is countable:

Hast du **ein** Haustier?

Do you have a pet?

Ich möchte **eine** Tasse Tee.

I'd like a cup of tea.

Compare also the use of the articles when the noun appears for the first and for the second time:

Ich lese **ein** Buch. **Das** Buch ist sehr interessant.

I'm reading a book. The book is very interesting.

There are two other grammar references that contain interesting information about the indefinite articles:

§ 11 Negation informs you about the negated indefinite article **kein**.

§ 3 Article – Definite informs you about cases where you don't use an article at all.

 5 COMPARISON

Regular forms

Basic form	Comparative	Superlative
klein *(small)*	kleiner	**am** kleinsten
laut *(loud)*	lauter	**am** lautesten
alt *(old)*	älter	**am** ältesten
dunkel *(dark)*	dunk**ler** (!)	**am** dunkelsten
teuer *(expensive)*	teu**rer** (!)	**am** teuersten

The comparative is formed by adding the ending **-er**.

The superlative ends in **-sten**. The ending **-esten** is used for adjectives in **-d, -t, -s, -ß, -sch** and **-z**.

Irregular forms

Basic form	Comparative	Superlative
groß *(big)*	größer	am größten
hoch *(high)*	höher	am höchsten
nah *(near)*	näher	am nächsten
gut *(good)*	**besser**	am **besten**
viel *(much)*	**mehr**	am **meisten**

Umlauts in the comparative and superlative

Especially one-syllable adjectives often take an umlaut:

a ▸ ä: alt *(old)* ▸ **ä**lter, am **ä**ltesten
Also: hart *(hard)*, lang *(long)*, nah *(near)*, kalt *(cold)*, warm *(warm, hot)*,

o ▸ ö: groß *(big)* ▸ gr**ö**ßer, am gr**ö**ßten
Also: hoch *(high)*

u ▸ ü: jung *(young)* ▸ j**ü**nger, am j**ü**ngsten
Also: kurz *(short)*, gesund *(healthy)*

Use

1. Expressing that two items or qualities are similar:

so / genauso + basic form + **wie**

Bananen sind **so** teuer **wie** Äpfel.

Bananas are as expensive as apples.

Maria ist **genauso** alt **wie** du.

Maria is just as old as you are.

2. Comparing one person, thing or quality to another:

comparative + **als**

Ich bin **älter als** meine Schwester.

I'm older than my sister.

Im Garten ist es **schöner als** auf dem Balkon.

In the garden it's nicer than on the balcony.

§ 6 DEMONSTRATIVE PRO-NOUNS

Dieser, diese, dieses

The demonstrative pronoun **dieser** *(this)* has the same endings as the definite article.

Singular	Masculine	Feminine	Neuter
Nom.	dies**er** Mann	dies**e** Frau	dies**es** Kind
Acc.	dies**en** Mann	dies**e** Frau	dies**es** Kind
Dat.	dies**em** Mann	dies**er** Frau	dies**em** Kind

Plural	All Gender
Nom.	dies**e** Personen
Acc.	dies**e** Personen
Dative	dies**en** Personen

Use

The demonstrative pronoun **dieser** is used if you want to point to something or someone close to you:

Was kostet **diese** Tasche?
How much does this bag cost?

It is used when you want to point to something or someone mentioned shortly before:
Neanderstraße ... ? Ich kenne **diese** Straße nicht.
Neander Street ... ? I don't know this street.

Der, die, das **emphasized**

	Singular			Plural
	Masc.	Fem.	Neuter	All Gender
Nom.	**der**	**die**	**das**	**die**
Acc.	**den**	**die**	**das**	**die**
Dat.	**dem**	**der**	**dem**	**denen**

The forms of the demonstrative pronoun and the definite article are identical apart from the dative plural.
Article: **den** – demonstrative pronoun: **denen**.

Use

The demonstrative pronoun refers to a noun mentioned before and it is used to avoid the repetition of the noun.

Wo ist <u>der Papagei</u>? – **Der** ist in seinem Käfig.
Where is the parrot? – It is in its cage.
Gefällt dir <u>der Schrank</u>? – **Den** finde ich hässlich.
Do you like the cupboard? – I find it ugly.

Special use of **das**: to refer to the complete information given before you use the pronoun **das**.
<u>Er ist nicht gekommen</u>. **Das** verstehe ich nicht.
He didn't come. I don't understand that.
<u>Du bist schüchtern</u>. **Das** glauben wir nicht.
You are shy. We don't believe that.

Note that the demonstrative pronoun is placed in front of the verb and it is emphasized.

§ 7 IMPERATIVE

The imperative forms are quite regular, apart from the verb **sein**.

Conjugation

	gehen	nehmen	sein
du:	geh!	nimm!	sei!
ihr:	geht!	nehmt!	seid!
Sie:	gehen Sie!	nehmen Sie!	seien Sie!

The regular forms of the imperative are derived from the present tense.
Du-form: You have to drop the ending **-st** and the personal pronoun.
Ihr-form: You just have to drop the personal pronoun.
Sie-form: This form is just inverted.

Verbs ending in **-gen**, **-den** or **-ten** form the 2nd person singular (**du**-form) by adding an **-e**:
entschuldigen ▶ entschuldig**e**! – *Excuse me!*
reden   ▶ red**e**! – *Speak!*
warten   ▶ wart**e**! – *Wait a moment!*

1

GRAMMAR OVERVIEW

Verbs with irregularities in the **du**-form:

fahren	▶ **fahr**! – *go!*
lesen	▶ **lies**! – *read!*
haben	▶ **hab**! – *have!*

Use

The imperative is used to give commands or make requests.

Geh nach Hause! – *Go home!*
Kommt mit! – *Come along!*
Seien Sie pünktlich! – *Be punctual!*

The imperative sounds less harsh when you add words like **bitte**, **doch** or **mal**.
Sei bitte pünktlich! – *Please be punctual!*
Geht doch nicht weg! – *Please don't go away!*
Geben Sie mir mal das Buch! –
Give me the book!

Watch out for the word order: The imperative is the first word in the sentence!

 8 INTERROGATIVE PRO-NOUNS

Here is a list of the interrogative pronouns from our course:

Wer ist dieser Mann?	*Who is this man?*
Was machst du heute?	*What are you doing today?*
Wen besuchst du?	*Who are you visiting?*
Wem gehört das?	*To whom does it belong?*
Wo wohnen Sie?	*Where do you live?*
Wohin gehst du?	*Where are you going?*
Woher kommst du?	*Where do you come from?*
Wann treffen wir uns?	*When do we meet?*
Wie geht es dir?	*How are you?*
Warum gehst du schon?	*Why are you going already?*

Another interrogative pronoun is **welcher** (*which*). The endings of welcher are the same as of the definite article.

Welches Haus gefällt dir?
Which house do you like?
Welche Sprachen sprechen Sie?
Which languages do you speak?

Word order: In sentences with an interrogative pronoun, the verb is in the second position followed by the subject and the complements:
Wann kommst du nach Hause?
When are you coming home?

 9 MASCULINE NOUNS IN *-E*

Masculine nouns ending in **-e** follow another declination pattern than all other nouns.
Masculine nouns in **-e** are:
der Deutsche (*German*), der Pole (*Pole*), der Russe (*Russian*), der Türke (*Turkish*), der Kollege (*colleague*), der Neffe (*nephew*), der Name (*name*)

Only the nominative singular ends in **-e**. All other cases, singular and plural, take the ending **-n**.

Nearly the same declination is also valid for der **Herr** (*sir, mister*) and **der Nachbar** (*neighbour*).

Singular

Nom.	der Türke	der Herr	der Nachbar
Acc.	den Türke**n**	den Herr**n**	den Nachbar**n**
Dat.	dem Türke**n**	dem Herr**n**	dem Nachbar**n**

Plural

Nom.	die Türke**n**	die Herr**en**	die Nachbar**n**
Acc.	die Türke**n**	die Herr**en**	die Nachbar**n**
Dat.	den Türke**n**	den Herr**en**	den Nachbar**n**

Some examples:
Meine Kollege**n** Mehmet und Dilek sind Türke**n**.
My colleagues Mehmet and Dilek are Turkish.
Wie sind deine Nachbar**n**? Sind sie nett?
How are your neighbours? Are they nice?

Ich muss Herr**n** Schmidt anrufen.
I have to call Mr. Schmidt.

Pay attention to the following important exception. In the nominative singular and plural you say:

der Deutsche	die Deutsch**en**
but: **ein** Deutsch**er**	Deutsch**e**

 10 MODAL VERBS

In German, there are six modal auxiliaries:

können	*to be able to, can*
wollen	*to want to*
müssen	*to have to, must*
dürfen	*to be allowed to, may*
sollen	*should, shall, to be supposed to*
mögen	*to like*

Conjugation

	können	wollen	müssen
ich	kann	will	muss
du	kannst	willst	musst
er/sie/es	kann	will	muss
wir	können	wollen	müssen
ihr	könnt	wollt	müsst
sie	können	wollen	müssen
Polite form:			
Sie	können	wollen	müssen

	dürfen	sollen	mögen
ich	darf	soll	mag
du	darfst	sollst	magst
er/sie/es	darf	soll	mag
wir	dürfen	sollen	mögen
ihr	dürft	sollt	mögt
sie	dürfen	sollen	mögen
Polite form:			
Sie	dürfen	sollen	mögen

The modal verbs are conjugated and they are usually followed by another verb in the infinitive form.
Ich will ausgehen. – *I want to go out.*

Use and word order

1. The modal is in the usual verb position: It comes second in assertions and in questions with interrogatives. In yes/no-questions it comes first.

The infinitive form of the second verb is always at the very end of the sentence.

Er **kann** nicht **schwimmen**.
He cannot swim.
Wir **wollen** nach Bonn **fahren**.
We want to go to Bonn.
Musst du heute **arbeiten**?
Do you have to work today?
Hier **darf** man nicht **weitergehen**.
Here it's not allowed to go on.
Wo **sollen** wir es **suchen**?
Where should we look for it?
Ich **mag** nicht Fußball **spielen**.
I don't like playing soccer.

2. The infinitive can be dropped when it is already mentioned before.

Willst du **mitkommen**? – Nein, ich **will** nicht.
Do you want to come along? – No, I don't want to.

3. The modals **können**, **wollen** and **mögen** can also be used as full verbs without an infinitive.

Er **kann** Französisch.	*He can speak French.*
Ich **will** einen Kaffee.	*I would likea coffee.*
Sie **mag** Kuchen.	*She likes cake.*

4. If you want to have something, it's more polite to use the subjunctive form of **mögen**.

Ich **möchte** ein Bier. – *I'd like a beer.*
Ich **möchte** ein Bier **trinken**.
I'd like to drink a beer.

The forms are regular:

Singular:	ich möchte, du möchtest, er/sie/es möchte
Plural:	wir möchten, ihr möchtet, sie möchten
Polite form:	Sie möchten.

Grammar overview

1

GRAMMAR OVERVIEW

 11 NEGATION

Nein and *doch*

To answer a negated question you can use **nein** *(no)* or **doch** *(yes, I do)*. Compare:
Kommen Sie **nicht** mit?
– **Nein**, ich habe keine Zeit. *(negative answer)*
– **Doch**, ich komme mit. *(positive answer)*
Aren't you coming along?
– No, I don't have time.
– Yes, I'm coming.

Negation with *nicht*

To negate a sentence or a part of it you add **nicht** *(not)*. The position of **nicht** depends on whether you negate (a) only a word of the sentence or (b) the whole sentence. Compare:
(a) Ich besuche **nicht** meine Tante.
   I'm not visiting my aunt (but another person).
(b) Ich besuche meine Tante **nicht**.
   I don't visit my aunt.

If you want to negate the whole sentence, you have to place **nicht** at the end of the sentence.

But there are exceptions:
– **sein** + adjective:
  Das ist **nicht** möglich! – *That isn't possible!*
– **sein** + noun:
  Das ist **nicht** meine Tasche.
  That isn't my bag.
– Separable verb:
  Ich komme **nicht** mit. – *I don't come along.*
– Modal verb + infinitive:
  Ich kann **nicht** kommen. – *I can't come.*
– Perfect tense:
  Er hat **nicht** geschlafen. – *He didn't sleep.*
– Prepositional phrase:
  Ich fahre **nicht** nach Köln.
  I'm not going to Cologne.

Negation with *kein*

Kein is used to negate (a) a noun with an indefinite article and (b) a noun without an article. Compare:
(a) Ich habe ein Auto. – *I've got a car.*
   Ich habe **kein** Auto. – *I haven't got a car.*
(b) Sie ist Lehrerin. – *She's a teacher.*
   Sie ist **keine** Lehrerin. – *She isn't a teacher.*

Declination

Singular	Masculine	Feminine
Nom.	kein Hund	keine Katze
Acc.	keinen Hund	keine Katze
Dat.	keinem Hund	keiner Katze

Singular	Neuter	Plural All Gender
Nom.	kein Pferd	keine Tiere
Acc.	kein Pferd	keine Tiere
Dat.	keinem Pferd	keinen Tieren

In the singular, **kein** is declined like the indefinite article **ein**. Unlike the indefinite article there are plural forms of **kein**.
Ich habe **keine** Haustiere.
I don't have got any pets.
Zwei Schiffe? Ich sehe **keine** Schiffe.
Two ships? I don't see any ships.

 12 NOUNS – GENDER

All nouns are either masculine, feminine or neuter. If there is an article it is easy to recognize the gender.

Masculine	Feminine	Neuter
der Hund	**die** Katze	**das** Pferd
der Fluss	**die** Straße	**das** Haus
der Wein	**die** Cola	**das** Bier

You need to know what gender a noun is, otherwise you can't choose the correct forms of …
– … the article:

der, **die** or **das**?

– ... the personal pronoun:
der Fluss ▶ **er** heißt Rhein,
die Straße ▶ **sie** ist lang,
das Haus ▶ **es** ist alt.

– ... the possessive pronoun:
die Katze ▶ **meine** Katze.

– ... the adjective ending:
der Hund ▶ ein braun**er** Hund.

Unfortunately, in most cases you cannot recognise the gender from the noun itself. So it's advisable that you always learn the definite article together with the noun.

However, there are some features like typical endings or word groups that help you to recognise the gender.

Masculine nouns

Features	Examples
-er	der Bäcker, der Lehrer
Seasons	der Frühling, der Sommer
Months	der Januar, der Februar
Days of the week	der Montag, der Dienstag
Directions	der Norden, der Süden

Feminine nouns

Features	Examples
-e	die Katze, die Blume
	but: **der** Name, **der** Kollege
-in	die Freundin, die Schülerin, die Bäckerin, die Lehrerin
-frau	die Geschäftsfrau
-ei	die Bäckerei, die Metzgerei
-ung	die Bestellung, die Verbindung
Foreign words in **-ät**, **-ik**, **-ion**, **-ie** and **-ur**	die Universität, die Musik, die Information, die Biologie, die Kultur

Neuter nouns

Features	Examples
-chen	das Brötchen, das Küsschen
-um	das Zentrum, das Museum
Colours	das Rot, das Blau
Countries	Deutschland, Österreich etc. (used without article) but: **die** Schweiz, **die** Türkei (always used with the article)

 13 NOUNS – SINGULAR

The noun itself isn't declined in the singular. Only the article shows up the case and the gender of the noun.

	Masculine	Feminine	Neuter
Nom.	der Fluss	die Stadt	das Land
Acc.	den Fluss	die Stadt	das Land
Dat.	dem Fluss	der Stadt	dem Land

But: Masculine nouns in **-e** follow another declination (see § **Masculine nouns in** -e):

	Masculine in -e
Nom.	der Kollege
Acc.	den Kolleg**en**
Dat.	dem Kolleg**en**

 14 NOUNS – PLURAL

Declination

	Masculine	Feminine	Neuter
Nom.	die Flüsse	die Städte	die Länder
Acc.	die Flüsse	die Städte	die Länder
Dat.	den Flüsse**n**	den Städte**n**	den Länder**n**

Note: The dative plural always ends in **-n**.
Exception: Foreign words have the ending **-s**: den Clown**s**, den Café**s**, den Foto**s** etc.

Masculine nouns ending in **-e** follow another declination pattern. See § **Masculine nouns in** -e.

Endings of the plural

Depending on the gender of the noun and their singular ending there are six different endings for the plural:

-e, -n, -en, -er, -s or no ending

If there's a vowel **a, o, u** in the noun, it is mostly changed to **ä, ö, ü.**
Here are the rules:

1. Masculine or neuter nouns in **-el, -en, -er** don't have any plural ending:

der Spiegel	die Spiegel
das Brötchen	die Brötchen
das Fenster	die Fenster

2. Other masculine or neuter nouns end in **-e**:

der Fluss	die Fl**ü**s**s**e
das Regal	die Regal**e**

3. Neuter nouns with one syllable end in **-er**:

das Dorf	die D**ö**rf**er**
das Bild	die Bild**er**

4. Feminine nouns in **-e** end in **-n**:

die Banane	die Banane**n**
die Straße	die Straße**n**

5. Feminine nouns ending in consonant or another vowel than **-e** have the plural ending **-en**:

die Tür die Tür**en**	
die Frau	die Frau**en**
die Kollegin	die Kollegin**n**en

6. Foreign words (all gender) end in **-s**:

das Foto	die Foto**s**
die Party	die Party**s**

Exceptions:
Unfortunately, there are a lot of exceptions. Here are only some of the most common ones:

der Mann	die Männer
der Vater	die Väter
die Mutter	die Mütter
die Tochter	die Töchter

Irregular plural forms:

das Material	die Materialien
das Museum	die Museen
das Praktikum	die Praktika

 15 WORD ORDER

Basic word order patterns

Depending on the position of the verb there are two basic word order patterns: the normal and the inverted word order.

1. Normal word order

Verb = 2nd position

This structure is used for assertions and questions with interrogatives.

Assertions:

Subject	Verb	Complements
Herr Müller	**lebt**	in Deutschland.
Ich	**komme**	aus Köln.

If you put another word than the subject into the first position, the subject is placed behind the verb. Compare:

Ich **besuche** heute meine Tante.
I'm visiting my aunt today.
Heute **besuche** ich meine Tante.
Today I'm visiting my aunt.

After **und** (*and*), **oder** (*or*) and **aber** (*but*) you always have the normal word order:
Sie mag Wein, aber er trinkt lieber Bier.
She likes wine, but he prefers drinking beer.

Questions with interrogatives:

Interrogative	Verb	Subject	Complements
Wo	**lebt**	Peter	jetzt?
Wann	**kommst**	du	nach Hause?

2. Inverted word order

Verb = 1st position

Yes/No-questions:

Yes/no-questions start with the verb followed by the subject.

Verb	Subject	Complements
Kommst	du	aus Italien?
Sind	Sie	Fotografin?

Imperative:

Verb	Subject	Complements
Kommen	Sie	bitte pünktlich!
Komm		bitte pünktlich!
Kommt		bitte pünktlich!

Note that only in the polite form of the imperative you'll encounter a subject.

Sentences with various complements

Apart from the word order patterns above that point out the position of the verb and the subject, we have to focus also on the complements.

Complements can be:	Examples:
Accusative objects:	Ich schreibe **einen Brief**.
Dative objects:	Ich schreibe **meiner Oma**.

Prepositional phrases
of location: Ich wohne **in Düsseldorf**.
of direction: Ich fahre **nach Berlin**.
of origin: Ich komme **aus Italien**.
of time: Ich komme **am Sonntag**.

All these complements come behind the verb. When you combine them in one sentence watch out for the following word order rules.

Rules for dative and accusative objects

If you have got a dative and an accusative object in one sentence the dative comes first.

Dative – Accusative (noun)
Ich schreibe **meiner Oma** einen Brief.
I'm writing a letter to my grandma.

This rule is also valid if the dative object is a pronoun (**mir, dir, ihm, ihr** etc.).

Ich schreibe **ihr** einen Brief.
I'm writing a letter to her.

But: If you replace the accusative object with a pronoun (**mich, dich, ihn, sie** etc.) the word order changes.

Accusative (pronoun) – Dative
Ich schreibe **ihn** meiner Oma.
Ich schreibe **ihn** ihr.

Rules for prepositional phrases

In general, prepositional phrases are placed at the end of the sentence:

Dative /Accusative – Prepositional phrases
Ich schreibe ihr einen Brief **zum Geburtstag**.
I'm writing her a letter to her birthday.
Ich besuche meine Oma **in Berlin**.
I'm visiting my grandma in Berlin.

Prepositional phrase of time – Other prepositional phrase

If there are two or more prepositional phrases in one sentence and if one of them is an expression of time like **am Donnerstag** (*on Thursday*), **um 10 Uhr** (*at 10 o'clock*), **im Januar** (*in January*) etc. the prepositional phrase of time comes first.
Ich fahre am Donnerstag mit Peter nach Berlin.
I'll be going to Berlin on Thursday with Peter.
Wir heiraten am 23. August in München.
We're going to get married in Munich on 23rd August.

When looking at the word order rules, these references might also be interesting:
§ **Adverbs** informs you about the position of the adverb in the sentence.
§ **Modal verbs** informs you about the different positions of modal verbs in the sentence.
§ **Perfect tense** informs you about the word order within a present perfect sentence.
§ **Subordinate clauses** informs you about the word order within subordinate clauses.

§ 16 PAST PARTICIPLE

You need the past participle to form the perfect tense (see § **Perfect tense**).

Regular verbs

ge- unchanged present stem **-t**

lernen *(to learn)*	**ge**lern**t**
suchen *(to look for)*	**ge**such**t**
machen *(to make)*	**ge**mach**t**

Verbs in **-den** or **-ten** get the ending **-et**:

reden *(to talk)*	**ge**red**et**
arbeiten *(to work)*	**ge**arbeit**et**

Irregular verbs

ge- often a changed stem **-en**

kommen *(to come)*	**ge**komm**en**
gehen *(to go)*	**ge**gang**en**
treffen *(to meet)*	**ge**troff**en**

but:

bringen *(to bring)*	**ge**brach**t** (!)
denken *(to think)*	**ge**dach**t** (!)

Verbs with separable prefixes

The most common separable prefixes are:
ab-, an-, auf-, aus-, ein-, hin-, los-, mit-, teil-, um-, vor-, weg-, weiter- and **zurück-**.

Verbs with separable prefixes can be regular or irregular:

Prefix **-ge-** unchanged present stem **-t**

vorhaben *(to have planned)*	vor**ge**hab**t**
auspacken *(to unwrap)*	aus**ge**pack**t**

Prefix **-ge-** often a changed stem **-en**

einladen *(to invite)*	ein**ge**lad**en**
aussteigen *(to get off)*	aus**ge**stieg**en**

Verbs beginning with *be-, ent-, er-, ver-*
These verbs don't have the marker **ge** and can be regular or irregular:

unchanged present stem **-t**

erzählen *(to tell)*	erzähl**t**
bestellen *(to order)*	bestell**t**

often a changed stem **-en**

bekommen *(to get)*	bekomm**en**
verstehen *(to understand)*	verstand**en**

Verbs in *-ieren*
Verbs in **-ieren** are regular, but they don't have the marker **ge**:

unchanged present stem **-t**

studieren *(to study)*	studier**t**
probieren *(to try)*	probier**t**

If you aren't sure whether a verb is irregular or not look at the glossary.

§ 17 PAST TENSE

Conjugation

	haben		sein
ich	hatte		**war**
du	hattest		**war**st
er/sie/es	hatte		**war**
wir	hatten		**war**en
ihr	hattet		**war**t
sie	hatten		**war**en
Polite form:			
Sie	hatten		**war**en

	können	wollen	müssen
ich	konnte	wollte	musste
du	konntest	wolltest	musstest
er/sie/es	konnte	wollte	musste
wir	konnten	wollten	mussten
ihr	konntet	wolltet	musstet
sie	konnten	wollten	mussten
Polite form:			
Sie	konnten	wollten	mussten

The marker of the past tense is the **-t-** for the regular forms. The irregular verb **sein** has the past stem **war**.
The personal endings are the normal endings for the present tense. Exception: The

3rd person singular of the regular forms is given an **-e** and the forms **ich/er war** are irregular.

Use

Written language:

The past tense is used especially in the written language, when a story starts and ends in the past. A typical beginning of a fairy-tale is:

Es **war** einmal ein kleines Kind. Es **hatte** keine Eltern und **musste** ...

Once upon a time there was a little child. It had no parents and had to ...

Spoken language:

It is much more common to use the perfect tense when talking about the past (see **§ 18 Perfect tense**). In the spoken language, only the past tense of a few verbs like **haben** and **sein** and the past of modals is really used.

Als Kind **wollte** ich Zahnärztin **werden**.
As a child I wanted to become a dentist.
Wir **mussten** gestern nach Wien **fahren**.
We had to go to Vienna yesterday.
Warum **konntest** du nicht **kommen**?
Why couldn't you come?
Hatten Sie 1964 schon ein Auto?
Did you already have a car in 1974?
Früher **war** ich oft allein.
I used to be alone a lot.

§ 18 PERFECT TENSE

The perfect tense is the most important past tense in German. It's used in the spoken language, in conversations. Note that the use of the German perfect tense doesn't automatically correspond with the present perfect in English or the perfect tense in your native language.

The perfect tense is a compound tense consisting of two parts:

present tense of + past participle of the verb **haben** or **sein**

Conjugation

	lernen	kommen
ich	habe gelernt	bin gekommen
du	hast gelernt	bist gekommen
er/sie/es	hat gelernt	ist gekommen
wir	haben gelernt	sind gekommen
ihr	habt gelernt	seid gekommen
sie	haben gelernt	sind gekommen
Polite form:		
Sie	haben gelernt	sind gekommen

Rules about the participle forms are explained in the section § Past participle.

Haben **or** *sein*?

Most verbs take **haben** to form the perfect tense. Reflexive verbs always take **haben**.

Sein is used for verbs that indicate ...
(a) motion:
kommen *(to come)*   ich bin gekommen
gehen *(to go)*   ich bin gegangen
fahren *(to go, to drive)* ich bin gefahren
schwimmen *(to swim)* ich bin geschwommen

(b) a change of condition:
aufstehen *(to get up)*   ich bin aufgestanden
einsteigen *(to get on)*   ich bin eingestiegen

(c) an event:
geschehen *(to happen)* es ist geschehen
(only the 3rd person singular is used)

Two exceptions:
sein *(to be)*   ich **bin** gewesen
bleiben *(to stay)*   ich **bin** geblieben

Word order

The conjugated verb **haben** or **sein** is in the usual verb position (second position in assertions and questions with interrogative pronouns first position in yes/no-questions).

Grammar overview

1

The past participle is always placed at the very end of the sentence.

Er	**ist**	nicht	**gekommen**.
Ich	**habe**	dort Englisch	**gelernt**.
Wo	**bist**	du am Montag	**gewesen**?
	Sind	Sie nach Köln	**gefahren**?

§ 19 PERSONAL PRONOUNS

Forms

Singular	Nom.	Acc.	Dat.
1st p.	ich	mich	mir
2nd p. (familiar)	du	dich	dir
2nd p. (polite)	Sie	Sie	Ihnen
3rd persons	er	ihn	ihm
	sie	sie	ihr
	es	es	ihm

Plural	Nom.	Acc.	Dat.
1st p.	wir	uns	uns
2nd p. (familiar)	ihr	euch	euch
2nd p. (polite)	Sie	Sie	Ihnen
3rd p.	sie	sie	ihnen

The polite forms **Sie** (you) and **Ihnen** (to you) are capitalised.

Use

Subject and object

The personal pronouns are used ...
(a) ... as subject (nominative case):
Er lebt in Berlin.
He lives in Berlin.
Wir sind aus Wien, und **ihr**?
We are from Vienna, and you?
Sind **Sie** Frau Müller?
Are you Mrs. Müller?
(b) ... as direct object (accusative case):
Peter, hier ist ein Anruf für **dich**.
Peter, there is a phone call for you.
Ich kann **ihn** nicht sehen.
I can't see him.

(c) ... as indirect object (dative case):
Wie geht es **Ihnen**? Wie geht es **dir**?
How are you?
Können Sie **mir** bitte helfen?
Can you help me, please?

Special uses of *es*

The pronoun **es** is used as a formal subject in sentences about the weather and the time.
Es regnet.   *It's raining.*
Es ist 8 Uhr. *It's 8 o'clock.*

The expression **es gibt** (there is, there are) is only used in the singular, even if the direct object is in the plural. Compare:
Es gibt nur einen Turm.
There is only one tower.
Es gibt nur zwei Türme.
There are only two towers.

§ 20 POSSESSIVE PRONOUNS

Every time you talk about belongings you need possessive pronouns like **mein** (my), **dein** (your) etc. Here are the possessive pronouns without endings:

Singular		
ich	**mein**	*my*
du	**dein**	*your (familiar)*
Sie	**Ihr**	*your (polite)*
er	**sein**	*his*
sie	**ihr**	*her*
es	**sein**	*its*

Plural		
wir	**unser**	*our*
ihr	**euer**	*your (familiar)*
Sie	**Ihr**	*your (polite)*
sie	**ihr**	*their*

Note that the polite form **Ihr** is capitalised.

GRAMMAR OVERVIEW

Declination

Depending on gender, case and number of the noun the possessive pronouns are given the following endings:

Singular	Masculine	Feminine
Nom.	mein Hund	meine Katze
Acc.	meinen Hund	meine Katze
Dat.	meinem Hund	meiner Katze

Singular	Neuter	Plural (all genders)
Nom.	mein Pferd	meine Tiere
Acc.	mein Pferd	meine Tiere
Dat.	meinem Pferd	meinen Tieren

The singular forms have the same endings as the indefinite article **ein** and the plural forms have the same endings as the negated indefinite article **kein**.

Kommt **dein** Bruder auch?
Is your brother coming, too?
Frau Müller, ist das **Ihre** Tasche?
Mrs. Müller, is this your bag?
Wir treffen uns mit **unseren** Kollegen am Freitag.
We are meeting our colleagues on Friday.
The declined forms of **euer** drop the second **e**:
Wo sind **eure** Eltern?
Where are your parents?

Use of *sein* and *ihr*

Watch out for the use in the 3rd person singular. **Sein** *(his)* refers to a male "owner" and **ihr** *(her)* to a female "owner". Compare:
Er besucht **seine** Eltern und **seinen** Bruder.
He's visiting his parents and his brother.
Sie besucht **ihre** Eltern und **ihren** Bruder.
She's visiting her parents and her brother.

 21 PREPOSITIONS

Prepositions are used without an article in front of proper names (exception: names of streets):

Ich fahre **zu** Peter / **nach** Bonn / **nach** Polen.
I'm going to Peter's / to Bonn / to Poland.
but:
Ich fahre **in die** Bäckerstraße.
I'm going to Baker Street.

With exception of proper names, prepositions are in general followed by an article, a possessive pronoun or demonstrative pronoun, which are declined in the case that the preposition governs.
Ich fahre **immer** mit de**m** Bus. (▶ dative)
I always go by bus.
Ich fahre nicht **ohne** mein**en** Freund.
(▶ accusative)
I'm not going without my friend.

Prepositions with accusative

bis *(till, to)*, **durch** *(through)* **entlang** *(along)*, **für** *(for)*, **gegen** *(against, about)*, **ohne** *(without)*, **um** *(at)*

bis (zu)	Fahren Sie **bis** zur Bäckerstraße.
	Go until you get to Baker street.
	Tschüss! **Bis** Montag!
	Bye-bye. Till Monday!
durch	Ich gehe gern **durch** den Park.
	I like walking through the park.
entlang	Geh diese Straße **entlang**.
	Go along this street.
für	Ein Geschenk **für** Lisa.
	A gift for Lisa.
gegen	Das Auto ist **gegen** das Haus gefahren.
	The car drove into the house.
	Es ist **gegen** 4 Uhr.
	It's about 4 o'clock.
ohne	Eine Wohnung **ohne** Balkon.
	A flat without a balcony.
um	Der Zug kommt **um** 3 Uhr an.
	The train arrives at 3 o'clock.

Note: The preposition **entlang** is placed behind the noun.

Grammar overview

1

Prepositions with dative

aus *(from, of)*, **bei** *(with, near, at)*, **gegenüber** *(opposite, across the road)*, **mit** *(with)*, **nach** *(after, to, past)*, **seit** *(since, for)*, **von** *(from, by, of)*, **zu** *(to)*

aus Woher kommst du? – **Aus** Österreich.
Where are you from? – From Austria.
Der Tisch ist **aus** Holz.
The table is made of wood.

bei Er wohnt **bei** seinen Eltern.
He lives with his parents.
Wir treffen uns **bei** der Kirche.
We meet near the church.

gegenüber **Gegenüber** dem Kiosk ist die Post.
The post office is opposite the kiosk.

mit Einen Apfelkuchen **mit** Sahne, bitte.
An apple pie with whipped cream, please.

nach Morgen fahre ich **nach** Berlin.
Tomorrow I'm going to Berlin.
Wie spät ist es? – Es ist 10 **nach** 2.
What time is it? – It's 10 past 2.
Was machst du **nach** dem Frühstück?
What do you do after breakfast?

seit Ich bin **seit** 1998 verheiratet.
I'm married since 1998.

von Er kommt **vom** Arzt zurück.
He's coming back from the doctor.
Hast du einen Stadtplan **von** Bonn?
Do you have a map of Bonn?

zu Wie komme ich **zum** Bahnhof?
How do I get to the railway station?

The following prepositions are usually contracted with the definite article:
bei, von, zu + dem ▶ **beim, vom, zum**
zu + der ▶ **zur**

Prepositions with accusative and dative

an *(at, on, to)*, **auf** *(at, in, on)*, **hinter** *(behind)*, **in** *(in, into, to)*, **neben** *(beside, next to)*, **über** *(over)*, **unter** *(under)*, **vor** *(in front of)*, **zwischen** *(between)*.

Rules and use

Wohin? *(Where to?)*	**Wo?** *(Where?)*
Direction, destination, motion	Position, location
Accusative	**Dative**
Wohin geht er?	Wo ist er?
– Ins Bett. *(To bed.)*	– Im Bett. *(In bed.)*

Compare the use of the accusative (A) and the dative (D) in the following examples:

an Er hängt das Bild **an die** Wand. (A)
He's hanging the picture on the wall.
Das Bild hängt **an der** Wand. (D)
The picture is (hanging) on the wall.

auf Er legt die Jacke **auf das** Sofa. (A)
He's putting the jacket on the sofa.
Die Jacke liegt **auf dem** Sofa. (D)
The jacket is (lying) on the sofa.

in Wir gehen **in den** Park. (A)
We go into the park.
Das Kind spielt **im** Park. (D)
The child is playing in the park.

über Häng die Lampe **über den** Tisch! (A)
Hang the lamp over the table!
Die Lampe hängt **über dem** Tisch. (D)
The lamp is hanging over the table.

vor Geht **vor das** Haus! (A)
Go in front of the house.
Vor dem Haus ist ein Garten. (D)
In front of the house there is a garden.

Note that the preposition **auf** (instead of **in**) is used with offices or institutions:
Ich gehe **auf die Bank**.
I'm going to the bank.
Er ist **auf der Post**.
He's at the post office.

The prepositions **an** and **in** have a temporal meaning, too. In this meaning they govern the dative case:
Wir heiraten **im** August.
We are getting married in August.

GRAMMAR OVERVIEW

Am Freitag fahre ich nach Wien.
On Friday I'm going to Vienna.
Ich bin **am** 12. Juli 1974 geboren.
I was born on 12 th July 1974.
Meine Tante kommt **am** Nachmittag.
My aunt is coming in the afternoon.
but:
Ich bin 1974 geboren. (without preposition!)
I was born in 1974.

The following prepositions are usually contracted with the definite article:
in, an + dem ▶ **im, am**
in, an, auf +das ▶ **ins, ans, aufs**

 22 PRESENT TENSE

Regular verbs

	wohnen		arbeiten	heißen
ich	wohne	-e	arbeite	heiße
du	wohnst	-st	arbeitest	heißt
er/sie/es	wohnt	-t	arbeitet	heißt
wir	wohnen	-en	arbeiten	heißen
ihr	wohnt	-t	arbeitet	heißt
sie	wohnen	-en	arbeiten	heißen
Polite form:				
Sie	wohnen	-en	arbeiten	heißen

The present tense of most German verbs is formed by dropping the infinitive ending **-en** and adding a personal ending to the stem (**wohn-, arbeit-, heiß-**).

If the stem ends in **-d** or **-t** (**baden, arbeiten**) you insert an **e** between stem and ending.
Lisa bad**et** gern.
Lisa likes having a bath.
Arbeit**et** ihr morgen?
Are you working tomorrow?

If the stem ends in **-s**, **-ß** or **-z**, the 2 nd person singular gets the ending **-t**.
Du tan**zt** sehr gut. – *You dance very well.*
Wie hei**ßt** du? – *What's your name?*

Verbs with stem-vowel changes

A number of verbs change the stem-vowel, but luckily only in the 2 nd and 3 rd person singular.

e ▶ i ("short i")
sprechen: ich spreche, du sprichst, er spricht
geben: ich gebe, du gibst, er gibt
essen: ich esse, du isst, er isst
treffen: ich treffe, du triffst, er trifft
helfen: ich helfe, du hilfst, er hilft
nehmen: ich nehme, du nimmst, er nimmt (!)

e ▶ ie ("long i")
sehen: ich sehe, du siehst, er sieht
lesen: ich lese, du liest, er liest

a ▶ ä
fahren: ich fahre, du fährst, er fährt
schlafen: ich schlafe, du schläfst, er schläft
halten: ich halte, du hältst, er hält

Note that not all verbs with **e** or **a** change the stem-vowel. In the glossary you can find the paradigm of the verbs which change the stem-vowel.

Irregular verbs

Some of the most frequently used verbs are irregular, e.g. **sein** *(to be)*, **haben** *(to have)*, **werden** *(to become)* and **wissen** *(to know)*:

	sein	haben	werden	wissen
ich	bin	habe	werde	weiß
du	bist	hast	wirst	weißt
er/sie/es	ist	hat	wird	weiß
wir	sind	haben	werden	wissen
ihr	seid	habt	werdet	wisst
sie	sind	haben	werden	wissen
Polite form:				
Sie	sind	haben	werden	wissen

Grammar overview

1

Use of the present tense

The present tense has a very broad usage. You can use it ...

(a) for a temporary situation:

Ich **gehe** jetzt ins Bett. Gute Nacht!

I'm going to bed now. Goodnight!

(b) for a permanent situation and event:

Meine Eltern **leben** in München.

My parents live in Munich.

(c) for a situation in the future:

Peter **kommt** morgen.

Peter will be arriving tomorrow.

 23 REFLEXIVE VERBS

A verb is called reflexive because the reflexive pronoun refers back to the subject and is identical with it.

The marker for the infinitive of a reflexive verb is the pronoun **sich** *(oneself)*.

Present tense

sich interessieren

ich	interessiere	mich
du	interessierst	dich
er /sie /es	interessiert	sich
wir	interessieren	uns
ihr	interessiert	euch
sie	interessieren	sich

Polite form:

Sie	interessieren	sich

Use and word order

In assertions and questions with an interrogative, the reflexive pronoun is placed behind the verb, in yes /no-questions it is placed behind the subject.

Ich interessiere mich für Kunst.

I'm interested in art.

Das Wetter ändert sich.

The weather is changing.

Freust du dich auf die Party?

Are you looking forward to the party?

Many German verbs can be reflexive and not reflexive:

sich anziehen	Ich ziehe mich an.
	I'm getting dressed.
anziehen	Ich ziehe die Jacke an.
	I'm putting on the jacket.

Perfect tense

The perfect tense of reflexive verbs is always formed by the auxiliary verb **haben**:

ich habe mich geändert

du hast dich gefreut

er hat sich angezogen *etc.*

 24 SEPARABLE VERBS

In German, there are a lot of verbs with a separable prefix. The infinitive of a separable verb like **ankommen** *(to arrive)* is written as one word. But to form a correct sentence in the present tense and in the imperative, the prefix **an-** must be removed and placed at the very end of the sentence.

ankommen:	Wir **kommen** um 8 Uhr **an**.
	We're arriving at 8 o'clock.
abfahren:	Um wie viel Uhr **fährt** der Zug **ab**?
	At what time does the train leave?
vorbereiten:	Susanne **bereitet** das Picknick **vor**.
	Susanne is preparing the picnic.
wegwerfen:	**Wirf** die Tüte nicht **weg**!
	Don't throw the bag away!

About the separable prefix

The separable prefix is always stressed: **ab**fahren, ich fahre **ab**.

The most common separable prefixes are:
ab-, an-, auf-, aus-, ein-, hin-, los-, mit-, teil-, um-, vor-, weg-, weiter- and **zurück-**.
Examples:

abfahren (*to leave*), anrufen (*to call*), aufstehen (*to get up*), ausgehen (*to go out*), einsteigen (*to get on*), hinfahren (*to go there*), losgehen (*to set off*), mitnehmen (*to bring along*), teilnehmen (*to take part*), umsteigen (*to change*), vorhaben (*to have planned*), wegwerfen (*to throw away*), weitergehen (*to go on*), zurückgehen (*to go back*)

Don't forget that these little prefixes change the meaning of a verb. Compare:

kommen	*to come*
ankommen	*to arrive*
mitkommen	*to go along*
zurückkommen	*to return*

Prefix and verb reunited

Watch out for the writing of the verb with a separable prefix in the following cases:

Sentences with modals:
The verb with a separable prefix is written together because it occurs in the infinitive form:
Meine Frau kann nicht **mitkommen**.
My wife can't come along.

Perfect tense:
The **ge-** of the past participle is inserted between the prefix and the stem of the verb.
Wir sind gestern **angekommen**.
We arrived yesterday.

Subordinate clauses:
The prefix and the verb are reunited.
Ich denke, dass er nicht **teilnimmt**.
I think he won't take part.

 25 SUBORDINATE CLAUSES

In German, subordinate clauses have two markers:
1. they are introduced by a conjunction,
2. the word order changes.

Note that there is a comma between the main clause and the subordinate clause:

You already know the conjunctions:
wenn   1. *if, in case,* 2. *when*
dass *that*
weil *because*

The conjunctions

wenn
The conjunction **wenn** introduces a subordinate clause with a conditional (*if, in case*) or a temporal meaning (*when*):
Wir gehen spazieren, **wenn** das Wetter schön ist.
We'll go for a walk if the weather is fine.
Er liest die Zeitung, **wenn** er frühstückt.
He reads the newspaper when he has breakfast.

weil
In order to give a reason for something you use a subordinate clause introduced by **weil** (*because*).
Ich kann nicht mitkommen, **weil** ich arbeiten muss.
I cannot come along because I have to work.

To answer a question beginning with **warum?** (*why?*) you can use a **weil**-clause without the main clause.
Warum fährst du nicht mit dem Auto?
– **Weil** ich lieber zu Fuß gehe.
Why don't you go by car?
– *Because I prefer walking.*

Grammar overview

1

dass

The conjunction **dass** *(that)* is used to report a thought, a speech, a supposition or an opinion etc. of yourself or of somebody else. The exact function depends on the meaning of the verb of the main clause, e.g.:

Ich vermute, **dass** er bald kommt.
(Supposition)
I suppose he'll be arriving soon.
Ich denke, **dass** du Recht hast. *(Opinion)*
I think you are right.
Sie hat mir erzählt, **dass** sie einen neuen Freund hat. *(Reported speech)*
She told me that she has a new boyfriend.

Word order

The conjugated verb is always at the end of the subordinate clause. Verbs with separable prefixes are reunited.

Compare the word order of the main clause and the corresponding subordinate clause in the following examples:

Ich habe keine Zeit.
Ich komme nicht mit, weil ich keine Zeit **habe**.
I'm not coming along because I don't have any time.

Er kommt um 3 Uhr an.
Er sagt, dass er um 3 Uhr **ankommt**.
He says that he'll be arriving at 3 o'clock.

Er muss nicht arbeiten.
Er freut sich, wenn er nicht **arbeiten muss**.
He's glad when he doesn't have to work.

 26 VERBS WITH PREPOSI-TIONS

Many verbs are followed by a preposition plus an accusative (A) or dative (D) and they have to be learnt by heart:

einladen zu + D	*to invite to*
halten von + D	*to think of*
sich bedanken für + A	*to thank for*
sich freuen auf + A	*to look forward to*
sich freuen über + A	*to be pleased about*
sich interessieren für + A	*to be interested in*
sich treffen mit + D	*to meet*
teilnehmen an + D	*to take part in*
warten auf + A	*to wait for*

2

....

UNIT 1

Exercise 3 – CD 1, Track 3

Herr Braun:	Guten Morgen, Herr Kowalski.
Thomas:	Guten Morgen, Herr Braun.
Herr Braun:	Wie geht es Ihnen?
Thomas:	Ganz gut, danke. Und Ihnen?
Herr Braun:	Gut. Herr Kowalski, das ist Frau Moser. Sie ist Fotografin.
Thomas:	Freut mich.
Herr Braun:	Frau Moser, das ist Herr Kowalski.
Sylvia:	Grüß Gott.
Herr Braun:	Und das ist Frau Hartmann.
Thomas:	Guten Morgen. Sie sind Studentin, oder?
Aynur:	Ja, ich studiere Journalismus und ich mache hier ein Praktikum.
Thomas:	Aha! Herzlich willkommen!
Sylvia, Aynur:	Danke.
Herr Braun:	Entschuldigen Sie bitte, ich muss weg. Auf Wiedersehen!
Thomas, Sylvia, Aynur:	Auf Wiedersehen, Herr Braun.

...

Thomas:	Alle Kollegen hier duzen sich. Können wir auch „du" sagen?
Sylvia:	Ja gerne. Ich heiße Sylvia. Und du bist ...?
Thomas:	Ich bin Thomas. Und du, wie heißt du mit Vornamen?
Aynur:	Ich heiße Aynur.
Thomas:	Wie bitte? Aynur? Wie schreibt man das?
Aynur:	A-y-n-u-r. Das ist türkisch.
Thomas:	Interessant!

Mister Braun:	Good morning. Mr. Kowalski.
Thomas:	Good morning, Mr. Braun.
Mister Braun:	How are you?
Thomas:	Not bad, thank you. And you?
Mister Braun:	I'm fine. Mr. Kowalski, this is Mrs. Moser. She's a photographer.
Thomas:	Nice to meet you.
Mister Braun:	Mrs. Moser, this is Mr. Kowalski.
Sylvia:	Pleased to meet you.
Mister Braun:	And this is Mrs. Hartmann.
Thomas:	Good morning. You're a student, aren't you?
Aynur:	Yes, I study journalism and I'm here for a work placement.
Thomas:	I see! Welcome!
Sylvia, Aynur:	Thank you.
Mister Braun:	Excuse me, I have to go. Goodbye!
Thomas, Sylvia, Aynur:	Goodbye, Mr. Braun.

...

Thomas:	All the colleagues here use the informal form of address. Can we also say "du" to each other?
Sylvia:	Yes, of course. My name is Sylvia. And you are ...?
Thomas:	Thomas. And what's your first name?
Aynur:	My name's Aynur.
Thomas:	Pardon? Aynur? How do you spell that?
Aynur:	A-y-n-u-r. It's Turkish.
Thomas:	Interesting!

Exercise 14 – CD 1, Track 11

Hallo Klaus!
Oh, hallo Thomas, wie geht es dir?
Ganz gut. Und dir?
Super.
Tschüss!
Tschüss Thomas!

2

TAPESCRIPTS

· ·

UNIT 2

Exercise 3 - CD 1, Track 15

Thomas:	Du sagst, der Name „Aynur" ist türkisch.
Aynur:	Ja, meine Mutter ist Türkin, aber mein Vater ist Deutscher.
Thomas:	Aha. Wohnen sie in Düsseldorf?
Aynur:	Nur mein Vater. Meine Mutter lebt in der Türkei.
Sylvia:	Fährst du oft in die Türkei?
Aynur:	Nein, nicht sehr oft. Und du? Woher kommst du?
Sylvia:	Ich komme aus Österreich, aus Wien. Und du Thomas?
Thomas:	Aus Düsseldorf.
Sylvia:	Und wo wohnst du in Düsseldorf?
Thomas:	In der Wodanstraße, direkt am Rhein. Und ihr?
Aynur:	Ich wohne in Bilk.
Sylvia:	Bilk?
Aynur:	Das ist ein Stadtteil von Düsseldorf. Er liegt im Süden.
Sylvia:	Ach so. Und ich wohne in der Bäckerstraße. Hier ist meine Visitenkarte.
Aynur, Thomas: Danke.	
Thomas:	Hast du auch eine Handynummer?
Sylvia:	Ja, die Nummer ist 0172-88 ...
Thomas:	Moment! Langsam, bitte!
Sylvia:	0172-88634012.
Aynur:	Bäckerstraße? Dort ist ein Museum, oder?
Silvia:	Ja, das Stadtmuseum und ein Markt ...
Aynur:	Richtig, der Karlsmarkt.

Thomas:	You say the name "Aynur" is Turkish.
Aynur:	Yes, my mother is Turkish, but my father is German.
Thomas:	I see! Do they live in Dusseldorf?
Aynur:	Only my father. My mother lives in Turkey.
Sylvia:	Do you often go to Turkey?
Aynur:	No, not very often. And you? Where do you come from?
Sylvia:	I come from Austria, from Vienna. And you, Thomas?
Thomas:	From Dusseldorf.
Sylvia:	And where do you live in Dusseldorf?
Thomas:	In Wodan Street, right on the Rhine. And you?
Aynur:	I live in Bilk.
Sylvia:	Bilk?
Aynur:	It's a district of Düsseldorf. It's in the South.
Sylvia:	I see! And I live in Bäcker Street. Here is my business card.
Aynur, Thomas: Thank you.	
Thomas:	Do you have a mobile number, too?
Sylvia:	Yes, the number is 0172-88 ...
Thomas:	Wait a moment! Slowly, please!
Sylvia:	0172-88634012.
Aynur:	Bäcker Street? There is a museum there, isn't there?
Silvia:	Yes, the city museum and a market ...
Aynur:	Right, the "Karlsmarkt".

Exercise 10 - CD 1, Track 19

Sprechen Sie Englisch?

Exercise 12 - CD 1, Track 20

1. Woher kommst du?
   Aus England.
2. Wo wohnen Sie, Frau Müller?
   In der Goethestraße 8, in Bonn.
3. Welche Sprachen sprichst du?
   Ich spreche Deutsch und Französisch. Und du?
   Nur Deutsch.

4. Sind Sie Italiener?
   Nein, ich bin Schweizer, aber ich spreche auch Italienisch und Französisch.
5. Ich komme aus Erlangen.
   Wo ist das?
   In Bayern.
   Und wohin fahren Sie?
   Nach Hamburg.

Exercise 3 – CD 1, Track 25

Thomas:	Hmm, was nehmt ihr denn?		Thomas:	Hm, what are you going to have?

Thomas: Hmm, was nehmt ihr denn?
Sylvia: Ich nehme einen Kaffee.
Aynur: Ich nehme lieber einen Tee und ein Stück Kuchen. Möchtest du nichts essen?
Sylvia: Nein, nur etwas trinken. Und du Thomas?
Thomas: Hmm, mal sehen. Vielleicht einen Toast oder ein Sandwich ...?
...
Bedienung: Guten Tag. Was möchten Sie?
Thomas: Guten Tag. Die Damen möchten einen Kaffee, einen Tee und einen Kuchen. Und ich hätte gern einen Schinkentoast und ein Mineralwasser.
Bedienung: Wir haben Käsekuchen, Apfelkuchen und Schokoladentorte.
Aynur: Einen Apfelkuchen, bitte.
Bedienung: Gerne. Ist das alles?
Aynur: Ja.
Bedienung: Also, einen Apfelkuchen, einen Schinkentoast, einen Kaffee, ein Mineralwasser, einen Tee. Möchten Sie den Tee mit Zitrone oder mit Milch?
Aynur: Mit Zitrone, bitte.
...
Thomas: Hallo, wir möchten bitte zahlen!
Bedienung: Sofort. Getrennt oder zusammen?
Thomas: Zusammen.
Bedienung: Moment ... Das macht 19 Euro 10.
Thomas: Stimmt so!
Bedienung: Danke. Auf Wiedersehen!
Thomas: Auf Wiedersehen!

Thomas: Hm, what are you going to have?
Sylvia: A cup of coffee.
Aynur: I'd rather have a cup of tea and a piece of cake. Wouldn't you like something to eat?
Sylvia: No, just to drink. What about you, Thomas?
Thomas: Hm, let's see. Maybe some toast or a sandwich ...?
...
Waiter: Good afternoon. What would you like?
Thomas: Good afternoon. The ladies would like a cup of coffee, a cup of tea and a piece of cake. And I'd like some toast with ham and a mineral water.
Waiter: We've got cheesecake, apple pie and chocolate cake.
Aynur: A piece of apple pie, please.
Waiter: Of course. Is that all?
Aynur: Yes.
Waiter: Right, a piece of apple pie, some toast with ham, a cup of coffee, a mineral water, a cup of tea. Would you like the tea with lemon or milk?
Aynur: With lemon, please.
...
Thomas: Hello, can we have the bill, please?
Waiter: Right away! Are you paying separately or all together?
Thomas: Together.
Waiter: Just a moment ... That's 19 Euros 10.
Thomas: Keep the change!
Waiter: Thank you. Goodbye!
Thomas: Goodbye!

2

TAPESCRIPTS

Exercise 13 (der Gast = guest) – CD 1, Track 32

Bedienung: Guten Tag. Was möchten Sie?
Gast: Guten Tag. Ich hätte gern einen Tee.
Bedienung: Mit Milch oder mit Zitrone?
Gast: Mit Milch, bitte.
Bedienung: Ist das alles?
Gast: Nein, ich möchte auch etwas essen.
Bedienung: Ein Sandwich, einen Toast oder einen Kuchen?

Gast: Einen Kuchen. Haben Sie Apfelkuchen?
Bedienung: Ja.
Gast: Gut. Ich nehme ein Stück Apfelkuchen.
Bedienung: Gerne.

....

UNIT 4

Exercise 4 - CD 1, Track 37

Thomas:	Lokalredaktion „Blickpunkte", Kowalski am Apparat.
Anruferin:	Guten Tag! Mein Name ist Kundera.
Thomas:	Guten Tag! Was kann ich für Sie tun, Frau Kundera?
Anruferin:	Ich habe eine Geschichte für die Zeitung. Also ... im Rhein schwimmt ein Krokodil.
Thomas:	Ein Krokodil? Sind Sie sicher?
Anruferin:	Ja, das Tier ist groß, 1 Meter 50 lang ... Sind Sie interessiert?
Thomas:	Ich weiß nicht ... ja, vielleicht. Wo ist das Krokodil jetzt?
Anruferin:	Etwa 10 Kilometer südlich vom Hauptbahnhof. Sie fahren nach Benrath und gehen zum Rhein. Dort sind zwei Schiffe und das Krokodil. Und? Kommen Sie?
Thomas:	Ja, ich denke, wir kommen. Danke für den Anruf.

...

Sylvia:	Was ist los?
Thomas:	Eine Dame sagt, im Rhein ist ein Krokodil!
Aynur:	Wirklich? Das ist doch nicht möglich!
Sylvia:	Wie bitte? Im Rhein gibt es doch keine Krokodile! Fische, Schiffe, ja, aber Krokodile?
Thomas:	Ich weiß. Aber es ist eine super Geschichte für „Blickpunkte".
Aynur:	Und was machen wir? Fahren wir hin?
Thomas:	Ja, wir fahren nach Benrath und suchen das Krokodil. Sylvia, machst du die Fotos?
Sylvia:	Ja, klar!
Thomas:	Also los!

Exercise 7 - CD 1, Track 41

Thomas:	„Blickpunkte", Kowalski. Guten Tag.
Frau Kundera:	Guten Tag! Hier spricht Kundera.
Thomas:	Was kann ich für Sie tun?

...

Thomas:	Kowalski.
Klaus:	Hallo Thomas! Hier ist Klaus.
Thomas:	Oh, hallo Klaus! Wie geht's?

English translation (right column):

Thomas:	Local editorial office "Blickpunkte", Kowalski on the phone.
Caller:	Good morning! My name is Kundera.
Thomas:	Good morning! What can I do for you, Mrs Kundera?
Caller:	I've got a story for the newspaper. Well ... a crocodile is swimming in the Rhine.
Thomas:	A crocodile? Are you sure?
Caller:	Yes, the animal is tall, 1.5 meters long ... Are you interested?
Thomas:	I don't know ... yes, maybe. Where is the crocodile now?
Caller:	About 10 kilometres to the south of main station. You go to Benrath and walk to the Rhine. There are two ships and the crocodile. So? Will you come?
Thomas:	Yes, I think we'll come. Thanks for calling.

...

Sylvia:	What's up?
Thomas:	A lady said there is a crocodile in the Rhine!
Aynur:	Really? But that isn't possible!
Sylvia:	What? There aren't any crocodiles in the Rhine, are there? Fish, ships, yes, but crocodiles?
Thomas:	I know. But it's a great story for "Blickpunkte".
Aynur:	And what shall we do? Shall we go there?
Thomas:	Yes, we'll go to Benrath and we'll look for the crocodile. Sylvia, will you take the pictures?
Sylvia:	Yes, of course!
Thomas:	Well, come on!

REVISION 1

Exercise 3 – CD 1, Track 48

1. Sind Sie Italiener?
2. Was trinken wir?
3. Wo liegt Köln?

4. Woher kommt er?
5. Guten Tag! Hier spricht Franz Weber.
6. Gibt es Krokodile im Rhein?

· ·

UNIT 5

Exercise 3 – CD 1, Track 52

Thomas:	Wie spät ist es jetzt?
Sylvia:	10 Uhr.
Thomas:	Wann fährt der nächste Zug nach Benrath?
Aynur:	Die S-Bahn fährt um 10.11 Uhr.
Thomas:	Müssen wir umsteigen?
Aynur:	Nein, die Verbindung ist direkt.
Thomas:	Und um wie viel Uhr kommen wir in Benrath an?
Aynur:	Um 10.23 Uhr.
Sylvia:	Aber wir können auch den Regional-Express nach Köln nehmen. Er hält auch in Benrath.
Aynur:	Wie lange fahren wir?
Sylvia:	Nur sechs Minuten.
Thomas:	In Ordnung. Wir nehmen den Regional-Express.
Sylvia:	Und die Fahrkarten?
Thomas:	Wir müssen am Informationsschalter fragen.

... (Am Informationsschalter)

Bahnbeamter:	Guten Tag. Was kann ich für Sie tun?
Thomas:	Guten Tag. Wir wollen mit dem Regional-Express nach Benrath fahren.
Bahnbeamter:	Drei Personen? Hin und zurück?
Aynur:	Nein, nur zwei. Ich habe ein Semesterticket.
Bahnbeamter:	Also zwei Hin- und Rückfahrkarten. Dann nehmen Sie ein 4erTicket.
Sylvia:	Wo können wir das Ticket kaufen?
Bahnbeamter:	Dort am Fahrkartenautomaten.
Sylvia:	Und auf welchem Gleis fährt der Zug ab?

Thomas:	What time is it now?
Sylvia:	It's 10 o'clock.
Thomas:	When's the next train to Benrath?
Aynur:	The S-Bahn leaves at 10.11.
Thomas:	Do we have to change trains?
Aynur:	No, it's a direct connection .
Thomas:	And what time will we arrive in Benrath?
Aynur:	At 10.23.
Sylvia:	But we can also take the Regional-Express to Cologne. It stops in Benrath, too.
Aynur:	How long does that take?
Sylvia:	Only six minutes.
Thomas:	All right. We'll take the Regional-Express.
Sylvia:	And the tickets?
Thomas:	We'll have to ask at the information service.

... (At the information service)

Railway official:	Good morning. What can I do for you?
Thomas:	Good morning. We want to go to Benrath by the Regional-Express.
Railway official:	Three return tickets?
Aynur:	No, only two. I've got a Semesterticket.
Railway official:	OK. Two returns. You'd best buy a four journey ticket.
Sylvia:	Where can we buy that?
Railway official:	Over there from the ticket machine.
Sylvia:	I see! And which platform does the train leave from?

▼

▼

Bahnbeamter:	Auf Gleis 15.	*Railway official:*	15.
Sylvia:	Danke für die Informationen. Auf Wiedersehen.	*Sylvia:*	Thanks for the information. Goodbye.
Bahnbeamter:	Auf Wiedersehen.	*Railway official:*	Goodbye.

Exercise 14 – CD 1, Track 61

Auf Gleis 10.
Ja, in Köln und Mainz.
Nein, die nächste ist Düsseldorf Hauptbahnhof.

. . . .

UNIT 6

Exercise 4 – CD 1, Track 65

Thomas:	Siehst du das Krokodil?	*Thomas:*	Can you see the crocodile?
Aynur:	Nein, ich sehe es nicht. Was machen wir jetzt?	*Aynur:*	No, I can't. What shall we do now?
Thomas:	Ich weiß nicht. Wie spät ist es?	*Thomas:*	I don't know. What time is it?
Aynur:	Viertel vor eins.	*Aynur:*	A quarter to 1.
Thomas:	So spät! Wir suchen das Krokodil schon zwei Stunden!	*Thomas:*	So late! We have been looking for the crocrodile for two hours!
Aynur:	Ja, und die Leute hier wissen auch nichts.	*Aynur:*	Yes, and no one here knows anything.
Thomas:	Was meinst du, fahren wir ins Büro zurück?	*Thomas:*	What do you think, shall we go back to the office?
Aynur:	Einverstanden! Wo ist Sylvia? Ich sehe sie nicht.	*Aynur:*	Right! Where is Sylvia? I can't see her.
...		...	
Aynur:	Ah, hier bist du!	*Aynur:*	Ah, here you are!
Sylvia:	Ja, ich mache Fotos und gehe ein wenig spazieren.	*Sylvia:*	Yes, I'm just taking some pictures and going for a little walk.
Aynur:	Aber hier darfst du nicht weitergehen. Das ist privat.	*Aynur:*	But you're not allowed to go any further, here. It's private property.
Sylvia:	Oh!	*Sylvia:*	Oh!
Thomas:	Hör mal Sylvia, Aynur und ich möchten nach Düsseldorf zurückfahren. Kommst du mit?	*Thomas:*	Listen Sylvia, Aynur and me would like to go back to Düsseldorf. Are you coming?
Sylvia:	Ja, gerne.	*Sylvia:*	Yes, I'd like to.
...		...	
Sylvia:	Und was machen wir jetzt?	*Sylvia:*	And what shall we do now?
Thomas:	Naja, am Nachmittag müssen wir arbeiten.	*Thomas:*	Well, this afternoon we have to work.
Sylvia:	Und dann? Sollen wir das Krokodil noch suchen?	*Sylvia:*	And after that? Should we continue looking for the crocodile?
Aynur:	Ich habe eine Idee: Wir gehen heute Abend in den Zirkus und fragen dort. Vielleicht fehlt ein Krokodil. Was haltet ihr davon?	*Aynur:*	I have an idea: Let's go to the circus this evening and we'll ask there. Maybe they're missing a crocodile. What do you think?
▼		▼	

| Sylvia: | Gute Idee! Aber ich habe keine Zeit. Ich will in den Sportverein gehen. | Sylvia: | Good idea! But I'm busy. I want to go to the sports club. |
| Thomas: | Ich habe leider auch keine Zeit. Aber am Mittwoch oder am Donnerstag können wir vielleicht in den Zirkus gehen. | Thomas: | I'm afraid I haven't got time, either. But maybe we can go to the circus on Wednesday or Thursday. |

Exercise 6 – CD 1, Track 67

Marco:	Hallo Karin, was machst du heute?	Karin:	Mit Doris?
Karin:	Ich gehe in die Disco. Und du?	Marco:	Nein, sie geht in den Zirkus.
Marco:	Ich weiß nicht. Vielleicht gehe ich ins Café.		

. . . .

UNIT 7

Exercise 3 – CD 1, Track 74

Aynur:	Gehst du regelmäßig in den Sportverein?	Aynur:	Do you go to the the sports club regularly?
Sylvia:	Ja, einmal in der Woche.	Sylvia:	Yes, once a week.
Aynur:	Und was machst du dort?	Aynur:	And what do you do there?
Sylvia:	Eine Stunde Gymnastik. Und du, was machst du in deiner Freizeit?	Sylvia:	I exercise for one hour. And you, what do you do in your free time?
Aynur:	Ich fahre gern Fahrrad. Aber am liebsten treffe ich Freunde. Wir gehen zusammen aus, wir kochen oder wir hören Musik.	Aynur:	I like cycling. But most of all I like meeting friends. We go out together, cook or listen to music.
Sylvia:	Thomas, was ist mit dir? Hast du ein Hobby?	Sylvia:	Thomas, what about you? Do you have a hobby?
Thomas:	Ja, Computer. Ich surfe gern im Internet. Und ich interessiere mich für Kunst und Kultur. Meine Frau und ich besuchen oft Ausstellungen oder gehen in Konzerte.	Thomas:	Yes, the computer. I like to surf the internet. And I'm interested in art and culture. My wife and I often visit exhibitions or go to concerts.
Sylvia:	Auch heute Abend?	Sylvia:	This evening, too?
Thomas:	Nein. Heute Abend haben wir ein Familienfest.	Thomas:	No. This evening we are going to have a family party.
Sylvia:	Oh, wie schön! Was feiert ihr?	Sylvia:	Oh, that's nice! What are you celebrating?
Thomas:	Meine Tochter Lisa hat Geburtstag.	Thomas:	It's the birthday of my daughter Lisa.
Sylvia:	Wie alt wird sie?	Sylvia:	How old is she?
Thomas:	Sieben. Meine Frau bereitet eine Party vor, mit einer Torte und mit Geschenken.	Thomas:	Seven. My wife is preparing a party with cakes and gifts.
Sylvia:	Toll! Und was schenkst du deiner Tochter?	Sylvia:	Great! And what are you giving as a present to your daughter?
Thomas:	Ein Kartenspiel und ein paar Bilderbücher ... Und was machst du nach dem Sportverein?	Thomas:	A card game and a few pictures books ... And what are you going to do after the sports club?
▼		▼	

2

TAPESCRIPTS

Sylvia:	Oh, ich bekomme noch Familienbe-such.
Thomas:	Wer kommt denn?
Sylvia:	Meine Tante aus Berlin. Sie ist zum ersten Mal in Düsseldorf und ich will ihr die Stadt zeigen. Und du Aynur?
Aynur:	Heute Abend mache ich nichts Besonderes. Meine Freundin kommt. Sie bringt mir die neue CD von den „Fantastischen Vier" mit.
Sylvia:	Aha! Also dann, ich wünsche euch viel Spaß! Tschüss!
Aynur:	Danke, dir auch. Tschüss!
Thomas:	Tschüss!

Sylvia:	Oh, I'm having part of my family visiting.
Thomas:	Oh, who's coming?
Sylvia:	My aunt from Berlin. It'll be her first time to Düsseldorf and I want to show her the town. And you, Aynur?
Aynur:	This evening, I'm not doing anything special. My friend's coming. She'll bring along the new CD of Die fantastischen Vier for me.
Sylvia:	Oh, I see! Well, have a lot of fun! Bye!
Aynur:	Thanks, you too. Bye!
Thomas:	Bye!

Exercise 11 – CD 1, Track 80

1. – Was machst du in deiner Freizeit?
   – Ich treffe gern Freunde.
2. – Magst du Kunst?
   – Nein, ich interessiere mich nicht für Kunst.

3. – Ich esse nicht gern Kuchen, und du?
   – Ich auch nicht.

UNIT 8

Exercise 3 – CD 1, Track 86

Susanne:	Hallo Thomas, da bist du ja endlich!
Thomas:	Hallo. Wo ist denn unser Geburtstagskind?
Susanne:	Da kommt sie.
Thomas:	Hallo, mein Schatz.
Lisa:	Hallo Papa! Endlich! Ich will doch meine Geschenke haben.
Thomas:	Ja, sofort. Aber zuerst singen wir ein Lied für dich.
Lisa:	Au ja!
Thomas, Susanne:	Zum Geburtstag viel Glück, zum Geburtstag viel Glück, zum Geburtstag, liebe Lisa, zum Geburtstag viel Glück.
...	
Lisa:	Darf ich jetzt die Geschenke auspacken?
Thomas:	Aber ja. Herzlichen Glückwunsch zum Geburtstag!
Lisa:	Ui, ein Kartenspiel. Danke, Papa.
Susanne:	Und schau mal, hier ist eine Karte von Oma.
Lisa:	Kannst du mir die Karte bitte vorlesen?

Susanne:	Hello Thomas, you are here at last!
Thomas:	Hello. Where is our birthday girl?
Susanne:	Here she is.
Thomas:	Hello, my sweetheart.
Lisa:	Hello daddy! Finally! I just want to have my gifts.
Thomas:	Yes, soon. But first of all we'll sing a song for you.
Lisa:	Fine!
Thomas, Susanne:	Happy birthday to you, happy birthday to you, happy birthday, dear Lisa, happy birthday to you.
...	
Lisa:	Can I unwrap the gifts now?
Thomas:	Of course. Happy birthday!
Lisa:	Oh, a card game. Thanks, daddy.
Susanne:	And look, here is a card from grandma.
Lisa:	Can you read the card to me, please?

▼

Susanne:	Oma schreibt: „Liebe Lisa, alles Gute zu deinem Geburtstag! Das nächste Mal feiere ich mit dir. Küsschen von deiner Oma."		*Susanne:*	Grandma writes: "Dear Lisa, all the best for your birthday! Next time I'll celebrate with you. Kisses from your grandma."

Susanne: Oma schreibt: „Liebe Lisa, alles Gute zu deinem Geburtstag! Das nächste Mal feiere ich mit dir. Küsschen von deiner Oma."

Lisa: Und wo ist das Geschenk von Oma?

Susanne: Hier. Es ist eine Überraschung.

...

Lisa: Ui, das ist aber toll. Jetzt kann ich mit einem Krokodil baden.

Thomas: Das gibt es doch nicht! Nicht möglich!

Susanne: Was ist los? Das ist doch nur ein Schwimmtier!

Thomas: Ja, aber du weißt, wir suchen ein Krokodil im Rhein. Das ist wirklich lustig!

Susanne: Du meinst, „euer" Krokodil ist vielleicht ein Schwimmtier aus Plastik?

Thomas: Ja, genau. Das muss ich morgen meinen Kolleginnen erzählen. Sylvia und Aynur lachen sicher auch!

Susanne: Grandma writes: "Dear Lisa, all the best for your birthday! Next time I'll celebrate with you. Kisses from your grandma."

Lisa: And where is the gift from grandma?

Susanne: Here. It's a surprise.

...

Lisa: Oh, that's really great. Now I can have a bath with a crocodile.

Thomas: That can't be true! Not possible!

Susanne: What's the matter? That's just a bath toy!

Thomas: Yes, but you know we are looking for a crocodile in the Rhine. That's really funny!

Susanne: You mean, "your" crocodile is maybe a bath toy made of plastic?

Thomas: Yes, exactly. I have to tell that to my colleagues tomorrow. Sylvia and Aynur will surely laugh, too!

Exercise 12 - CD 1, Track 93

Lieber Max,
wie geht es dir? Ich bin in Berlin und besuche meine Eltern. Bis bald!
Viele liebe Grüße
deine Steffi

....

UNIT 9

Exercise 4 - CD 2, Track 03

Thomas: Guten Morgen, Frau Schmidt.

Frau Schmidt: Guten Morgen, Herr Kowalski. Und? Was haben Sie in den letzten Tagen gemacht? Haben Sie das Krokodil gesucht?

Thomas: Ja, am 1. Juni sind Sylvia, Aynur und ich nach Benrath gefahren. Wir haben dort das Krokodil gesucht und ein paar Leute gefragt, aber ohne Erfolg.

Frau Schmidt: Schade! Ach übrigens, gestern hat eine Frau für Sie angerufen.

Thomas: Was hat sie gesagt?

Frau Schmidt: Sie hat die Geschichte über das Krokodil in der Zeitung gelesen.

Thomas: Und weiter?

▼

Thomas: Good morning, Mrs. Schmidt.

Frau Schmidt: Good morning, Mr. Kowalski. Well, what did you do in the last few days? Did you look for the crocodile?

Thomas: Yes, on the 1st of June Sylvia, Aynur and I went to Benrath. There we looked for the crocodile and questioned a few people, but without any success.

Frau Schmidt: That's a pity! Oh, by the way, yesterday a woman called for you.

Thomas: What did she say?

Frau Schmidt: She read the story about the crocodile in the newspaper.

Thomas: And then?

▼

Frau Schmidt:	Und dann hat sie von ihrem Nachbarn erzählt. Dieser Nachbar ist ein Tierfreund und er hat viele Haustiere. Und nun ist ein Tier weg.	Frau Schmidt:	And then she spoke about her neighbour. This neighbour is a animal lover and he's got a lot of pets. And now one animal is missing.
Thomas:	Ja, und?	Thomas:	Yes, and what then?
Frau Schmidt:	Naja, diese Haustiere sind sehr exotisch und nun fehlt ein Krokodil. Wollen Sie hinfahren und den Tierfreund befragen? Er heißt Greiner und wohnt in ... Moment, ich habe seine Adresse auf einen Zettel geschrieben. Hier ist der Zettel.	Frau Schmidt:	Well, these pets are very exotic and now a crocodile is missing. Do you want to go there to question the animal lover? His name is Greiner and he lives in ... Just a moment, I wrote his address on a piece of paper. Here is the piece of paper.
Thomas:	Danke. Aha, Oskar Greiner, Neanderstraße ... Wo ist das? Kennen Sie diese Straße?	Thomas:	Thanks. I see, Oskar Greiner, Neander street ... Where is that? Do you know that street?
Frau Schmidt:	Ja, ich glaube, die Straße liegt im Stadtteil Flingern. Sie nehmen den Bus Nummer 834 und steigen an der vierten oder fünften Haltestelle aus.	Frau Schmidt:	Yes, I think, the street is situated in the district Flingern. You take the bus number 834 and you get off on the forth or fifth station.
Thomas:	Vielen Dank, Frau Schmidt.	Thomas:	Thanks a lot, Mrs. Schmidt.
Frau Schmidt:	Keine Ursache. Also dann, bis später!	Frau Schmidt:	Don't mention it. Well then, see you later!
Thomas:	Bis später! Tschüss, Frau Schmidt.	Thomas:	See you later! Bye, Mrs. Schmidt.

Exercise 13 – CD 2, Track 09

1. Was hast du gestern Abend gemacht?
2. Wann ist Peter gekommen?
3. Hast du Maria in den letzten Tagen gesehen?

UNIT 10

Exercise 2 – CD 2, Track 11

1. Er geht über die Brücke zum Bus.
2. Der Vogel ist auf der Mauer.
3. Das Kind spielt vor dem Haus.
4. Die Haltestelle liegt neben dem Kiosk.
5. Das Hotel liegt zwischen der Post und der Bank.
6. Das Schiff ist unter der Brücke.
7. Sie geht in die Disco.
8. Das Kind ist hinter dem Haus.
9. Das Auto fährt an der Ampel nach rechts.

Exercise 4 – CD 2, Track 13

Sylvia:	Wohin müssen wir jetzt gehen? Rechts oder links?	Sylvia:	Where do we have to go now? Right or left?
Thomas:	Ich habe keine Ahnung. Aynur, gib mir mal den Stadtplan.	Thomas:	I have no idea. Aynur, give me the city map.
Aynur:	Oh, tut mir leid. Ich habe ihn im Büro vergessen.	Aynur:	Oh, I'm sorry. I forgot it in the office.
Thomas:	Macht nichts! Wir fragen jemanden.	Thomas:	It doesn't matter! We'll ask somebody.
...		...	

Thomas:	Entschuldigen Sie bitte, wie kommen wir zur Neanderstraße?	Thomas:	Excuse me, please, how do we get to Neander Street?
Mann:	Tut mir leid, ich bin nicht von hier.	Man:	I'm sorry, I'm not from here.
Thomas:	Hmm. Da kann man nichts machen.	Thomas:	Hmm. Never mind.
Mann:	Fragen Sie doch in der Apotheke oder am Kiosk gegenüber.	Man:	Ask in the pharmacy or at the kiosk opposite.
Thomas:	Gute Idee! Danke.	Thomas:	Good idea! Thank you.
...		...	
Thomas:	Guten Tag, wir suchen die Neanderstraße.	Thomas:	Good morning, we are looking for Neander Street.
Mann im Kiosk:	Neanderstraße? Warten Sie ... Gehen Sie diese Straße entlang immer geradeaus, am Kindergarten und an der Schule vorbei bis zur Kreuzung. Dort gehen Sie nach rechts, dann wieder geradeaus. Dann die erste Straße links. Das ist die Neanderstraße.	Man in the kiosk:	Neander Street? Wait a second ... Go along this street always straight ahead, pass the kindergarten and the school until you get to a crossroad. There you turn right, then again straight ahead. Then the first street on the left. That's Neander Street.
Thomas:	Also, noch einmal. Wir gehen bis zur Kreuzung, dann rechts, dann geradeaus, dann links.	Thomas:	Well, once again. We go to the crossroad, then right, then straight ahead, then left.
Mann im Kiosk:	Genau!	Man in the kiosk:	Exactly!
Sylvia:	Ist es weit? Sollen wir mit dem Bus zurückfahren?	Sylvia:	Is it far? Should we go by bus?
Mann im Kiosk:	Nein, nein, es sind nur 10 Minuten zu Fuß.	Man in the kiosk:	No, no, it's only 10 minutes to walk.
Sylvia:	Ja, das ist wirklich nicht weit. Vielen Dank für die Auskunft.	Sylvia:	Yes, that's not really far. Thanks a lot for the information.
Mann im Kiosk:	Keine Ursache.	Man in the kiosk:	Don't mention it.

Exercise 9 - CD 2, Track 17

a. Am Kiosk gibt es Zeitungen.
b. Er geht auf die Post.
c. Die Kinder spielen im Park.
d. An der Ampel müssen Sie abbiegen.
e. Fahren Sie über die Kreuzung.
f. Geh in die Straße links.
g. Ich gehe auf den Platz.
h. Vor dem Hotel ist ein Auto.
i. Der Park liegt hinter dem Bahnhof.
j. Neben dem Kino ist ein Café.
k. Das Schiff fährt unter die Brücke.

Exercise 10 - CD 2, Track 019

Dialogue 1
– Entschuldigen Sie bitte, wie komme ich zur Post?
– Tut mir leid. Ich bin nicht von hier.

Dialogue 2
– Ich suche den Kindergarten. Ist es weit?
– Nein, nur 10 Minuten zu Fuß.

Exercise 15 - CD 2, Track 23

1. Sie sind an der Schule. Gehen Sie die Straße entlang und dann rechts. Dann geradeaus über die Kreuzung. Links sehen Sie die ...
2. Sie sind am Bahnhof. Gehen Sie links bis zur Kreuzung. Dort gehen Sie rechts, dann noch einmal rechts durch die Fußgängerzone. Dann gehen Sie links. Dort sehen Sie einen Kiosk. Neben dem Kiosk ist ein ...

··

UNIT 11

Exercise 3 - CD 2, Track 25

Thomas:	Sind wir hier richtig?
Aynur:	Ja, hier steht „Greiner". Er wohnt im 2. Stock.
Thomas:	Er ist noch nicht zu Hause. Dann warten wir eben.
...	
Sylvia:	Herr Greiner wohnt aber sehr schön!
Thomas:	Stimmt, die Straße ist ruhig gelegen, aber nicht zu weit vom Zentrum.
Aynur:	Das gelbe Haus von Herrn Greiner finde ich besonders schön. Die Tür ist grün, die Fensterrahmen sind blau ... Mir gefallen bunte Häuser.
Sylvia:	Du hast Recht. Dieses Haus ist wirklich schön. Ich mache ein paar Fotos.
...	
Aynur:	Hast du heute schon viel fotografiert?
Sylvia:	Ja, ich bin früh aufgestanden und sofort nach dem Frühstück bin ich losgegangen und habe Fotos in der Altstadt gemacht. Du weißt ja, ich wohne ganz zentral. Und was hast du heute schon gemacht?
Aynur:	Heute Morgen hat mein Vater angerufen und mich zum Abendessen eingeladen.
Thomas:	Apropos essen, habt ihr keinen Hunger? Es ist schon Mittag. Nach dem Gespräch mit Herrn Greiner können wir doch etwas essen gehen.
Sylvia:	Wo möchtest du denn essen?
Thomas:	Auf dem Weg zur Neanderstraße habe ich ein kleines Lokal gesehen.
Aynur:	Welches? Das kleine griechische?
Thomas:	Ja. Vielleicht können wir dort Mittag essen.
Sylvia, Aynur:	Einverstanden!
Thomas:	Hoffentlich kommt Herr Greiner bald!

Thomas:	Are we at the right house here?
Aynur:	Yes, here it says "Greiner". He lives on the 2nd floor.
Thomas:	He isn't at home yet. So we'll just wait.
...	
Sylvia:	Mr. Greiner lives in a very nice area
Thomas:	That's right, the street is quiet, but not too far from the centre.
Aynur:	I find Mr. Greiner's yellow house especially nice. The door is green, the window frames are blue ... I like colourful houses.
Sylvia:	You are right. This house is really nice. I'll take some photos.
...	
Aynur:	Have you already taken a lot of photos today?
Sylvia:	Yes, I got up early and immediately after breakfast I set off and took photos in the old town centre. As you know, I live quite central.- And what have you already done today?
Aynur:	This morning my father called and invited me for dinner.
Thomas:	Talking about food, aren't you hungry? It's noon already. After the conversation with Mr. Greiner we could go and eat something.
Sylvia:	Where would you like to eat?
Thomas:	On the way to Neander Street I saw a small pub.
Aynur:	Which one? That small greek one?
Thomas:	Yes. Maybe we can have some lunch there.
Sylvia, Aynur:	Agreed!
Thomas:	I hope Mr. Greiner will come soon!

Exercise 5 - CD 2, Track 26

1. aufstehen
2. ins Bett gehen
3. duschen
4. einkaufen
5. frühstücken

6. zu Mittag essen
7. zu Abend essen
8. die Kinder zur Schule bringen
9. zur Arbeit gehen
10. nach Hause kommen

Exercise 6 – CD 2, Track 28

1. • Du wohnst aber schön!
   ○ Ja, die Wohnung ist wirklich ruhig und nah am Zentrum gelegen.
2. • Wohnen Sie in der Stadt?
   ○ Nein, ich wohne außerhalb, auf dem Land.

3. • Wie ist deine Wohnung?
   ○ Meine Wohnung liegt im Erdgeschoss und ist laut. Aber es gibt eine Terrasse.

....

UNIT 12

Exercise 4 (*Hr. = Herr*) **– CD 2, Track 37**

Hr. Greiner:	Kommen Sie herein! Sie können Ihre Jacken hier an die Garderobe hängen.
Thomas:	Danke. Sylvia, Aynur, gebt mir eure Jacken.
Hr. Greiner:	Darf ich Ihnen alles zeigen?
Thomas:	Ja, gerne.
Hr. Greiner:	Wir gehen zuerst ins Wohnzimmer.

...

Hr. Greiner:	Also, hier stehen meine Terrarien. Schauen Sie, dort auf dem Regal stehen meine Schildkröten. Und dort über der Heizung sehen Sie zwei Schlangen.
Aynur:	Über der Heizung?
Hr. Greiner:	Ja. Schlangen brauchen viel Wärme.
Aynur:	Aha! Sind die giftig?
Hr. Greiner:	Nein, nein, die sind ganz ungefährlich. Sie können sie gern streicheln.
Aynur:	Nein, danke!
Hr. Greiner:	Möchten Sie auch meine Papageien sehen?
Sylvia:	Oh ja, wo sind die denn?
Hr. Greiner:	Sie sind in der Küche. Kommen Sie!

...

Aynur:	Uj, die sind aber wunderschön!
Hr. Greiner:	Warten Sie, ich stelle die Käfige auf den Tisch. Dann können Sie die Papageien besser sehen.
Sylvia:	Sie haben wirklich viele exotische Tiere!
Hr. Greiner:	Ja, ich bin Lehrer für Biologie und interessiere mich für Tiere in Australien.
Sylvia:	Ach so! Ich habe schon gesehen, an der Wand im Wohnzimmer hängen viele Fotos von Australien. Mein Kompliment, es sind sehr schöne Fotos!
Hr. Greiner:	Danke.

▼

Mr. Greiner:	Come in! You can hang your jackets up here on the hall-stand.
Thomas:	Thank you. Sylvia, Aynur, give me your jackets.
Mr. Greiner:	Shall I show you everything?
Thomas:	Yes, that would be nice.
Mr. Greiner:	First we will go into the living-room.

...

Mr. Greiner:	Well, here are my terraria. Look, on the shelf over there are my turtles. And over the radiator you can see two snakes.
Aynur:	Over the radiator?
Mr. Greiner:	Yes. Snakes need warm temperatures.
Aynur:	I see! Are they poisonous?
Mr. Greiner:	No, no, they are quite harmless. If you like you can stroke them.
Aynur:	No, thanks!
Mr. Greiner:	Would you like to see my parrots, too?
Sylvia:	Oh yes, where are they?
Mr. Greiner:	They are in the kitchen. This way.

...

Aynur:	Oh, they are really beautiful!
Mr. Greiner:	Wait a moment, I'll put the cages on the table. So you can see the parrots better.
Sylvia:	You have many exotic animals indeed!
Mr. Greiner:	Yes, I'm a biology teacher and I'm interested in animals from Australia.
Sylvia:	I see! I already saw many pictures from Australia on the wall in the living-room. My compliment, they are very good pictures!
Mr.Greiner:	Thank you.

▼

2

Thomas:	Aber sagen Sie, ein Krokodil haben Sie nicht? Oder ist es im Badezimmer?
Hr. Greiner:	Ein Krokodil? Nein. Das ist zu groß für meine Wohnung!

Thomas:	But tell us, haven't you got a crocodile? Or is it in the bathroom?
Mr. Greiner:	A crocodile? No. That's too big for my flat!

Exercise 6 – CD 2, Track 39

1. In diesem Zimmer spielen die Kinder.
2. Hier kochen wir das Essen.
3. Hier stehen ein Sofa, zwei Sessel, ein Tisch und Regale.
4. In diesem Zimmer steht ein Bett und ein Schrank.

Exercise 10 – CD 2, Track 42

1. Wohin legst du die Fotos?
2. Wohin hängst du den Spiegel?
3. Wohin stellst du den Käfig?

....

REVISION 3

Exercise 9 – CD 2, Track 48

a. Gehen Sie an die Ecke und an der Ecke links.
b. Jetzt ist er auf dem Markt und dann geht er auf den Turm.
c. Ich gehe durch den Park.
d. Gehen Sie diesen Weg entlang.
e. Gegenüber dem Kiosk liegt die Bushaltestelle.
f. Hinter dem Haus spielt ein Kind. Gehen Sie hinter das Haus.

g. Was machen wir nach dem Frühstück?
h. Wir fahren ohne die Kinder nach Italien.
i. Er wartet seit einer Stunde.
j. Über der Heizung hängt ein Foto. Häng es bitte über das Sofa.
k. Vor der Tür ist ein Teppich. Leg ihn bitte vor die Kommode.
l. Wie komme ich zum Bahnhof?

....

UNIT 13

Exercise 4 – CD 2, Track 52

Susanne:	Thomas, ich möchte deine Kolleginnen endlich kennen lernen. Was meinst du, können wir uns am Samstag mit ihnen treffen?
Thomas:	Das ist eine gute Idee. Wann sollen wir sie treffen? Am Abend?
Susanne:	Nein, am Nachmittag. Dann kann Lisa auch dabei sein.
Thomas:	Gut. Was hältst du von einem Biergarten oder einem Café?
	▼

Susanne:	Thomas, I really would like to meet your colleagues. What do you think, could we meet them on Saturday?
Thomas:	That's a good idea. When shall we meet them? In the evening?
Susanne:	No, in the afternoon. That way Lisa can come , too.
Thomas:	Fine. What do you think of a beer garden or a café?
	▼

Susanne:	Nein, ich möchte sie lieber zu einem Picknick am Rhein einladen. Das Wetter ist so schön. Und Lisa freut sich schon sehr auf ein Picknick.	*Susanne:*	No, I'd prefer to invite them to a picnic at the Rhine. The weather is so lovely. And Lisa is already looking forward to a picnic.
Thomas:	Hm, und was machen wir, wenn es regnet?	*Thomas:*	Hm, and what shall we do, if it rains?
Susanne:	Dann gehen wir natürlich nicht an den Rhein. Aber ich habe im Radio gehört, das Wetter bleibt schön und die Sonne scheint.	*Susanne:*	Then, of course, we won't go to the Rhine. But I've heard on the radio, that the weather's going to stay fine und the sun's going to shine.
Thomas:	Also gut, ich frage mal Sylvia und Aynur und rufe dich dann zurück. Bis später!	*Thomas:*	Well then, I'll ask Sylvia and Aynur and I'll call you back. See you later!
Susanne:	Tschüss. Bis später!	*Susanne:*	Bye. See you later!
...		...	
Thomas:	Habt ihr am Samstagnachmittag schon etwas vor? Meine Frau und ich möchten euch zu einem Picknick einladen.	*Thomas:*	Do you have anything planned for Saturday afternoon? My wife and I would like to invite you to a picnic.
Sylvia:	Am Samstag? Ja, das passt mir gut. Aynur, kannst du auch?	*Sylvia:*	On Saturday? Yes, that suits me fine. Aynur, can you also make it?
Aynur:	Ja, für ein Picknick habe ich immer Zeit!	*Aynur:*	Yes, I always have time for a picnic!
Sylvia:	Wann und wo treffen wir uns?	*Sylvia:*	When and where shall we meet?
Thomas:	Um 3 Uhr an der Brücke nach Oberkassel. Von dort gehen wir noch etwa 5 Minuten zu Fuß. Ich kann euch abholen, wenn ihr wollt.	*Thomas:*	At 3 o'clock at the bridge to Oberkassel. From there we have to walk for about 5 minutes. I can pick you up, if you want.
Sylvia:	Ja.	*Sylvia, Aynur:*	Yes, that would be very nice.
Aynur:	Gerne.		
Sylvia:	Sollen wir etwas mitbringen? Vielleicht einen Kuchen? Oder eine Flasche Sekt?	*Sylvia:*	Shall we bring something along? Perhaps a cake? Or a bottle of sparkling wine?
Thomas:	Nein, nein, das ist nicht nötig. Susanne bereitet alles vor.	*Thomas:*	No, no, that's not necessary. Susanne is preparing everything.
Sylvia:	In Ordnung! Sag deiner Frau schon mal vielen Dank für die Einladung!	*Sylvia:*	All right! Say "thank you" to your wife for the invitation!

....

UNIT 14

Exercise 4 - CD 2, Track 64

Thomas:	Was bereitest du denn für das Picknick vor?	*Thomas:*	What are you going to prepare for the picnic?
Susanne:	Ich mache einen Obstsalat. Der schmeckt immer so lecker. Dann gibt es Wurst, Käse, Tomatensalat und natürlich Brot.	*Susanne:*	I'm going to make a fruit salad. It always tastes so delicious. Then we'll have sausage, cheese, tomato salad and of course bread.

▼ ▼

Thomas:	Brot? Ich finde Brötchen aber besser als Brot.		*Thomas:*	Bread? But I like rolls better than bread.
Susanne:	Also gut, dann nehmen wir Brötchen.		*Susanne:*	Well, o.k., let's have rolls then.
Thomas:	Musst du noch viel einkaufen? Ich kann dir helfen, wenn du willst.		*Thomas:*	Do still you have to buy a lot? I can help you if you like.
Susanne:	Oh, ja bitte. Kannst du die Getränke im Supermarkt besorgen? Dort sind sie am billigsten.		*Susanne:*	Oh yes, please. Can you get the beverages from the supermarket? There they are the cheapest.
Thomas:	Kein Problem. Kann ich dir sonst noch helfen?		*Thomas:*	No problem. Can I help you with anything else?
Susanne:	Nein, danke. Ich brauche nur noch frisches Obst und Gemüse, dann muss ich noch in die Metzgerei. Zum Bäcker gehe ich erst morgen.		*Susanne:*	No, thanks. I only need fresh fruit and vegetables and I need to go to the butcher's. I'm not going to the baker's until tomorrow.
Thomas:	Gut. Nimmst du Lisa zum Einkaufen mit?		*Thomas:*	Fine. Are you taking Lisa shopping with?
Susanne:	Ja. Lisa, kommst du? Wir gehen einkaufen!		*Susanne:*	Yes. Lisa, are you ready? We are going shopping!
Lisa:	Ich komme!		*Lisa:*	I'm coming!
Thomas:	Vergiss die Einkaufstaschen nicht!		*Thomas:*	Don't forget the shopping bags!
Susanne:	Oh ja, danke! Bis später dann.		*Susanne:*	Oh yes, thanks! See you later.
...			...	
Verkäuferin:	Guten Tag, was darf es sein?		*shop assistant:*	Good afternoon, what can I get you?
Susanne:	Ich hätte gern 10 kleine Bratwürste und 400 Gramm Salami.		*Susanne:*	I'd like 10 small fying sausages and 400 grams of salami.
Verkäuferin:	Die Salami am Stück oder geschnitten?		*shop assistant:*	The salami in one piece or sliced?
Susanne:	Geschnitten. Ganz dünne Scheiben, bitte.		*Susanne:*	Sliced. Very thin slices, please.
Verkäuferin:	Darf es sonst noch etwas sein? Wir haben heute Schinken im Angebot.		*shop assistant:*	Would you like anything else? Today we have got ham on offer.
Susanne:	Nein, danke. Das ist alles.		*Susanne:*	No, thank you. That's everything.
Verkäuferin:	Das macht dann 11 Euro und 45 Cent ... Danke. Einen schönen Tag noch!		*shop assistant:*	Then it's 11 Euro and 45 Cent ... Thank you. Have a nice day!
Susanne:	Gleichfalls. Auf Wiedersehen!		*Susanne:*	The same to you. Goodbye!
Lisa:	Und wohin gehen wir jetzt?		*Lisa:*	And where are we going now?
Susanne:	Zum Markt. Wir brauchen noch Tomaten, Gurken und etwas Obst.		*Susanne:*	To the market. We still need tomatoes, cucumbers and some fruit.

Exercise 9 – CD 2, Track 68

1. Möchten Sie den Schinken am Stück oder geschnitten?
2. Was darf es sein?
3. Ist das alles?

Exercise 4 – CD 2, Track 75

Susanne:	Sylvia, hast du den Obstsalat schon probiert?
Sylvia:	Ja, ich hatte schon eine Portion, aber ich nehme gern noch etwas.
Susanne:	Aynur, was kann ich dir noch anbieten?
Aynur:	Oh, danke, ich bin satt. Es war wirklich alles sehr lecker.
Susanne:	Und du, Lisa? Noch etwas Nachtisch?
Lisa:	Nein.
Susanne:	Was ist los mit dir? Du bist heute aber schüchtern!

...

Sylvia:	Lisa, erzähl doch mal. Gehst du schon in die Schule?
Lisa:	Ja, in die erste Klasse.
Aynur:	Macht es dir Spaß?
Lisa:	Oh ja, besonders Malen und Sport.
Aynur:	Und wie ist deine Lehrerin? Ist sie streng?
Lisa:	Nein, sie ist nett. Ich mag sie.
Aynur:	Das ist prima. Ich bin früher nie gern in die Schule gegangen. Ich war auch eine schlechte Schülerin. Und du, Sylvia?
Sylvia:	Ich war ganz gut. Hattest du eigentlich als Kind einen Traumberuf?
Aynur:	Ja, Ärztin.
Sylvia:	Und du, Lisa? Was möchtest du später einmal werden?
Lisa:	Ich möchte Künstlerin werden.
Thomas:	Sagt mal, wollen wir nicht langsam gehen? Es ist schon spät.
Sylvia:	Ja, in Ordnung.

...

Lisa:	Hier, Papa, die Flaschen!
Thomas:	Nein, das sind Pfandflaschen. Die werfen wir nicht weg.
Susanne:	Thomas, hier ist noch mehr Abfall!
Thomas:	Ich hole ihn gleich. Lisa, bring doch die Flaschen zurück zu Mama.
Lisa:	Gut. Aber dann ...

Susanne:	Sylvia, have you already tried the fruit salad?
Sylvia:	Yes, I have already had a portion, but I'd like to have a bit more.
Susanne:	Aynur, what else can I offer you?
Aynur:	Oh, thanks, I'm really full. Everything was really delicious.
Susanne:	And you, Lisa? More dessert?
Lisa:	No.
Susanne:	What's the matter with you? You are a bit shy today!

...

Sylvia:	Lisa, tell me. Do you already go to school?
Lisa:	Yes, I'm in my first year.
Aynur:	Do you enjoy it?
Lisa:	Oh yes, especially painting and sports.
Aynur:	And what is your teacher like? Is she strict?
Lisa:	No, she's nice. I like her.
Aynur:	That's great. I never used to like going to school. And I was not very good either. And you, Sylvia?
Sylvia:	I was quite good. By the way, did you have a dream job when you were a child?
Aynur:	Yes, doctor.
Sylvia:	And you, Lisa? What would you like to become later?
Lisa:	I'd like to become an artist.
Thomas:	Tell me, isn't it just about time to go? It's already late.
Sylvia:	Yes, all right.

...

Lisa:	Here, daddy, the bottles!
Thomas:	No, these are refundable bottles. We don't throw them away.
Susanne:	Thomas, there's still some more waste here!
Thomas:	I'll get it in a minute. Lisa, take the bottles back to mummy.
Lisa:	Okay. But then ...

2

Exercise 13 – CD 2, Track 81

Frau Kramer: Als Kind war ich sehr schüchtern und ich war oft allein. Am liebsten habe ich mit meinem Hund gespielt. Ich bin aber sehr gern in die Schule gegangen. Ich war eine fleißige und sehr gute Schülerin. Meine Lehrer waren nicht streng und die Schule hat mir immer Spaß gemacht. Ich hatte auch einen Traumberuf: Ärztin.

Herr Kolb: Auch ich bin gern in die Schule gegangen und ich hatte viele Freunde in der Schule. Nach der Schule sind wir oft mit dem Fahrrad an den Rhein gefahren und haben dort Fußball gespielt. Ich war sehr sportlich und mein Traumberuf war Sportler. Naja, früher habe ich wirklich viel Sport gemacht und leider wenig gelernt. (lacht) Ich war wirklich faul und ein schlechter Schüler.

....

UNIT 16

Exercise 4 – CD 2, Track 86

Lisa:	Papa, Papa! Schau mal! Was ist das hier?
Thomas:	Wo denn?
Lisa:	Hier! Da schwimmt etwas im Fluss.
Thomas:	Was denn?
Lisa:	Es sieht aus wie ein Tier. Es ist so grün und braun wie mein Schwimmtier zu Hause.
Thomas:	Wie bitte?
...	
Sylvia:	Nicht möglich! Das ist wirklich ein Krokodil!
Aynur:	Ein echtes?
Sylvia:	Nein, es sieht echt aus, aber es ist aus Holz und Styropor.
Thomas:	Ja, aber wie kommt es hierher? Wem kann es gehören? Was meint ihr?
Sylvia:	Ich vermute, dass es dem Theater gehört.
Aynur:	Aber warum schwimmt das Krokodil im Rhein?
Sylvia:	Vielleicht, weil jemand einen Spaß machen wollte.

▼

Lisa:	Daddy, Daddy! Look! What is that over there?
Thomas:	Oh, where?
Lisa:	There! There is something floating in the river.
Thomas:	What is it?
Lisa:	It looks like an animal. It's as green and brown as my bath toy at home.
Thomas:	Pardon?
...	
Sylvia:	Not possible! That's a crocodile indeed!
Aynur:	A real one?
Sylvia:	No, it looks like real, but it is made of wood and polystyrene.
Thomas:	Yes, but how did it get here? To whom does it belong? What do you think?
Sylvia:	I suppose it belongs to the theatre.
Aynur:	But why is the crocodile floating in the Rhine?
Sylvia:	Maybe, because somebody wanted to play a joke.

▼

Thomas:	Das ist gut möglich. Ich denke aber, dass es jemand für den Karneval gemacht hat.	Thomas:	That's quite possible. But I think that somebody built it for the carnival.
Sylvia:	Für den Karneval? Das verstehe ich nicht. Karneval war im Februar. Warum ist das Krokodil jetzt im Juni hier?	Sylvia:	For the carnival? I don't understand that. Carnival was in February. Why is the crocodile here now, in June ?
Thomas:	Der Karneval ist bei uns so wichtig wie Ostern oder Weihnachten. Man bereitet ihn das ganze Jahr vor, auch im Juni.	Thomas:	The carnival is as important for us as Easter or Christmas. They prepare it all year long, also in June.
Aynur:	Ja, man plant sehr früh die Masken und Kostüme und man baut schon jetzt Figuren für den nächsten Umzug. Hast du den Umzug im Februar nicht gesehen?	Aynur:	Yes, they plan the masks and costumes very early and are now already building the figures for the next parade. Didn't you see the parade in February?
Sylvia:	Nein, ich musste nach Wien fahren. Und ich habe noch nie an einem Karneval in Düsseldorf teilgenommen.	Sylvia:	No, I had to go to Vienna. And I've never attended a carnival in Düsseldorf.
Susanne:	Entschuldigt die Unterbrechung, aber kann es sein, dass ihr genau dieses Krokodil für eure Zeitung sucht? Nehmt es doch mit und schreibt eure Geschichte zu Ende!	Susanne:	Sorry to interrupt you, but could it be that you are looking for exactly this crocodile for your newspaper? Take it with you and finish writing your story!
Thomas:	Eine ausgezeichnete Idee!	Thomas:	Excellent idea!

....

REVISION 4

Exercise 5 – CD 2, Track 95

1. Ich ziehe mich erst nach dem Frühstück an.
2. Freust du dich über das Geschenk?
3. Vielleicht ändert sich das Wetter.
4. Wir treffen uns um 3 Uhr mit unserem Chef.
5. Warum duzt ihr euch nicht?
6. Die Kinder verkleiden sich gern als Clowns.
7. Frau Müller, interessieren Sie sich für Kunst?
8. Moment, ich habe mich noch nicht angezogen!

Answer key + tips

TIP 1 / 13

Of course you can learn the verbs with all their endings by repeating only the forms. But there is another way to help you remember words: create a context for each form, such as **Wie heißt du?** or **Aynur ist Studentin.**

UNIT 1

2

1. Ich bin Thomas Kowalski. Ich bin Redakteur.

2. Ich bin Herr Braun. Ich bin Chefredakteur.

3. Ich heiße Aynur Hartmann. Ich bin Studentin.

4. Ich heiße Sylvia Moser. Ich bin Fotografin.

5. Ich bin Susanne Kowalski.

4

1. F; **2.** T; **3.** T; **4.** T; **5.** T; **6.** F; **7.** T; **8.** F

7

1. Ankara; **2.** Berlin; **3.** Budapest; **4.** Moskau; **5.** Paris; **6.** Wien

9

stress on the 1. syllable:
Radio, Technik, Disco
stress on the 2. syllable:
Musik, Computer, Hotel, Kassette
stress on the 3. syllable:
Telefon

10

1. er; **2.** ich; **3.** sie

12

1. ist; **2.** bin; **3.** sind

13 `TIP`

(du) studierst; (er, sie, es) studiert; (sie / Sie) studieren; (ich) heiße; (er, sie, es) heißt; (sie / Sie) heißen; (du) bist; (wir) sind; (sie / Sie) sind

15

6. A; **4.** B; **1.** C; **5.** D; **3.** E; **8.** F; **7.** G; **9.** H; **10.** I; **2.** J

16

1. Guten Tag, ich bin Frau Schmidt.

2. Guten Tag, ich heiße Aynur Hartmann.

3. Freut mich. Sie sind Fotografin, oder?

4. Nein. Sylvia Moser ist Fotografin.

5. Aha! Und Sie?

6. Ich bin Studentin. Ich mache hier ein Praktikum.

7. Und was studieren Sie?

8. Ich studiere Journalismus.

9. Interessant!

17

1. du; **2.** Sie; **3.** ich; **4.** er; **5.** ihr; **6.** sie; **7.** wir; **8.** es

UNIT 2

1

1. B; **2.** F; **3.** C; **4.** A; **5.** J; **6.** E; **7.** G; **8.** H; **9.** D; **10.** I

4

	Aynur	Sylvia	Thomas
1.	yes	no	no
2.	no	no	yes
3.	no	yes	no
4.	yes	yes	yes
5.	no	yes	no

5

1. Nachname; **2.** Sylvia; **3.** Beruf; **4.** Adresse; **5.** Telefonnummer

7

1. eins; **2.** neun; **3.** vier; **4.** fünf; **5.** acht; **6.** drei; **7.** zwei; **8.** sieben; **9.** null; **10.** sechs

9

1. Frau Müller ist aus Berlin.
2. Wo liegt die Wodanstraße?
3. Aynur fährt in die Türkei.
4. Sind Sie aus Österreich?
5. Fahren Sie nach Düsseldorf?

10

b

11

1. nach; 2. aus; 3. in

12

1. B; 2. C; 3. A; 4. A; 5. C

14 TIP

1. der; 2. die; 3. das; 4. die; 5. der;
6. die; 7. der; 8. die; 9. das; 10. das

······································

UNIT 3

1

1. Kaffee; 2. Kuchen; 3. Schokoladentorte; 4. Tee; 5. Bier; 6. Mineralwasser; 7. Cola; 8. Schinkentoast;
9. Orangensaft; 10. Wein

2

1. A; 2. D; 3. F; 4. C; 5. E; 6. B

4

zu Sylvia: einen Kaffee
zu Aynur: einen Apfelkuchen, einen Tee mit Zitrone
zu Thomas: ein Mineralwasser, einen Schinkentoast

7

1. zehn; 2. sechzehn; 3. zwölf

8

1. i; 2. a

9

1. nimmst; 2. möchte; 3. zahlt;
4. fährt; 5. isst; 6. hätte; 7. hast

10

1. möchte; 2. hätte; 3. nehme

12

1. C; 2. F; 3. A; 4. D; 5. G; 6. B; 7. E

14

1. einen; 2. den; 3. ein

15

1. ein; 2. einen; 3. einen; 4. die *(or)*
eine; 5. die; 6. eine; 7. das; 8. den;
9. der

······································

UNIT 4

2

1. groß; 2. möglich; 3. keine;
4. gefährlich

3

1. B; 2. D; 3. E; 4. A; 5. C

5 TIP

1. F; 2. T; 3. T; 4. F; 5. T; 6. F

8

1. B; 2. E; 3. A; 4. D; 5. F; 6. C

10

1. Zeitungen; 2. Fotos; 3. Kuchen;
4. Frauen; 5. Fische; 6. Schiffe;
7. Häuser; 8. Tiere

12

1. groß; 2. heiß; 3. lang; 4. schlecht;
5. alt

13

1. keine; 2. kein; 3. keine; 4. keinen

14 TIP

1. keinen; 2. nicht; 3. kein;
4. keinen; 5. nicht; 6. keine

16

1. vierundzwanzig;
2. hundert / einhundert;
3. dreiundsechzig; 4. siebzig;
5. achthundertfünfzig

3

ANSWER KEY + TIPS

Answer key + tips

TIP 5 / 8

Typical separable pre-fixes are: **ab-, an-, auf-, aus-, ein-, hin-, um-, zu-, zurück-**
In most dictionaries, separable verbs are marked like this: **ein|steigen**. So you know that you have to say **ich steige ein**. The prefix is always stressed: **ab**fahren – ich fahre **ab**.

TIP 5 / 10

Learn the irregular forms of the modals this way: start with the 1st and 3rd person singular and then plural. That's easy be-cause the forms are the same: ich will – er will (*I/he want(s)*) and wir wollen – sie wollen (*we/they want*). Then go to the 2nd person.

REVISION 1

1
1. H; **2.** I; **3.** A; **4.** F; **5.** D; **6.** J; **7.** E;
8. C; **9.** G; **10.** B

2
1. Spricht er Deutsch?
2. Möchtest du ein Bier? / Möchten Sie ein Bier?
3. Gibt es Kaffee und Kuchen?
4. Wie heißen Sie? / Wie heißt du?
5. Woher kommt er? / Woher kommt Mario?/Woher ist Mario?
6. Wo leben Rita und Max? / Wo leben sie? / Wer lebt in Frank-reich?

3
1. A; **2.** B; **3.** B; **4.** C; **5.** B; **6.** A

4
1. A; **2.** C; **3.** B

5
(1) **1.** st; **2.** t; **3.** en; **4.** en
(2) **5.** nimmt; **6.** fährst; **7.** fährt
(3) **8.** sind; **9.** hat

6
die; eine; kein; einen / keinen

7
1. die Computer; **2.** die Telefone;
3. die Gläser; **4.** die Tassen;
5. die Bedienungen; **6.** die Hotels

8
1. du; **2.** Sie; **3.** Wir

9
1. C; **2.** D; **3.** A; **4.** D; **5.** C; **6.** B; **7.** C;
8. D

11
(1) **1.** C; **2.** A; **3.** B
(2) **1.** A; **2.** C; **3.** B
(3) **1.** B; **2.** A; **3.** C
(4) **1.** B; **2.** C; **3.** A
(5) **1.** B; **2.** A; **3.** C

12
1. sehr; **2.** groß / super; **3.** Kirchen / Burgen / Städte / Häuser; **4.** wir;
5. trinken; **6.** sind

13
1. fünf Flaschen; **2.** drei Häuser;
3. zwei Kuchen; **4.** sieben Frauen

UNIT 5

1
1. Haltestelle; **2.** aussteigen;
3. Straßenbahn; **4.** Fahrkarten-auto-mat; **5.** entwerten; **6.** U-Bahn; **7.** ein-steigen; **8.** Gleis

2
1. Intercity; **2.** S-Bahn; **3.** Regional-Express; **4.** um; **5.** umsteigen;
6. direkt

4
1. F; **2.** F; **3.** T; **4.** F; **5.** T; **6.** T

5
1. C; **2.** G; **3.** D; **4.** F; **5.** B; **6.** A; **7.** E

6
1. wie viel; **2.** lange; **3.** Minuten;
4. um

7
1. 7; **2.** 3; **3.** 8; **4.** 2; **5.** 6; **6.** 1; **7.** 5

8 `TIP`
1. steigen; **2.** aus; **3.** kommst;
4. zurück; **5.** fährt; **6.** ab

9
1. C; **2.** A; **3.** J; **4.** H; **5.** G; **6.** E; **7.** B;
8. D; **9.** I; **10.** F

10 `TIP`
1. wollt; **2.** müssen; **3.** umsteigen;
4. kann; **5.** kaufen

11 `TIP`

1. Ich kann nicht kommen.
2. Peter will den Bus nehmen.
3. Sie können mit dem IC um 11 Uhr fahren.
4. Ich muss hier aussteigen.
5. Wohin willst du fahren?

12

1. Rückfahrkarte; **2.** Klasse;
3. zurück; **4.** einfache; **5.** Zuschlag;
6. Erwachsene

13

1. Zwei Fahrkarten hin und zurück nach Köln.
2. Wo kann ich Fahrkarten für die S-Bahn kaufen?
3. Ich möchte eine Einzelfahrkarte.
4. Muss ich die Fahrkarte entwerten?
5. Ich brauche einen Zuschlag für den ICE.
6. Eine einfache Fahrt zweiter Klasse nach Bonn.

14

a. question 5; **b.** question 4;
c. question 2

15

1. kann; **2.** ab; **3.** hin; **4.** fragen;
5. hält; **6.** Minuten

16

1. Der ICE nach München fährt auf Gleis 16 ab.
2. Um wie viel Uhr kommt Peter an?
3. Fährst du um 10 Uhr zurück?
4. Ich will nicht mit der Straßenbahn fahren. / Ich will mit der Straßenbahn nicht fahren.
5. Wo können wir Fahrkarten kaufen?
6. Muss ich in Köln umsteigen?

UNIT 6

2

1. a; **2.** b; **3.** c; **4.** d; **5.** e

5

1. a, c, d, g; **2.** b, e, f, h

6

1. Disco; **2.** Café; **3.** Zirkus

7

1. ins; **2.** in die; **3.** ins; **4.** in den;
5. in die; **6.** ins; **7.** ins

8

1. dich; **2.** es; **3.** uns

9

1. sie; **2.** mich; **3.** ihn; **4.** uns; **5.** es

11

1. Morgen; **2.** Mittag; **3.** Abend

12

1. Montag; **2.** Donnerstag;
3. Mittwoch; **4.** Wochenende;
5. Freitag; **6.** Samstag; **7.** Sonntag;
8. Dienstag

13

1. Montag; Dienstag; Mittwoch; Donnerstag; Freitag; Samstag; Sonntag
2. acht Uhr morgens; elf Uhr vormittags; sieben Uhr abends
3. Morgen; Vormittag; Mittag; Nachmittag; Abend; Nacht
4. zwei Uhr; fünf nach zwei; Viertel nach zwei; halb drei; drei Uhr
5. halb vier; Viertel vor vier; vier Uhr; Viertel nach vier; halb fünf

14

1. soll; **2.** darfst; **3.** mag

15

1 b; **2** c; **3** a; **4** b

TIP 5 / 11

In sentences with modal verb and infinitive put always the infinitive at the end.

The infinitive form of verbs with separable prefixes is written in one word.

3

ANSWER KEY + TIPS

Answer key + tips

TIP 7 / 7

There are little signs that indicate the dative case: the **m** and the **r** in the singular: You have **wem?** (to whom?) and the masculine and neuter articles are **dem** and **einem**. You'll also find a **m** in **ihm** (to him, to it). Or the letter **r** in the feminine articles **der** and **einer** and in some of the personal pronouns: **mir, dir, ihr.**

TIP 8 / 11

Try to learn and repeat words by combining nouns and verbs. One way is to start with the verb and to make chains like **ich schreibe einen Brief, eine Postkarte, eine Geschichte** etc. (In our example you would practise the accusative case at the same time). Another way is to start with the noun and to think about what you can do with it, e.g. **eine Geschichte lesen, vorlesen, erzählen, schreiben, hören** etc.

TIP 8 / 15

In a sentence the verb is always in the 2nd position.

The word order changes if there is an accusative pronoun. You have to place it in front of the dative.

UNIT 7

2
1. B; **2.** C, D, F, G; **3.** A, E, H

4
1. T; **2.** F; **3.** F; **4.** T; **5.** F; **6.** T

5
1. H; **2.** F; **3.** C; **4.** B; **5.** G; **6.** E; **7.** I;
8. A; **9.** D

7 TIP
1. einem; **2.** einer; **3.** einem; **4.** den;
5. dem

9
1. D; **2.** A; **3.** F; **4.** E; **5.** B; **6.** C

10
1. zweimal; **2.** immer; **3.** manchmal

11
1. yes; **2.** no; **3.** no

13
1. e; **2.** en; **3.** e; **4.** em; **5.** er; **6.** em

15
1. A; C; D; **2.** A; B; D; **3.** B; D; **4.** B; C

UNIT 8

1
1. Liebe; **2.** Glückwunsch; **3.** bei;
4. Papa; **5.** Küsschen; **6.** Überraschung

2
1. D; **2.** A; **3.** B; **4.** E; **5.** C

4
1. yes; **2.** no; **3.** yes; **4.** no; **5.** yes;
6. yes; **7.** no; **8.** yes; **9.** yes; **10.** no

7
1. Herzlichen Glückwunsch!;
2. Gute Besserung!; **3.** Viel Erfolg!

8
1. B; **2.** G; **3.** F; **4.** C; **5.** A; **6.** D; **7.** E

9
1. mit; **2.** bei; **3.** zum

10
1. von; **2.** mit einem; **3.** zur;
4. aus der; **5.** bei meiner

11 TIP
1. schreiben; **2.** gratulieren;
3. vorlesen; **4.** auspacken;
5. wünschen; **6.** erzählen

13
1. Lieber; **2.** dir; **3.** deinen;
4. kommen; **5.** mit; **6.** Herzliche;
7. deine

14
1. dir; **2.** eine Geschichte; **3.** es

15 TIP
1. Ich schreibe ihr einen Brief.
2. Sie wünscht ihnen viel Glück.
3. Anna schenkt sie dem Kind.
4. Wir erzählen es ihm.

16
1. Mama; **2.** Papi; **3.** Großmutter; **4.** Opa

REVISION 2

1
1. E; **2.** G; **3.** J; **4.** A; **5.** C; **6.** I; **7.** H;
8. F; **9.** D; **10.** B

2
Lieber Herr Holzmann,
ich wünsche Ihnen alles
Gute zum Geburtstag!
Viele herzliche Grüße
von Ihrer Kollegin Inge Munz
PS: Treffe ich Sie am Montag im
Büro?

3
1. a2; b3; c1
2. a3; b2; c1
3. a1; b3; c2

4
1. Ja, ich habe eine Schwester, aber keinen Bruder.
2. Meine Schwester lebt in Bayern, meine Eltern in Berlin.
3. Mit Freunden, Geschenken und einer Torte.
4. Meine Hobbys sind Computer und Musik.
5. Nein, aber manchmal jogge ich oder spiele Fußball.
6. Ich koche gern.
7. Ich treffe meine Freunde und wir kochen zusammen.
8. Ich gehe nicht gern in die Disco.

5
1. meine; **2.** unsere; **3.** ihrem; **4.** seine

6
1. können, **2.** will, **3.** e, **4.** arbeitet, **5.** ab (oder) zurück, **6.** vor

7
1. ihm; **2.** ihnen; **3.** ihn; **4.** sie; **5.** ihr

8
1. zum; **2.** von; **3.** bei

9
1. kann; **2.** willst; **3.** sollt; **4.** muss

11
1. Töchter; **2.** Schwester; **3.** Thomas; **4.** Tante; **5.** Enkelin; **6.** Schwiegermutter

12
1. Hochzeit, Oma, Herzlichen Glückwunsch!
2. Abfahrt, umsteigen, Hin- und Rückfahrkarte
3. fernsehen, Ausstellungen besuchen

13
1. D; **2.** A; **3.** A; **4.** D; **5.** C; **6.** B

14
1. A; **2.** B; **3.** B

15
1. A; **2.** C; **3.** C; **4.** B; **5.** A; **6.** B

....

UNIT 9

1
1. E; **2.** D; **3.** A; **4.** B; **5.** C

2
1. E, H; **2.** A, C, F, G; **3.** B, D

3
1. B; **2.** D; **3.** G; **4.** F; **5.** A; **6.** E; **7.** C

5
1. F; **2.** F; **3.** T; **4.** F; **5.** T; **6.** T; **7.** F; **8.** T

7
1. 25. 8.; **2.** 7. 9.

8
1. B; **2.** A; **3.** B; **4.** C

9
1. dieser; **2.** dieses; **3.** diesen; **4.** diese

11 `TIP`
1. gefragt; **2.** gekauft; **3.** gehört; **4.** gelernt

12 `TIP`
1. gemacht; **2.** haben; **3.** gehört; **4.** gelernt; **5.** habe; **6.** gelesen; **7.** gewesen; **8.** bin; **9.** gefahren; **10.** gespielt; **11.** ist; **12.** gekommen

TIP 9 / 11

How do you know that a verb is irregular and the past participle is formed by **ge-...-en**? Well, look at 2nd and 3rd person singular of the present tense. If there is a change of the stem vowel (**ich sehe, du siehst, er sieht**) the verb is irregular and the past participle ends in **-en** (**ich habe gesehen**). For many other verbs this tip doesn't work and it can be only recommended to learn new verbs together with the past participle, e.g. **schreiben: ich schreibe, ich habe geschrieben.**

TIP 9 / 12

Remember that a verb which indicates a motion always takes **sein** as an auxiliary verb.

3

ANSWER KEY + TIPS

Answer key + tips

TIP 11 / 6

A good way to learn words is to look for the opposite. You can do this for single words like mit ◆ ohne (*with* ◆ *without*), **nah** ◆ **weit** (*near* ◆ *far*), **schwarz** ◆ **weiß** (*black* ◆ *white*), but also for longer expressions like **in der Stadt** ◆ **auf dem Land** (*in town* ◆ *in the country*).

13
1. Ich habe gelesen.; **2.** Vorgestern.; **3.** Nein.

14
1. Mai – Juni – Juli – August – September
2. vor einem Monat – letztes Wochenende – vorgestern – gestern
3. geboren – verheiratet – geschieden
4. im letzten Jahr – letzten Monat – letzte Woche – in den letzten Tagen
5. am 5. März – am 11. 3. – am 9. 4. – am 15. April – am 3. 11.

15
1. NACHBAR; **2.** MÄRZ; **3.** SCHADE; **4.** VOGEL; **5.** GEWESEN; **6.** ZETTEL; **7.** GESCHIEDEN

16
1. kann; **2.** weiß; **3.** kenne; **4.** weißt; **5.** kann; **6.** kennen

UNIT 10

2
1. über; **2.** auf; **3.** vor; **4.** neben; **5.** zwischen; **6.** unter; **7.** in; **8.** hinter; **9.** an

3
1. D; **2.** G; **3.** A; **4.** F; **5.** B; **6.** E; **7.** C

5
Reihenfolge: c h f d a e g b

7
1. Buchhandlung; **2.** Kiosk; **3.** Post; **4.** Reisebüro; **5.** Metzgerei; **6.** Bäckerei

8
1. dem; **2.** die; **3.** der

9
1. b; e; f; g; k
2. a; c; d; h; i; j

11
1. Kreuzung; **2.** rechts; **3.** die erste links

12
1. Geben; **2.** komm; **3.** schaut

13
1. bring; **2.** kommt; **3.** geh; **4.** Gib; **5.** biegen (…) ab; **6.** lies (…) vor

15
1. zur Bank; **2.** zum Café

UNIT 11

1
1. B; **2.** E; **3.** A; **4.** C; **5.** D

2
1. D, F, H, J; **2.** B, C, G, K; **3.** A, E, I

4

	Aynur	Sylvia	Thomas
1.	yes	yes	yes
2.	no	yes	no
3.	yes	no	no
4.	no	no	yes
5.	yes	yes	yes

6 **TIP**
1. F; **2.** F; **3.** T

8
1. C; **2.** F; **3.** A; **4.** B; **5.** G; **6.** E; **7.** D

10
1. bestellen, **2.** studieren, **3.** auspacken, **4.** umsteigen, **5.** ausgehen, **6.** einladen, **7.** aufstehen

12

1. rot; **2.** gelb; **3.** weiß; **4.** braun;
5. blau; **6.** lila; **7.** grün

13

1. kleine; **2.** italienisches; **3.** helle;
4. bitterer

14

1. gefallen; **2.** schönes; **3.** große;
4. welches; **5.** mir; **6.** lustige

15

1. G; **2.** A; **3.** H; **4.** B; **5.** C; **6.** I; **7.** D;
8. E; **9.** F

....

UNIT 12

2

1. A, B, D, G, I
2. C, E, F, H, J

3

1. C; **2.** A; **3.** D; **4.** E; **5.** B

5

1. F; **2.** T; **3.** F; **4.** T; **5.** T; **6.** F; **7.** F; **8.** F

6

1. Kinderzimmer / das Kinderzimmer; **2.** Küche / die Küche;
3. Wohnzimmer / das Wohnzimmer;
4. Schlafzimmer / das Schlafzimmer

8

1. legt; **2.** sitzt; **3.** liegt

9

1. an der; **2.** über der; **3.** neben der;
4. auf dem; **5.** unter dem; **6.** im;
7. in der; **8.** hinter dem

10

1. Ich lege die Fotos in den Schrank.
Ich lege sie in den Schrank.
2. Ich hänge den Spiegel an die
Wand.

Ich hänge ihn an die Wand.
3. Ich stelle den Käfig auf die Kommode.
Ich stelle ihn auf die Kommode.

11

1. Wand; **2.** Mitte; **3.** hinten

14

1. OBEN; **2.** RAUM; **3.** MIETE;
4. VORNE; **5.** STREICHELN;
6. EIGENTUMSWOHNUNG;
7. LEHRER; **8.** NEBENKOSTEN

....

REVISION 3

1

1. f; **2.** h; **3.** i; **4.** d; **5.** g; **6.** a; **7.** j;
8. b; **9.** c; **10.** e

2

1. Mein Geburtstag ist am 16. April.
2. Ich bin 1967 geboren.
3. Nein, ich bin nicht verheiratet. / Ja, ich bin seit 1995 verheiratet.
4. Nein, ich habe keine Haustiere. / Ja, ich zwei Katzen und einen
Papagei.
5. Sie hat 2 Zimmer, eine Küche und
ein Bad.
6. Sie ist ruhig gelegen, nicht weit
vom Zentrum.
7. Mir gefallen Rot und Dunkelblau.
Rosa und Lila finde ich nicht schön.
8. Ich habe meine Freunde getroffen
und wir sind ins Kino gegangen.
9. Ich habe nicht gekocht, ich habe
nicht gearbeitet, ich bin nicht ausgegangen.

3

1. C; **2.** B; **3.** D; **4.** A

4

1. B; **2.** C; **3.** A

TIP 13 / 5

For checking your understanding ask yourself questions beginning with **w** *(W-questions), e.g.* **wer?** *(who is mentioned?),* **was?** *(what is happening?),* **wo?** *(where does it take place?),* **wann?** *(when does it take place?),* **warum?** *(why is it happening?).*

5

1. getanzt; **2.** gegangen; **3.** eingekauft; **4.** erzählt; **5.** studiert; **6.** sein; denken; bringen

6

1. Wir haben eine Ausstellung in Köln besucht.
2. Peter hat viel Bier getrunken.
3. Ich habe gestern sieben Briefe geschrieben.
    (oder) Gestern habe ich sieben Briefe geschrieben.
4. Er ist schon um 5 Uhr weggefahren.
5. Sie hat die Kinder in die Schule gebracht.

7

1. diese; **2.** Welche; **3.** rote; **4.** weiße; **5.** weißer; **6.** dieses; **7.** Welches; **8.** gelbe

8

1. Leg / leg, **2.** Geh / geh, **3.** Bringen Sie / bringen Sie, **4.** Warte / warte / Wart / wart, **5.** Entschuldige / entschuldige, **6.** Gebt / gebt, **7.** Seien Sie / seien Sie

9

1. durch; entlang; ohne
2. gegenüber; nach; seit; zu
3. an; auf; hinter; über; vor

10

1. an; **2.** auf; **3.** unter

11

1. C; **2.** A; **3.** D; **4.** B; **5.** A; **6.** C; **7.** B; **8.** D

12

1. das Frühstück – das Mittagessen – das Abendessen
2. zu Hause frühstücken – im Büro arbeiten – nach Hause kommen – ins Bett gehen
3. im letzten Jahr – vor einer Woche – gestern – heute – morgen
4. Januar – Februar – März – April – Mai – Juni – Juli
5. am 11. 6. – am 3. September – am 6. 11. – am Tag vor Weihnachten

13

1. A; **2.** C; **3.** B

14

1. B; **2.** A; **3.** D

15

1. links; **2.** laut; **3.** weit; **4.** oben

16

1. B, C; **2.** A, C; **3.** A, B, D; **4.** C, D; **5.** A, B, D; **6.** B, C, D

....

UNIT 13

1

1. A; H; **2.** B; E; **3.** C; G; **4.** D; F

2

1. D; **2.** A; **3.** E; **4.** F; **5.** B; **6.** C

3

1. E; **2.** C; **3.** A; **4.** B; **5.** D

5 `TIP`

1. B; **2.** B; **3.** A; **4.** C; **5.** C; **6.** A

8

1. Wir machen ein Picknick, wenn die Sonne scheint.
2. Ich gehe aus, wenn ich gegessen habe.
3. Er kommt um 12 Uhr an, wenn der Zug pünktlich ist.

9 TIP

1. Er freut sich, wenn er Geschenke bekommt.
2. Ich komme gern, wenn ich Zeit habe. / Ich komme gerne, wenn ich Zeit habe.
3. Bring ihm das Buch mit, wenn du ihn morgen siehst.
4. Wir gehen spazieren, wenn das Wetter schön bleibt.
5. Sie geht in die Disco, wenn sie ihre Freunde treffen will.

10
1. passt; **2.** geht; **3.** kann

12
1. dich; **2.** uns; **3.** sich

13:
1. freue; **2.** mich; **3.** bedanken; **4.** sich; **5.** treffen; **6.** uns; **7.** ändert; **8.** sich; **9.** Freust; **10.** dich

14
1. b; **2.** c; **3.** b; **4.** a

15
1. Ich habe mich über deinen Besuch gefreut.
2. Was machen wir am Wochenende, wenn es regnet?
3. Ich gebe dir das Buch, wenn ich es gelesen habe.
4. Er hat sich nie für Kunst interessiert.
   (oder) Er hat sich für Kunst nie interessiert.
5. Schneit es bei euch im Norden?
6. Sie hat endlich seine Freunde kennen gelernt.
   (oder) Sie hat seine Freunde endlich kennen gelernt.
7. Es passt mir gut, wenn wir uns am Freitag treffen.

UNIT 14

2
1. C; **2.** E; **3.** A; **4.** D; **5.** B

3
1. vier Brötchen, das Brot
2. frisches Obst, der Salat, das Gemüse
3. die Salami, drei Scheiben Schinken, die Bratwurst

5
1. B, C; **2.** B, C, D; **3.** A, C

7
1. Kilo (oder) Kilogramm; **2.** Stück; **3.** Liter

8
1. Liter; **2.** Kilo (oder) Kilogramm; **3.** Gramm; **4.** Nudeln; **5.** Tüte (oder) Packung; **6.** Bäcker; **7.** Stück; **8.** –

9
1. Am Stück.; **2.** 4 Bratwürste.; **3.** Ja.

11
1. am hellsten; **2.** jünger; **3.** kälter

12
1. billiger als; **2.** wärmer als; **3.** lieber als

13
1. TEUER; **2.** GLEICHFALLS; **3.** EINKAUFSKORB; **4.** GESUND; **5.** SCHNEIDEN

14
1. C; **2.** A; **3.** B

UNIT 15

2
1. A; **2.** B; **3.** C; **4.** D; **5.** E

3
1. C; **2.** F; **3.** E; **4.** D; **5.** A; **6.** B

TIP 13 / 9

In subordinate clauses, the conjugated verb is placed at the end.

3

ANSWER KEY + TIPS

TIP 16 / 11

What do you do if you want to say something but you don't know the exact word? A very simple solution is to use the word das **Ding** (*thing*). For example: **Wie heißt dieses Ding?** (*What's the name of this thing?*) or **Gib mir mal das Ding!** (*Give me that thing!*). To clarify what you mean you can point at the item with your finger.

5
1. yes; **2.** no; **3.** no; **4.** yes; **5.** no; **6.** yes; **7.** yes; **8.** no; **9.** yes; **10.** no

8
1. unfreundliche; **2.** unhöflich; **3.** unsympathisch

9
1. unfreundlich; **2.** satt; **3.** faul; **4.** höflich; **5.** schüchtern; **6.** schlank; **7.** unsympathisch

11
1. hatte; **2.** waren; **3.** hatte

12
1. war; **2.** hatten; **3.** warst; **4.** wart; **5.** hatte; **6.** waren

13

	Frau Kramer	Herr Kolb
1.	yes	no
2.	yes	yes
3.	yes	no
4.	yes	yes
5.	no	yes
6.	no	yes

14
1. Pfand; **2.** weg; **3.** sortieren

....

UNIT 16

1
1. d; **2.** b; **3.** e; **4.** a; **5.** c

2
1. kann; **2.** Clown; **3.** sieht nicht aus; **4.** vermute; **5.** so (...) wie

3
1. b; **2.** e; **3.** f; **4.** a; **5.** g; **6.** d; **7.** c

5
1. yes; **2.** no; **3.** no; **4.** yes; **5.** yes; **6.** yes; **7.** no

6
1. ausziehen; **2.** an

8
1. A, B, D, F, G; **2.** C, E, H, I, J

9
(ich) wollte, (du) wolltest, (er, sie, es) wollte, (wir) wollten, (ihr) wolltet, (sie) wollten, (Sie) wollten

11 **TIP**
1. B, C; **2.** A, B, C, D; **3.** A, C,D

12
1. Es kann sein, dass sie sich als Clown verkleidet hat.
2. Wir vermuten, dass er schon nach Hause gegangen ist.

13
1. Du siehst wie mein Freund aus.
2. Das Tier sieht aus wie eine kleine Schlange.

14
1. C; **2.** D; **3.** D; **4.** A

15
1. D; **2.** A; **3.** C; **4.** H; **5.** F; **6.** G; **7.** B; **8.** E

....

REVISION 4

1
1. F; **2.** J; **3.** B; **4.** G; **5.** A; **6.** I; **7.** H; **8.** D; **9.** C; **10.** E

2

1. Als Kind wollte ich Ärztin oder Zahnärztin werden.
2. Ich arbeite als Krankenschwester.
3. Ich war fleißig und eine gute Schülerin. Die Schule hat mir immer Spaß gemacht.
4. Ich lerne Deutsch, weil mir die Sprache gefällt und weil ich im nächsten Jahr nach Berlin fahren will.
5. Ich denke, dass frisches Obst und Gemüse gesund ist.
6. Heute ist es sonnig und warm. Die Temperatur liegt bei 24 Grad.
7. Der Karneval ist sehr wichtig bei uns. Man macht einen Umzug mit Festwagen, die Leute tragen Verkleidungen oder Masken.
8. Man bringt Pralinen, ein Buch oder Blumen mit.

3

1. A, **2.** C, **3.** B, **4.** C, **5.** B, **6.** A

4

1. hoch; **2.** wie; **3.** am; **4.** größten; **5.** lieber; **6.** als

5

1. ziehe; **2.** dich; **3.** sich; **4.** treffen (...) uns; **5.** euch; **6.** verkleiden (...) sich; **7.** interessieren (...) sich; **8.** habe

6

1. für; **2.** auf; **3.** zum; **4.** auf; **5.** über; **6.** am; **7.** vom; **8.** für

7

1. waren; **2.** Mussten; **3.** wollte; **4.** konnte; **5.** hatten; **6.** war

8

1. G; **2.** H; **3.** B; **4.** C; **5.** E; **6.** K; **7.** N; **8.** M

10

1. Ich freue mich, wenn du mitkommst.
2. Er schreibt ihr, dass er ein Auto gekauft hat.
3. Er kommt zu spät, weil er sich noch umziehen muss.
4. Es ist schade, dass er nicht teilnimmt.
5. Wir essen nur frisches Obst, weil das gesünder ist.
6. Sie hört Musik, wenn sie zu Hause arbeitet.

11

1. C; **2.** A; **3.** B; **4.** C; **5.** A; **6.** D; **7.** B; **8.** A

12

1. A, E; **2.** D, F, G; **3.** B, C, H

13

1. B; **2.** A; **3.** A; **4.** B; **5.** C; **6.** B; **7.** B; **8.** A

14

1. Maler (oder) Künstler; **2.** Lehrerin; **3.** Bäcker

15

1. C; **2.** B; **3.** A

16

1. A; **2.** D; **3.** C

Glossary

das	4erTicket	four journey ticket

....

A

	abbiegen	to turn off, to turn
der	Abend	evening
das	Abendessen	dinner
	abends	in the evening
	aber	but, really
	abfahren	to leave, depart
die	Abfahrt	departure
der	Abfall	waste, rubbish, garbage
der	Abfalleimer	rubbish bin, garbage can
	abholen	to pick up
	ach	oh
	acht	eight
	achte / r /s	eighth
	achtzehn	eighteen
	achtzehnte / r /s	eighteenth
	achtzig	eighty
	achtzigste / r /s	eightieth
	Adieu	bye
die	Adresse	address
	aha	I see
die	Ahnung	idea
	alkoholfrei	non-alcoholic
	alkoholisch	alcoholic
	alle	all, each
	allein	alone
	alles	all, everything
	alles Gute	all the best
	alles Liebe	lots of love!
	als	than, as
	also	well
	alt	old
das	Alt	type of beer
die	Altstadt	old town centre
	am	see preposition an
	am besten	best
	am Ende	at the end
	am meisten	most
die	Ampel	traffic light
	an	at, in, on, to
	anbieten	to offer

sich	ändern	to change (oneself)
	ändern	to change (s.th.)
das	Angebot	offer
	Ankara	Ankara
	ankommen	to arrive
der	Anruf	phone call
	anrufen	to call, phone
der	Anrufer	caller
	anziehen	to put on
sich	anziehen	to get dressed
der	Apfel	apple
der	Apfelkuchen	apple pie
die	Apfelsine	orange
die	Apotheke	pharmacy
der	Apparat	machine, phone
der	April	April
	apropos	by the way
die	Arbeit	job, work
	arbeiten	to work
das	Arbeitszimmer	study
der	Arzt	doctor
der	Aschermitt-woch	Ash Wednesday
	attraktiv	attractive
	auch	also, ...,too
	auf	in, on, at, to
	Auf Wieder-hören	goodbye
	Auf Wieder-luege	goodbye
	Auf Wieder-sehen	goodbye
	aufstehen	to get up
der	August	August
	aus	from, made of
	ausgehen	to go out
	ausgezeichnet	excellent
die	Auskunft	information
	auspacken	to unwrap
	aussehen	to look (like)
	außerhalb	outside
	aussteigen	to get off
die	Ausstellung	exhibition
	Australien	Australia

4

GLOSSARY

	ausziehen	to take off
sich	ausziehen	to undress
das	Auto	car
der	Auto-mechaniker	car mechanic

B

	Ba-ba	bye
der	Bäcker	baker
die	Bäckerei	baker's
das	Bad	bathroom
	Baden	region in South Germany
	baden	to have a bath
das	Badezimmer	bathroom
der	Bahnbeamte	railway official
der	Bahnhof	railway station
der	Bahnsteig	platform
	bald	soon
der	Balkon	balcony
die	Banane	banana
die	Bank	bank
	bauen	to build
sich	bedanken	to thank
sich	bedienen	to help oneself
die	Bedienung	waiter / waitress
	befragen	to question
	bei	at, with
	bekommen	to receive
	Benrath	district of Düsseldorf
	berichten	to report
	Berlin	Berlin
der	Beruf	profession
	beruflich	professional
	besitzen	to own
das	Besondere	unique, particular
	besonders	especially
	besorgen	to provide
	besser	better
die	Besserung	improvement
die	Bestellung	order
der	Besuch	visit
	besuchen	to visit
das	Bett	bed
	bewölkt	cloudy

das	Bier	beer
der	Biergarten	beer garden
das	Bild	picture
das	Bilderbuch	picture book
	Bilk	district of Düsseldorf
	billig	cheap
die	Biologie	biology
die	Birne	pear
	bis	till, see you ..., to
	bitte	please, pardon
	bitter	bitter
	blau	blue
	bleiben	to remain, to stay
die	Blume	flower
der	Blumenkohl	cauliflower
der	Blumenladen	florist's
die	Bohne	bean
die	Bratwurst	frying sausage
	brauchen	to need
	braun	brown
der	Brief	letter
	bringen	to take, to bring
das	Brot	bread
das	Brötchen	roll, sandwich
die	Brotzeit	snack time
die	Brücke	bridge
der	Bruder	brother
das	Buch	book
die	Buchhandlung	book shop
	buchstabieren	to spell out
	Budapest	Budapest
der	Bundesfeiertag	national day in Switzerland
	bunt	colourful
die	Burg	castle
das	Büro	office
der	Bus	bus
die	Bushaltestelle	bus stop

C

das	Café	café
der	Cappuccino	cappuccino
die	CD (Compact Disc)	CD
der	Cent	cent

Glossary

	Charlottenburg	district in Berlin
der	Chefredakteur	editor-in-chief
der	Chip	crisp, potato chip
	Christi Himmelfahrt	Ascension Day
der	Clown	clown
die	Cola	coke
der	Computer	computer
der	Computerladen	computer shop
der	Container	container
die	Couch	sofa
der	Cousin	cousin

D

	da	there
	dabei sein	to participate, to take part
die	Dame	lady
der	Dank	gratitude
	danke	thank you
	dann	then
	das	this, it, these, the
	dass	that
	dauern	to take
die	Decke	ceiling
	dein / e	your
das	Deka(gramm)	10 gram(me)s
	dem	the, to which
	den	the, this
	denen	to which
	denken	to think
	denn (conjunction)	because
	denn (intensifying term)	normally not translated
	der	the, this
	deutsch	German
das	Deutsch	German
der	Deutsche	German
	Deutschland	Germany
der	Dezember	December
	dich	you
	dick	thick, fat
	die	the

der	Dienstag	Tuesday
	dienstags	on Tuesdays
	diese / r / s	this, that
das	Ding	thing
	dir	you
	direkt	right by, direct
die	Disco	disco
	doch	normally not translated, yes
der	Donnerstag	Thursday
das	Dorf	village
	dort	there
die	Dose	tin, can
	drei	three
	dreißig	thirty
	dreißigste / r / s	thirtieth
	dreizehn	thirteen
	dreizehnte / r / s	thirteenth
	dritte / r / s	third
die	Drogerie	drugstore
	du	you
	dunkel	dark
	dünn	thin
	durch	through
	dürfen	to be allowed to, may, in a question about a wish
	duschen	to take a shower
	Düsseldorf	Düsseldorf
	(sich) duzen	to use the informal form

E

	eben	just, simply
	echt	real
die	Ecke	corner
das	Ei	egg
	eigentlich	by the way
die	Eigentumswohnung	owner-occupied flat
	ein paar	a few
	ein wenig	a little
	ein / e	a
	einfach	single
das	Einfamilienhaus	detached house
die	Einheit	reunification

	einkaufen	to do the shopping
	einkaufen gehen	to go shopping
der	Einkaufskorb	shopping basket
die	Einkaufstasche	shopping bag
	einladen	to invite
die	Einladung	invitation
	einmal	once, one day
	eins	one
	einsteigen	to get on
	einverstanden	agreed
die	Einzelfahrkarte	single journey ticket
der	Eiskaffee	iced coffee
	elf	eleven
	elfte / r / s	eleventh
die	Eltern	parents
das	Ende	end
	endlich	finally, at last
	England	Great Britain
der	Engländer	English
	englisch	English
der	Enkel	grandson
das	Enkelkind	grandchild
	entlang	along
	entschuldigen	to excuse
	Entschuldigung	Excuse me.
	entwerten	to cancel (the ticket)
	er	he
der	Erdapfel	potato
das	Erdgeschoss	ground floor
der	Erfolg	success
	erste / r / s	first, not until
der	Erwachsene	adult
	erzählen	to tell
	es	it
	es gibt	there's, there are
der	Espresso	espresso
das	Essen	meal
	essen	to eat
das	Esszimmer	dining-room
	etwa	about
	etwas	something, some
	euch	you
	euer /eure	your

der	Euro	euro
der	Eurocity	eurocity train
	exotisch	exotic

F

	fahren	go
der	Fahrer	driver
die	Fahrkarte	ticket
der	Fahrkarten-automat	ticket machine
der	Fahrkarten-schalter	ticket office
der	Fahrplan	time table
das	Fahrrad	bycicle
	Fahrrad fahren	to ride a bike
die	Fahrt	journey
die	Familie	family
der	Familien-besuch	family visit
das	Familienfest	family party
	fantastisch	fantastic
die	Farbe	colour
der	Fasching	carnival
die	Fasnacht	carnival
	faul	lazy
der	Februar	February
	fehlen	to be missing
	feiern	to celebrate
der	Feiertag	bank holiday
das	Fenster	window
der	Fensterrahmen	window frame
	fernsehen	to watch TV
der	Festwagen	carnival float
die	Figur	figure
	finden	to find
der	Fisch	fish
	Fl.	abbreviation of *Flasche*
die	Flasche	bottle
das	Fleisch	meat
	fleißig	diligent
	Flingern	district in Düsseldorf
der	Flughafen	airport
das	Flugzeug	airplane

4

GLOSSARY

Glossary

der	Flur	corridor
der	Fluss	river
das	Foto	picture
der	Fotograf	photographer
	fotografieren	to take a picture
die	Frage	question
	fragen	to ask
der	Franken	Franc
	Frankfurt	Frankfurt
	Frankreich	France
der	Franzose	French
	französisch	French
die	Frau	Mrs, wife
das	Fräulein	Miss
der	Freitag	Friday
die	Freizeit	leisure time
	freuen	to be glad
sich	freuen (auf)	to look forward (to)
sich	freuen (über)	to be pleased about
der	Freund	friend, boyfriend
	freundlich	friendly, kind
	frisch	fresh
der	Friseur	hairdresser
der	Frisör	hairdresser
	früh	early
	früher	in the past, used to do, earlier
der	Frühling	spring
das	Frühstück	breakfast
	frühstücken	to have breakfast
	fünf	five
	fünfte / r / s	fifth
	fünfzehn	fifteen
	fünfzehnte / r / s	fifteenth
	fünfzig	fifty
	fünfzigste(r, s)	fiftieth
	für	for
	furchtbar	terrible
der	Fuß	foot
der	Fußball	soccer
der	Fußboden	floor
die	Fußgänger-zone	pedestrian precinct

G

	g	Abbreviation of Gramm
	ganz	quite, very, whole
die	Garderobe	hall-stand
der	Garten	garden
der	Gast	guest
der	Gastgeber	host
das	Gebäck	pastries
	geben	to give
	geboren	born
der	Geburtstag	birthday
das	Geburtstags-kind	birthday girl / boy
	gefährlich	dangerous
	gefallen	to like
	gegen	against, about
	gegenüber	opposite, over there
	gehen	to be, to go, to work
	gehören	to belong to
	gelb	yellow
die	Gelberübe	carrot
das	Geld	money
	gelegen sein	to be situated
das	Gemüse	vegetable
	genau	exact
	genauso ... wie	as ... as
das	Gepäck	luggage
	geradeaus	straight ahead
	gern /e	with pleasure
etw	gern /e haben	to like
etw	gern /e machen	to like doing sth.
die	Geschäftsfrau	businesswoman
die	Geschäftsleute	businesspeople
der	Geschäfts-mann	businessman
	geschehen	to happen
das	Geschenk	gift
die	Geschichte	story
	geschieden	divorced
die	Geschwister	brothers and sisters
das	Gespräch	conversation
	gestern	yesterday
	gesund	healthy

4

GLOSSARY

das	Getränk	drink, beverage
	getrennt	separate
	giftig	poisonous
das	Glas	glass
	glauben	to believe
	gleich	at once
	gleichfalls	the same to you
das	Gleis	rails
das	Glück	luck
der	Glückwunsch	congratulations
das	Gold	gold
der	Goldfisch	gold fish
das / der	Grad	degree
das	Gramm	gram(me)
	gratulieren	to congratulate
der	Grieche	Greek
	Griechenland	Greece
	groß	tall, big, great, adult
	Großbritannien	Great Britain
die	Großeltern	grandparents
die	Großmutter	grandmother
der	Großvater	grandfather
	Grüezi	hello
	grün	green
der	grüne Punkt	a green dot on the packaging
der	Gruß	greeting
	Grüß Gott!	good morning, hello, good afternoon
die	Gurke	cucumber
	gut	good
	Gute Nacht!	good night
	Guten Morgen!	good morning
	Guten Tag!	good morning, hello, good afternoon
das	Guten-Abend-Ticket	Good Night Ticket
die	Gymnastik	gymnastics

....

H

	haben	to have
	halb	half
	hallo	hello

	halten	to stop, to think of
die	Haltestelle	stop
	Hamburg	Hamburg
der	Hamster	hamster
die	Handynummer	mobile number
	hängen	to hang sth up
	hart	hard
der	Hase	rabbit
der	Hasi	darling
	hässlich	ugly
der	Hauptbahnhof	central station
das	Haus	house
die	Hausnummer	house number
das	Haustier	pet
	heiraten	to marry
	heiß	hot
	heißen	to be called, to be
die	Heizung	heating
	helfen	to help
	hell	light
	hellblau	light blue
das	Helle	type of beer
der	Herbst	autumn
	herein	come in
	hereinkommen	to come in
der	Herr	Mister
	herrlich	wonderful
	herzlich	hearty, warm
	heute	today
	hier	here
	hierher	over there
der	Himmel	sky
die	Hin- und Rückfahrkarte	return ticket
	hin und zurück	there and back again
	hinfahren	to go there
	hingehen	to go there (on foot)
	hinten	behind, in the back
	hinter	behind
das	Hobby	hobby
	hoch	high
die	Hochzeit	wedding
	hoffentlich	hopefully, I hope (so)

4

GLOSSARY

Glossary

	höflich	*polite*
	holen	*to get, to fetch*
das	Holz	*wood*
	hören	*to hear, to listen*
das	Hotel	*hotel*
	hübsch	*pretty*
der	Hund	*dog*
	hundert	*hundred*
	hundertste / r / s	*hundredth*
der	Hunger	*hunger*
	hungrig	*hungry*

....

I

der	IC	train connecting cities nationwide
der	ICE	very fast and high-tech train
	ich	*I*
die	Idee	*idea*
	ihm	*him*
	ihn	*him*
	ihnen	*them*
	Ihnen	*you*
	ihr	*you, her, their, her*
	Ihr	*your*
	im	see preposition *in*
	immer	*always*
	in	in, to, into
die	Information	*information*
der	Informations- schalter	*information office*
	ins	see preposition *in*
der	Intercity	train connecting cities nationwide
der	Intercity- express	very fast and high-tech train
	interessant	*interesting*
sich	interessieren	*to be interested*
	interessiert	*interested*
das	Internet	*Internet*
	inzwischen	*in the meantime*
	Italien	*Italy*

der	Italiener	*Italian*
	italienisch	*Italian*

....

J

	ja	*yes*
die	Jacke	*jacket*
das	Jahr	*year*
der	Jänner	*January*
der	Januar	*January*
die	Jause	*snack*
	jemand	*somebody*
	jetzt	*now*
	joggen	*to jog*
der	Journalismus	*journalism*
der	Juli	*July*
	jung	*young*
der	Juni	*June*

....

K

der	Kaffee	*coffee*
das	Kaffeehaus	*café*
der	Käfig	*cage*
	kalt	*cold*
die	Kaltmiete	*rent without extra costs*
der	Karfiol	*cauliflower*
der	Karlsmarkt	a market in Düsseldorf
der	Karneval	*carnival*
der	Karnevals- verein	*carnival society*
die	Karotte	*carrot*
die	Karte	*card*
das	Kartenspiel	*card game*
die	Kartoffel	*potato*
der	Käse	*cheese*
der	Käsekuchen	*cheese cake*
die	Kassette	*cassette*
die	Katze	*cat*
	kaufen	*to buy*
	kein / e	*no, any*
	Keine Ursache!	*Don't mention it!*
der	Keller	*cellar*
	kennen	*to know*
	kennen lernen	*to get to know, to meet*

4

GLOSSARY

	kg	abbreviation of *Kilogramm*
das	Kilo(gramm)	*kilogram(me)*
der	Kilometer	*kilometre*
das	Kind	*child*
der	Kindergarten	*kindergarten*
das	Kinderzimmer	*child's room, children's room*
das	Kino	*cinema, movie*
der	Kiosk	*kiosk*
die	Kirche	*church*
	klar	*clear, yes*
die	Klasse	*class*
	klein	*small, little*
	Koblenz	*Koblenz*
	kochen	*to cook*
der	Kollege	*colleague*
	Köln	*Cologne*
	kommen	*to come*
die	Kommode	*chest of drawers*
das	Kompliment	*compliment*
	können	*can, to know*
das	Konzert	*concert*
der	Kopfsalat	*lettuce*
	kosten	*to cost*
das	Kostüm	*costume, suit (for women)*
der	Krankenpfleger	*male nurse*
die	Kranken-schwester	*nurse*
	Kreuzberg	*district in Berlin*
die	Kreuzung	*crossroad*
das	Krokodil	*crocodile*
die	Küche	*kitchen*
der	Kuchen	*cake*
die	Kultur	*culture*
die	Kunst	*art*
der	Künstler	*artist*
der	Kunststoff	*plastic*
	Kurfürsten-damm	*street in Berlin*
	kurz	*short*
der	Kuss	*kiss*
das	Küsschen	*little kiss*

L

	l	abbreviation of *Liter*
	lachen	*to laugh*
die	Lampe	*lamp, light*
das	Land	*country*
der	Landwirt	*farmer*
	lang	*long*
	langsam	*slowly, just about time*
	langweilig	*boring*
	laut	*loud, noisy*
	leben	*to live*
das	Lebensmittel	*food*
	lecker	*delicious*
das	Leder	*leather*
	legen	*to put*
der	Lehrer	*teacher*
	leidtun	*to be sorry*
	leider	*unfortunately*
	lernen	*to learn*
	lesen	*to read*
	letzte / r / s	*last*
die	Leute	*people*
die	Liebe	*love*
	liebe / r / s	*dear*
	lieber nehmen	*to prefer*
der	Liebling	*darling*
das	Lied	*song*
	liegen	*to be situated, to lay, to be laying*
	lila	*purple*
	links	*left*
der	Liter	*liter*
das	Lokal	*pub*
die	Lokalredaktion	*local editorial department*
	los sein	*to happen*
	losgehen	*to set off*
	Ltr.	abbreviation of *Liter*
die	Lust	*joy, pleasure*
	lustig	*funny*

4

Glossary

M

	machen	to do, to make, to be
	macht nichts	it doesn't matter
der	Mai	may
der	Maifeiertag	1. may day
	Mainz	Mainz
das	Mal	time
	mal	often not translated
	malen	to paint
das	Malen	painting (school subject)
der	Maler	painter
die	Mama	mum, mom
die	Mami	mum, mom
	man	they, one, you
	manchmal	sometimes
der	Mann	man
der	Markt	market
der	März	March
die	Maß	1 liter mug
das	Material	material
die	Mauer	wall
die	Maus	mouse
das	Mäuschen	darling (literally: little mouse)
das	Meerschwein-chen	guineapig
	mehr	more
die	Mehrfahrten-karte	multiple journey ticket
	mein / e	my
	meinen	to think, to mean
das	Metall	metal
der	Meter	meter
die	Metzgerei	butcher's
	mich	me
die	Miete	rent
die	Mietwohnung	rented flat
die	Milch	milk
der	Milchkaffee	white coffee
das	Mineralwasser	mineral water
	minus	here: below zero
die	Minute	minute
	mir	me
	mit	with

	mitbringen	to bring along
	mitkommen	to come along
	mitnehmen	to take along
der	Mittag	noon
	mittagessen	to have lunch
das	Mittagessen	lunch
	mittags	midday
die	Mitte	middle
der	Mittwoch	Wednesday
das	Möbel	furniture
das	Möbelstück	piece of furniture
	möbliert	furnished
	mögen	to like
	möglich	possible
die	Möhre	carrot
	mollig	plump
der	Moment	moment
der	Monat	month
der	Montag	Monday
	montags	on Mondays
der	Morgen	morning
	morgen	tomorrow
	morgens	in the morning
	Moskau	Moskow
der	Müll	waste
die	Mülltonne	trashcan
das	Museum	museum
die	Museumsinsel	district of Berlin with many historical museums and architectural highlights
die	Musik	music
	müssen	must
die	Mutter	mother
die	Mutti	mom, mum

N

	nach	to, past, after
der	Nachbar	neighbour
der	Nachmittag	afternoon
der	Nachname	surname
	nächste / r / s	next
die	Nacht	night
der	Nachtisch	dessert
die	Nähe	near

	naja	well
der	Name	name
der	Namenstag	name day
der	Nationalfeier-tag	national bank holiday
	natürlich	of course
der	Nebel	fog
	neben	near, beside, next to
die	Nebenkosten	extra costs
	neblig	foggy
der	Neffe	nephew
	nehmen	to take
	nein	no
	nett	nice
	neu	new
das	Neujahr	New Year's Day
	neun	nine
	neunte / r / s	ninth
	neunzehn	nineteen
	neunzehnte / r / s	nineteenth
	neunzig	ninety
	neunzigste / r / s	ninetieth
	nicht	not
die	Nichte	niece
	nichts	nothing
	nie	never
	noch	still
	noch einmal	once more, again
	noch nicht	not ... yet
der	Norden	north
	Nordrhein-Westfalen	North-Rhine-Westphalia
	nötig	necessary
der	November	November
die	Nudel	noodle
	null	zero
die	Nummer	number
	nun	now
	nur	just, only

....

O

	oben	up, at the top, upstairs
	Oberkassel	district of Düsseldorf
das	Obst	fruit
der	Obstkuchen	fruit cake
der	Obstsalat	fruit salad
	oder	question tag, or
	oft	often
	ohne	without
der	Oktober	October
die	Oma	grandma
die	Omi	grandma
der	Onkel	uncle
der	Opa	grandpa
der	Opi	grandpa
die	Orange	orange
	orange	orange
der	Orangensaft	orange juice
die	Ordnung	order
der	Osten	east
der	Osterhase	easter bunny
	Ostern	Easter
	Österreich	Austria
der	Österreicher	Austrian
	österreichisch	Austrian

....

P

	paar	a few
die	Packung	packet
der	Papa	dad
der	Papagei	parrot
der	Papi	dad
das	Papier	paper
der	Paradeiser	tomato
	Paris	Paris
der	Park	park
die	Party	party
	passen	to suit
	Pckg.	abbreviation of Packung
der	Perron	platform
das	Perron	platform
die	Person	person
die	Pfalz	Palatinate
das	Pfand	deposit

4

GLOSSARY

Glossary

die	Pfandflasche	returnable bottle
das	Pferd	horse
	Pfiat' Di	Goodbye
	Pfingsten	Whitsun
das	Pfund	pound
das	Picknick	picnic
das	Pils	type of beer
	planen	to plan
das	Plastik	plastic
der	Platz	square
der	Pole	Pole
	Polen	Poland
	polnisch	Polish
der	Polterabend	eve-of-wedding ceremony
die	Portion	portion
die	Post	post office
die	Postkarte	postcard
das	Praktikum	work placement
die	Praline	chocolate candy
	prima	great
	privat	private
	pro	per
	probieren	to try
das	Problem	problem
	Prost!	cheers!
das	PS (Post-skriptum)	PS
	pünktlich	on time

Q

der	Quadratmeter	square meter

R

das	Rad	bike
das	Radio	radio
das	Radler	beer diluted with lemon soda
der	Rappen (1/100 Franken)	centime, rappen
das	Rathaus	town hall
der	Raum	room, space
die	Rechnung	bill
das	Recht	right

	rechts	right
der	Redakteur	editor
	reden	to talk
das	Regal	shelf
	regelmäßig	regularly
der	Regen	rain
der	Regional-Express	regional train
	regnen	to rain
	regnerisch	rainy
der	Reichstag	seat of the German government
der	Reis	rice
das	Reisebüro	travel agency
die	Reise	journey
das	Restaurant	restaurant
der	Restmüll	waste that cannot be recycled
der	Rhein	Rhine
	Rheinhessen	region in the southwest of Germany
	richtig	right
die	Richtung	direction
	Rom	Rome
	rosa	pink
der	Rosenmontag	Shrove Monday
	rot	red
der	Rotwein	red wine
	ruhig	quite
der	Russe	Russian
	russisch	Russian
	Russland	Russia

S

	sagen	to say
die	Sahne	cream
die	Salami	salami
der	Salat	lettuce, salad
der	Samstag	Saturday
der	Samstagnach-mittag	Saturday afternoon
das	Sandwich	sandwich
der	Sänger	singer

4

	satt	*full*	die	Schwieger-mutter	*mother-in-law*
die	S-Bahn	*rapid suburban train*	der	Schwiegersohn	*son-in-law*
	schade	*it's a pity!*	die	Schwieger-tochter	*daughter-in-law*
der	Schatz	*sweetheart*	der	Schwiegervater	*father-in-law*
	schauen	*to look*		schwimmen	*to swim*
die	Scheibe	*slice*	das	Schwimmtier	*bath toy*
	scheinen	*to shine*		sechs	*six*
	schenken	*to give as present*		sechste / r / s	*sixth*
das	Schiff	*boat*		sechzehn	*sixteen*
die	Schildkröte	*turtle*		sechzehnte / r / s	*sixteenth*
der	Schinken	*ham*		sechzig	*sixty*
der	Schinkentoast	*toast with ham*		sechzigste / r / s	*sixtieth*
	schlafen	*to sleep*		sehen	*to see*
das	Schlafzimmer	*bedroom*		sehr	*very*
die	Schlagsahne	*whipped cream*		sein	*to be*
die	Schlange	*snake*		sein / e	*his, its*
	schlank	*slim*		seit	*since, for*
	schlecht	*bad*	der	Sekt	*sparkling wine*
	schmecken	*to taste*		selbstbewusst	*self-confident*
der	Schnaps	*liquor*		selten	*seldom*
der	Schnee	*snow*	das	Semesterticket	*reduced price ticket (for students only)*
	schneiden	*to slice*			
	schneien	*to snow*	die	Semmel	*roll*
die	Schokolade	*chocolate*	der	September	*September*
die	Schokoladen-torte	*chocolate tart*	der	Sessel	*chair*
	schon	*already*		setzen	*to set (down)*
	schön	*beautiful, nice, fine, lovely*		sich	*reflexive pronoun*
der	Schrank	*cupboard*		sicher	*sure*
	schreiben	*to write*		sie	*she, they, her, them*
der	Schreiner	*carpenter*		Sie	*you*
	schüchtern	*shy*		sieben	*seven*
die	Schule	*school*		siebte / r / s	*seventh*
der	Schüler	*pupil, schoolboy*		siebzehn	*seventeen*
der	Schwager	*brother-in-law*		siebzehnte / r / s	*seventeenth*
	schwarz	*black*		siebzig	*seventy*
die	Schweiz	*Switzerland*		siebzigste / r / s	*seventieth*
der	Schweizer	*Swiss*	das	Silber	*silver*
	schweizer-deutsch	*Swiss German*		singen	*to sing*
	schweizerisch	*Swiss*		sitzen	*to sit*
die	Schwester	*sister*		so	*so*
die	Schwieger-eltern	*parents-in-law*			

Glossary

	so ... wie	as ... as
	sofort	coming!, immediatly
der	Sohn	son
	sollen	to be supposed to, should, shall
der	Sommer	summer
der	Sonnabend	Saturday
die	Sonne	sun
	sonnig	sunny
der	Sonntag	Sunday
	sonst	else
	sortieren	to sort
	Spanien	Spain
der	Spanier	Spaniard
	spanisch	Spanish
der	Sparpreis	budget price
der	Spaß	fun
	Spaß machen	to enjoy
	spät	late
der	Spatz	sparrow
der	Spatzi	honey, darling
	spazieren gehen	to go for a walk
die	Speise	dish
die	Speisekarte	menu
der	Spiegel	mirror
das	Spiel	game
	spielen	to play
der	Sportler	sportsman
die	Sportlerin	sportswoman
	sportlich	sporty
der	Sportverein	sports club
die	Sprache	language
	sprechen	to speak
	St.	abbreviation of Stück
die	Stadt	city, town
das	Stadtmuseum	city museum
der	Stadtplan	city street map
der	Stadtteil	district
	stehen	to be written, to stand, to be (standing)
der	Stein	stone
	stellen	to put sth
	stimmen	to be right
	stimmt so	keep the change
der	Stock	floor
der	Stoff	cloth, fabric
die	Straße	street, road
die	Straßenbahn	tram
	streicheln	to caress
	streng	strict
das	Stück	piece
der	Student	student
das	Studentenwohnheim	halls of residence
	studieren	to study
der	Stuhl	chair
die	Stunde	hour
das	Styropor	polystrene
	suchen	to search
der	Süden	south
	südlich	southern
	super	super, great
der	Supermarkt	supermarket
	surfen	to surf
	süß	sweet
	sympathisch	pleasant

T

der	Tag	day
die	Tante	aunt
	tanzen	to dance
die	Tasche	bag
die	Tasse	cup
die	Taufe	baptism
	tausend	thousand
das	Taxi	taxi
die	Technik	technology
der	Tee	tea
	teilnehmen	to attend
das	Telefon	phone
die	Telefonnummer	phone number
die	Temperatur	temperature
das	Tennis	tennis
der	Teppich	carpet
das	Terrarium	terrarium
die	Terrasse	terrace

4

GLOSSARY

	teuer	expensive
das	Theater	theatre
das	Ticket	ticket
das	Tier	animal
der	Tierfreund	animal lover
der	Tisch	table
der	Toast	toast
das	Toastbrot	toast
die	Tochter	daughter
die	Toilette	toilet
	toll	great
die	Tomate	tomato
der	Tomatensalat	tomato salad
die	Torte	tart (with layer cream)
die	Trafik	kiosk (in Austria)
	tragen	to carry, to wear
die	Tram	tram
der	Traumberuf	dream job
	treffen	to meet
sich	treffen mit	to meet somebody
	trinken	to drink
das	Trinkgeld	tip
die	Trinkhalle	kiosk
	tschüss	bye
	tun	to do
die	Tür	door
der	Türke	Turkish
die	Türkei	Turkey
	türkisch	Turkish
der	Turm	tower
die	Tüte	bag

U

die	U-Bahn	underground
	über	about, over
die	Überraschung	surprise
	übrigens	by the way
die	Uhr	time
	um	at
	umsteigen	to change (train, bus or tram)
sich	umziehen	to change one's clothes
der	Umzug	parade, procession

	unattraktiv	unalluring
	und	and
	unfreundlich	unfriendly
	ungefährlich	harmless
	ungesund	unhealthy
	unhöflich	impolite
die	Universität	university
	unmöglich	impossible
	uns	(to) us
	unser/e	our
	unsportlich	unathletic
	unsympathisch	disagreable, unpleasant
	unten	down, at the bottom, downstairs
	unter	under
	unterwegs	on the way
die	Unterbrechung	interruption
die	Ursache	reason

V

der	Vater	father
der	Vati	father
die	Verbindung	connection
der	Verein	club
	vergessen	to forget
	verheiratet	married
der	Verkäufer	seller, shop assistant
sich	verkleiden	to dress up (as)
die	Verkleidung	dressing up
die	Verlobung	engagement
	vermuten	to suppose
	verrückt	crazy
	verstehen	to understand
	viel	much
	vielleicht	perhaps, maybe
	vier	four
	vierte/r/s	fourth
das	Viertel	quarter
	vierzehn	fourteen
	vierzehnte/r/s	fourteenth
	vierzig	fourty
	vierzigste/r/s	fourtieth
die	Visitenkarte	business card

Glossary

der	Vogel	bird
	vom	see preposition von
	von	of, from
	vor	to, ago, in front of
	vorbeigehen	to pass
	vorbereiten	to prepare
	vorgestern	the day before yesterday
	vorhaben	to have planned
	vorlesen	to read (something to somebody)
der	Vormittag	morning (time from nine to noon)
	vormittags	in the morning
der	Vorname	first name
	vorne	in the front

w

die	Wand	wall
	wann	when
	war	was
	warm	warm, hot
die	Wärme	heat
die	Warmmiete	rent including extra costs
	warten	to wait
	warum	why
	was	what
	wechselhaft	changeable
der	Weg	way, path
	weg	away
das	Weggli	roll
	wegwerfen	to throw away
	weich	soft, tender
	Weihnachten	Christmas
	weil	because
der	Wein	wine
der	Weinberg	wineyard
	weiß	white
der	Weißwein	white wine
	weit	far
	weiter	then
	weitergehen	to go on
das	Weizen	type of beer
	welche / r / s	which

	welchem	which
	wem	to whom
	wen	whom
	wenig	a little
	weniger	less
	wenn	if, when
	wer	who
	werden	to become
	werfen	to throw
der	Westen	West
das	Wetter	weather
die	WG	short form for Wohngemeinschaft
	wichtig	important
	wie	how, as
	wie lange	how long
	wie viel /e	how much, what
	wieder	again
	Wien	Vienna
	willkommen	welcome
der	Wind	wind
	windig	windy
der	Winter	winter
	wir	we
	wirklich	really, indeed
	wissen	to know
	wo	where
die	Woche	week
das	Wochenende	weekend
	woher	where ... from?
	wohin	where ...(to)?
	wohnen	to live
die	Wohngemein-schaft	people sharing a flat
die	Wohnung	flat
das	Wohnzimmer	living-room
die	Wolke	cloud
	wollen	to want
	wunderschön	wonderful
	wünschen	to wish
die	Wurst	sausage, salami

4

GLOSSARY

Z

	zahlen	*to pay*
der	Zahnarzt	*dentist*
	zehn	*ten*
	zehnte / r / s	*tenth*
	zeigen	*to show*
die	Zeit	*time*
die	Zeitung	*newspaper*
	zentral	*central*
das	Zentrum	*center*
der	Zettel	*piece of paper*
das	Zimmer	*room*
der	Zirkus	*circus*
die	Zitrone	*lemon*
das	Zmorge	*breakfast*
	zu	*to, too*
	zu Abend essen	*to have dinner*
	etwas zu Ende schreiben	*to end*
	zu Fuß	*walking*
	zu Mittag essen	*to have lunch*
der	Zucker	*sugar*
	zuerst	*at first*
der	Zug	*train*
	zurück	*back*
	zurückbringen	*to bring back*
	zurückfahren	*to go back (by means of transport)*
	zurückgehen	*to go back (on foot)*
	zurückkommen	*to return*
	zurückrufen	*to call back*
	zusammen	*together*
der	Zuschlag	*additional charge*
	zwanzig	*twenty*
	zwanzigste / r / s	*twentieth*
	zwei	*two*
	zweimal	*twice*
	zweite / r / s	*second*
die	Zwiebel	*onion*
	zwischen	*between*
	zwölf	*twelve*
	zwölfte / r / s	*twelvth*

GLOSSARY

Bildnachweis

Illustrationen: Walter Uihlein

S. 10: © davis - Fotolia.com

S. 11, Übung 1, Hallo: shutterstock/ Stephen Coburn, Auf Wiedersehen: thinkstock (Digital Vision), Grüß Gott: © Jeanette Dietl - Fotolia.com, Guten Morgen: istockphoto.com/ Cristian Lazzari, Gute Nacht: © st-fotograf - Fotolia.com Übung 2, 1: thinkstock (Stockbyte), 2: © Robert Kneschke - Fotolia.com, 3: fotolia.de/ Yuri Arcurs, 4: thinkstock (Feverpitched), 5: © goodluz - Fotolia.com

S. 12: fotolia/ pressmaster

S. 20, 1: © katatonia - Fotolia.com, 2: thinkstock (Ingram Publishing), 3: thinkstock (Olaf Bender), 4: thinkstock (Prill Mediendesign & Fotografie), 5: thinkstock (claudiodivizia), 6: thinkstock (Design Pics), 7: thinkstock (villy_yovcheva), 8: istock/36clicks

S. 22: shutterstock.com/ Villedieu Christophe

S. 27, 1: fotolia/ karandaev, 2: © unpict - Fotolia.com, 3: © Corinna Gissemann - Fotolia.com, 4: fotolia/ gtranquillity, 5: istockphoto.com/ Sebastian Vera, 6: thinkstock (Evgeny Karandaev), 7: fotolia/ Celso Pupo, 8: thinkstock (GooDween123), 9: shutterstock/ ifong, 10: fotolia.de/ Mikko Pitkänen

S. 28, Speisekarte: thinkstock (Michael Blann), Bestellung: fotolia/ shotsstudio, Zahlen: © Jürgen Fälchle - Fotolia.com

S. 30, Bier: fotolia.de/ Nitr und thinkstock (olm26250), Kuchen: fotolia.de/ sorcerer11 und thinkstock (olm26250), Rechnung: thinkstock (Brian Jackson) und thinkstock (olm26250)

S. 33: © Marina Grau - Fotolia.comS

S. 35, erste Reihe, von links nach rechts: © Kara - Fotolia.com, © K.Weissfloch - Fotolia.com, © cbpix - Fotolia.com, fotolia.de/ daniel sainthorant; Reihe 2: thinkstock (jackryan89), thinkstock (itakefotos4u), © fotografci - Fotolia.com, © fire foto - Fotolia.com

S. 36: fotolia.de/ Hanik

S. 38: © Minerva Studio - Fotolia.com

S. 39: thinkstock (dolgachov)

S. 40, 1: thinkstock (dolgachov), 2: thinkstock (Cameron Spencer), 3: thinkstock (claudiarndt), 4: thinkstock (Mattia Pelizzar), 5: thinkstock (Nikolay Pozdeev)

S. 48, 1: © SeanPavonePhoto - Fotolia.com, 2: fotolia/ shotsstudio, 3: thinkstock (Ryan McVay)

S. 49, Hamburg: © davis - Fotolia.com, Bier: © Anton Prado PHOTO - Fotolia.com, Häuser: thinkstock (StockSolutions), Kuchen: © ld1976 - Fotolia.com, Frauen: thinkstock (macniak)

S. 51, 1: PONS GmbH, 2: thinkstock (Monkey Business), 3: thinkstock (Marco Richter),

4: © Kaubo - Fotolia.com, 5: PONS GmbH, 7: © Sven Grundmann - Fotolia.com, 8: PONS GmbH

S. 52, links: © Lilyana Vynogradova - Fotolia.com, rechts: Deutsche Bahn AG

S. 54, Uhr: PONS GmbH

S. 59, Übung 1, 1: thinkstock (naumoid), 2: © Warren Goldswain - Fotolia.com, 3: © juniart - Fotolia.com, 4: istockphoto.com/ Catherine Yeulet, 5: thinkstock (swilmor), 6: shutterstock.com/ wavebreakmedia ltd, 7: fotolia.de/ Ferenc Szelepcsenyi, 8: fotolia/ Robert Kneschke, 9: fotolia.de/ Christian Schwier, 10: shutterstock.com/ Neale Cousland Übung 2, 1: thinkstock (Stockbyte), 2: © contrastwerkstatt - Fotolia.com, 3: © mangostock - Fotolia.com, 4: © habari - Fotolia.com, 5: © goodluz - Fotolia.com

S. 61, Bank: © JWS - Fotolia.com, Schild: © leuchtturm2013 - Fotolia.com

S. 62: fotolia.de/ Yuri Arcurs

S. 64: PONS GmbH

S. 66, 1: © habari - Fotolia.com, 2: © auremar - Fotolia.com, 3: © gilotyna - Fotolia.com, 4: thinkstock (Wavebreakmedia Ltd)

S. 67, Fahrradhelm: istockphoto.com/ Kati Molin, Mann: istockphoto.com/ Joselito Briones, Museum: thinkstock (Digital Vision), Konzert: © stokkete - Fotolia.com, Musik: shutterstock/ StockLite

S. 68, links: © ARochau - Fotolia.com, rechts: © apops - Fotolia.com

S. 71, 1: istockphoto.com/ Joselito Briones, 2: thinkstock (Digital Vision), 3: fotolia.de/ contrastwerkstatt, 4: fotolia.de/ Günter Menzl, 5: shutterstock/ Kzenon , 6: © apops - Fotolia.com, 7: © stokkete - Fotolia.com, 8: © ARochau - Fotolia.com, 9: thinkstock (Purestock), 10: fotolia.de/ Yuri Arcurs

S. 75, Kuchen: thinkstock (sodapix sodapix); Übung 2, 1: thinkstock (JupiterImages), 2: thinkstock (Jacob Wackerhausen), 3: © drubig-photo - Fotolia.com, 4: thinkstock (studiovespa), 5: thinkstock (Fuse)

S. 76, links: thinkstock (Andrew Olney), rechts: © Jürgen Fälchle - Fotolia.com

S. 80: thinkstock (RudolfT)

S. 82: EKS GmbH

S. 84, 1: Deutsche Bahn AG, 2: thinkstock (Fuse), 3: thinkstock (julief514)

S. 85, 1: shutterstock/Golden Pixels LLC, 2: thinkstock (Fuse), 3: thinkstock (Maria Yfanti), 4: shutterstock/ auremar

S. 88, Lisa: shutterstock/ Stephanie Frey, Verena: istockphoto.com/ Wilson Valentin, Susanne: shutterstock/ Golden Pixels LLC, Thomas: shutterstock/ Monkey Business Images, Oma: shutterstock/ Yuri Arcurs

S. 89, 1: © ARochau - Fotolia.com, 2: thinkstock (Monkey Business), 3: shutterstock/ Kzenon
S. 91, 1: © Michael Möller - Fotolia.com, 2: Walter Uihlein, 3: © mattkayusb - Fotolia.com, 4: © lightpoet - Fotolia.com, 5: © www.jh-photo.de - Fotolia.com
S. 92: thinkstock (hurricanehank)
S. 94, 1: © Eric Isselée - Fotolia.com, 2: fotolia.de/ liliya kulianionak, 3: © Vera Kuttelvaserova - Fotolia.com, 4: shutterstock.com/ dusan964, 5: © Eric Isselée - Fotolia.com, 6: © Iosif Szasz-Fabian - Fotolia.com, 7: fotolia.de/ Pavel Sazonov, 8: © Uros Petrovic - Fotolia.com, 9: © cynoclub - Fotolia.com, 10: © Irochka - Fotolia.com
S. 101, links: © maho - Fotolia.com, rechts: © ArTo - Fotolia.com
S. 102: PONS GmbH
S. 106, 1: shutterstock/ Mimadeo, 2: © Marcel Schauer - Fotolia.com, 3: © bluedesign - Fotolia.com, 4: © JR Photography - Fotolia.com, 5: fotolia/ P.C., 6: thinkstock (Sergei Poromov), 7: © mediagram - Fotolia.com, 8: fotolia/ Martina Berg, 9: © Laiotz - Fotolia.com, 10: © fuxart - Fotolia.com
S. 107, 1: istockphoto.com/ Cristian Lazzari, 2: fotolia/ fotoali, 3: fotolia.de/ Mark Stout, 4: fotolia/ Kzenon, 5: fotolia/ juniart
S. 108, links: © Kara - Fotolia.com, rechts: thinkstock (Fuse)
S. 109, von links nach rechts, Reihe 1: istockphoto.com/ Cristian Lazzari, fotolia/ juniart, fotolia/ fotoali, fotolia/ Kzenon, fotolia.de/ Mark Stout, shutterstock/erwinova, thinkstock (dziewul), thinkstock (LuminaStock), thinkstock (Keith Levit), © drubig-photo - Fotolia.com
S. 111, weiß: istockphoto.com/ pialhovik, gelb: shutterstock.com/ Elenapavlova, orange: shutterstock.com/ Gelpi, rosa: shutterstock.com/ Elnur, rot: shutterstock.com/ Elenapavlova, grün: shutterstock.com/ nito, lila: thinkstock (Jiripravda), braun: shutterstock.com/ Jennifer Stone, schwarz: shutterstock.com/ AndyTu;
S. 114: thinkstock (MayerKleinostheim)
S. 117, links: © swisshippo - Fotolia.com, rechts: thinkstock (reptiles4all)
S. 118, 1: thinkstock (MartinSarikov), 2: fotolia.de/ virtua73, 3: thinkstock (wasan gredpree), 4: shutterstock.com/ Alistair Cotton, 5: fotolia.de/ Asparuh Stoyanov, 6: istockphoto.com/ Bernd Klumpp, 7: istockphoto.com/ Jeff Irving, 8: thinkstock (AnikaSalsera), 9: thinkstock (Volodymyr Khomiakov), 10: thinkstock (KatarzynaBialasiewicz)
S. 127, 1: © sad dogg design - Fotolia.com, 2: thinkstock (theJIPEN), 3: thinkstock (GooDween123)
S. 129, 1: thinkstock (Choreograph), 2: thinkstock (LuckyBusiness), 3: © olly - Fotolia.com
S. 131, 1: shutterstock/ ultimathule, 2: shutterstock/ Ondacaracola, 3: shutterstock/ Botond Horváth, 4: fotolia/ silviaantunes
S. 132, 1: © Niklas Kratzsch - Fotolia.com, 2: PONS GmbH, 3: © Gina Sanders - Fotolia.com, 4: thinkstock (antikainen), 5: © Givaga - Fotolia.com
S. 133: © belahoche - Fotolia.com
S. 134, 1: © forkART Photography - Fotolia.com, 2: fotolia.de/ veneratio, 3: © magann - Fotolia.com, 4: fotolia/ JCVStock, 5: fotolia.de/ Leonid Nyshko, 6: fotolia.de/ Yury Zap, 7: fotolia/ af photo, 8: fotolia.de/ Armin Sepp
S. 138, 1: thinkstock (Purestock), 2: © forkART Photography - Fotolia.com, 3: fotolia.de/ Armin Sepp, 4: thinkstock (Fuse)
S. 141: © Minerva Studio - Fotolia.com
S. 142, 1: fotolia.de/ Denis Dryashkin, 2: fotolia/ valeriy555, 3: fotolia/ m.arc , 4: fotolia.de/ angelsimy, 5: fotolia.de/ volff, 6: fotolia/ valeriy555, 7: istockphoto.com/ peter chen, 8: shutterstock.com/ Dawn Gilfillan, 9: fotolia/ Leonid Nyshko, 10: © Jiri Hera - Fotolia.com
S. 144: © Christophe Fouquin - Fotolia.com
S. 147, Student: thinkstock (Digital Vision), Schüler: © pressmaster - Fotolia.com, Freunde: © pressmaster - Fotolia.com, kein Computer: © olly - Fotolia.com, Arzt: © Syda Productions - Fotolia.com, Geschäftsleute: shutterstock/ Marcin Balcerzak, Frau: thinkstock (Mallivan), Verkäufer: thinkstock (Digital Vision)
S. 148, 1: thinkstock (Ikonoklast_Fotografie), 2: thinkstock (David Pereiras Villagrá), 3: © eyetronic - Fotolia.com, 4: © Picture-Factory - Fotolia.com, 5: thinkstock (Monkey Business)
S. 149: thinkstock (Jochen Sand)
S. 150, von links nach rechts, Reihe 1: fotolia.de/ Brocreative, © CandyBox Images - Fotolia.com, © Karin & Uwe Annas - Fotolia.com, © Visionsi - Fotolia.com, © Rido - Fotolia.com; Reihe 2: fotolia.de/ AVAVA, © sumnersgraphicsinc - Fotolia.com, © Kzenon - Fotolia.com, thinkstock (Digital Vision), thinkstock (IPGGutenbergUKLtd)
S. 154: © eyetronic - Fotolia.com
S. 155, Übung 1, 1: shutterstock/ Pecold, 2: fotolia/ kids.4pictures, 3: thinkstock (Salih Kuelcue), 4: fotolia/ Picture-Factory, 5: fotolia/ rsester; Übung 2: shutterstock/ Benoit Daoust
S. 157: thinkstock (Maxim Bolotnikov)
S. 160, 1: fotolia/ carloscastilla, 2: © Aaron Amat - Fotolia.com (Fahrrad), © M. Schuppich - Fotolia.com (Geld), 3: thinkstock (Tom Le Goff)
S. 170, 1: © shootingankauf - Fotolia.com, 2: © Spofi - Fotolia.com, 3: thinkstock (andresrimaging)